PRAISE FOR RIANE EISLER'S
THE *REAL WEALTH OF NATIONS*

"Eisler shows how to value economically what is valuable human-ly—and what could be more revolutionary than that? To imagine money not as the root of all evil but the measure of all good, read *The Real Wealth of Nations*."

—Gloria Steinem

"This book should be mandatory reading for every CEO, every econ-omist, every government official, every student, and every citizen of our world."

—Jeffrey Hollender, President, Seventh Generation, Inc.

"In *The Real Wealth of Nations,* Riane Eisler, long a voice of sanity and clarity in an increasingly confusing world, does what has been desperately needed for a long time: she brings back a human- and nature-centric perspective to economics to show how ends and means can be integrated."

—Peter Senge, author of *The Fifth Discipline*

"In *The Real Wealth of Nations*, Riane Eisler lays out a comprehen-sive and compelling argument for why we must change national and global priorities about what work, and which workers, we value—including worldwide attitudes towards caring for our children."

—Marian Wright Edelman, President, Children's Defense Fund

"An essential tool for government leaders, politicians, economists, and everyone looking for ways to halt environmental destruction, eradicate poverty, stabilize population, and build a better future, *The Real Wealth of Nations* shows us how to construct a sustainable new economy—and a good quality of life for generations to come."

—The Honorable Vigdís Finnbogadóttir, President of Iceland, 1980–1996

"*The Real Wealth of Nations* is a call for nothing less than a ground shift in consciousness. I urge you to read this profound and important book."

—Eve Ensler, author of *The Vagina Monologues* and *Insecure at Last*

"In this brilliant new look at economic systems and how they interact with culture, Riane Eisler has created what is sure to be a classic and—hopefully—world-changing book."

—Thom Hartmann, author of *Screwed* and *The Last Hours of Ancient Sunlight*

"Riane Eisler is one of the most important and influential thinkers of our time. In *The Real Wealth of Nations* she turns her attention to the importance of caring and issues a clarion call for contemporary societies to recognize and value the essential contribution of caregiving to human well-being."

—David C. Korten, author of *The Great Turning* and *When Corporations Rule the World*

"Eisler has done it again—producing an exciting and urgently needed guide to the economic realities that face our society. Those of us who hope for a new direction in dealing with issues like poverty and global warming need to read and reread Eisler's analysis. *The Real Wealth of Nations* is a necessary handbook for the 21st century."

—Rabbi Michael Lerner, editor of *Tikkun* and author of *The Left Hand of God*

"The real wealth of nations has always been in people, yet the vast economy of caring (over half of all economic activity globally) is still ignored and unpaid—largely relegated to the world's women. Eisler sets the record straight, showing us an array of new options for creating sustainable, caring societies. Must reading!"

—Hazel Henderson, author of *Building a Win-Win World* and *Ethical Markets*

"This is a wonderful, hopeful book, not about where we have been economically, but about the potential for economics to reflect what we truly value—quality of life and quality of the environment."

—Daniel Kammen, Codirector, Berkeley Institute of the Environment, University of California

"Why has conventional economics been so slow to offer compelling, useful responses to our most threatening challenges, such as environmental degradation or raging inequalities? Riane Eisler answers this question, and in doing so, reinvents the dismal science, infusing it with the essential ingredients it needs to get us out of the terribly narrow box in which we've been stuck."

—Jared Bernstein, senior economist, Economic Policy Institute, author of *Crunch* and *All Together Now*

"Riane Eisler speaks from the heart, showing how we can make a better world for our children and our children's children. It is time to love our planet, love our neighbors, and heed Riane's call to action . . . it's time for a caring revolution."

—Joan Blades, cofounder, MoveOn.org, and author of *The Motherhood Manifesto*

"From third world poverty to climate change, it's become increasingly clear that traditional economic thinking is not only unable to solve today's myriad of problems, it's responsible for many of them. Riane Eisler's brilliant new book expands the scope and practice of economics beyond capitalism and socialism to a new economics in which equity, justice, and environmental sanity prevail. Must reading!"

—Morris Dees, cofounder, Southern Poverty Law Center

"In this brilliant new book, Riane Eisler hits the nail on the head. She points out exactly how and why the only sustainable economic systems are those that include the cost of human caring and happiness in the bottom line. Better yet, she provides us with practical steps toward implementing this crucial economic shift."

—Christiane Northrup, MD, author of *Women's Bodies, Women's Wisdom* and *Mother-Daughter Wisdom*

"*The Real Wealth of Nations* outlines a new economics—one that inspires us to fulfill the dream envisioned when the United States' Founders declared independence from that earlier empire."

—John Perkins, author of *Confessions of an Economic Hit Man*

"This book should be read by every member of Congress, and its practical ideas incorporated into economic policy."

—The Honorable Claudine Schneider, former member of the United States Congress

"This book is an essential, practical, and loving survival guide to the future."

—Margaret Wheatley, author of *Leadership and the New Science*

"Listen to Riane Eisler! No one is better at conveying the urgent message that we must abandon our economic double standard and start valuing the essential work of caring for and investing in ourselves and our environment."

—Ann Crittenden, author of *The Price of Motherhood*

"Riane Eisler is one of the great wisdom voices of our times. In *The Real Wealth of Nations*, she gives us the vision and understanding —and the tools we can use—to shift our economics to a path where greed and violence no longer prevail but are replaced by creativity and generosity. If you want to be part of the solution, read this magnificent book!"

—John Robbins, author of *Healthy at 100* and *Diet for a New America*

"Riane Eisler has provided an accessible, fascinating, and persuasive argument for a caring perspective on economics. Brilliant."

—Nel Noddings, Professor Emeritus, Stanford University, and author of *The Challenge to Care in Schools* and *Starting at Home*

"*The Real Wealth of Nations* will challenge you to reconsider not just where our nation is going but also what role you want to play in its future. This is a call to action that should be read and discussed by parents with their children, in our schools, and throughout any and all not-only-for-profit organizations."

—Mark Albion, cofounder, Net Impact, and author of *More Than Money, True to Yourself* and *Making a Life, Making a Living*

"Brilliant and inspiring! Riane Eisler is one of those few extraordinary people whose insight and ability to express complicated ideas in simple language help the rest of us to understand the human condition. *The Real Wealth of Nations* updates the dismal science of economics to the complex realities of the 21st century and points the way to a sustainable future."

—Mal Warwick, coauthor of *Values-Driven Business* and board chair, Social Venture Network

"What if the world's economic system supported everyone and Mother Earth, too? This is now possible thanks to Riane Eisler's *The Real Wealth of Nations*."

—Dr. Robert Muller, former United Nations Assistant Secretary General

"Riane Eisler has always been a revolutionary who has forced us to confront our conventional conceptions with unconventional thought. In her new book she applies her revolutionary insights to that most 'dismal science,' economics, and in the process shows us how, with a bit of caring and a great deal of imagination, it need not remain dismal for long. A tour de force!"

—William F. Schulz, former Executive Director, Amnesty International USA, and Fellow, Carr Center for Human Rights Policy, Kennedy School of Government, Harvard University

"*The Real Wealth of Nations* describes, illustrates, and animates a new perspective on economics. Chock full of examples and compelling facts on how to strengthen the quality of human and natural capital, it shows what is possible and necessary."

—Jane Dutton, Chair, Management and Organizations Department, University of Michigan School of Business, and author of *Energize Your Workplace*

"In this lively and wide-ranging book, Riane Eisler once again powerfully shows that we need to replace relations of domination with relations of partnership."

—Julie A. Nelson, Senior Research Associate, Global Development and Environment Institute, Tufts University, and author of *Economics for Humans*

THE
REAL
WEALTH
OF
NATIONS

OTHER WORKS BY RIANE EISLER

BOOKS

The Chalice and The Blade: Our History, Our Future

Sacred Pleasure: Sex, Myth, and the Politics of the Body—New Paths to Power and Love

Tomorrow's Children: A Blueprint for Partnership Education in the 21st Century

The Power of Partnership: Seven Relationships That Will Change Your Life

The Equal Rights Handbook: What ERA Means to Your Life, Your Rights, and the Future

Dissolution: No-Fault Divorce, Marriage, and the Future of Women

The Gate: A Memoir of Love and Reflection

The Partnership Way: New Tools for Living and Learning (with David Loye)

Women, Men, and the Global Quality of Life (with David Loye and Kari Norgaard)

Educating for a Culture of Peace (editor, with Ron Miller)

AUDIO

The Chalice and The Blade: Our History, Our Future

VIDEO/DVD

Tomorrow's Children: Partnership Education in Action

THE
REAL
WEALTH
OF
NATIONS

CREATING A
CARING ECONOMICS

RIANE EISLER

Berrett–Koehler Publishers, Inc.
San Francisco
a BK Currents book

Berrett-Koehler Publishers, Inc.
235 Montgomery Street, Suite 650
San Francisco, CA 94104-2916
Tel: (415) 288-0260   Fax: (415) 362-2512   www.bkconnection.com

Ordering Information
Quantity sales. Special discounts are available on quantity purchases by corporations, associations, and others. For details, contact the "Special Sales Department" at the Berrett-Koehler address above.
Individual sales. Berrett-Koehler publications are available through most bookstores. They can also be ordered directly from Berrett-Koehler: Tel: (800) 929-2929; Fax: (802) 864-7626; www.bkconnection.com
Orders for college textbook/course adoption use. Please contact Berrett-Koehler: Tel: (800) 929-2929; Fax: (802) 864-7626.
Orders by U.S. trade bookstores and wholesalers. Please contact Ingram Publisher Services, Tel: (800) 509-4887; Fax: (800) 838-1149; E-mail: customer.service@ingram publisherservices.com; or visit www.ingrampublisherservices.com/Ordering for details about electronic ordering.

Berrett-Koehler and the BK logo are registered trademarks of Berrett-Koehler Publishers, Inc.

Printed in the United States of America
Berrett-Koehler books are printed on long-lasting acid-free paper. When it is available, we choose paper that has been manufactured by environmentally responsible processes. These may include using trees grown in sustainable forests, incorporating recycled paper, minimizing chlorine in bleaching, or recycling the enrgy produced a the paper mill.

Library of Congress Cataloging-in-Publication Data

Eisler, Riane Tennenhaus.
  The real wealth of nations : creating a caring economics / by Riane Eisler.
    p. cm.
  Includes bibliographical references and index.
  ISBN 978-1-57675-388-0 (hardcover)
  ISBN 978-1-57675-629-4 (pbk.)
  1. Welfare economics. 2. Environmental economics. I. Title.
  HB99.3.E37 2007
  330.12'6--dc22   2006100211

First Edition
13 12 11 10 09 08   10 9 8 7 6 5 4 3 2 1

Cover Design: Karen Marquardt   Proofreader: Henrietta Bensussen
Interior Design: Seventeenth Street Studios   Indexer: Medea Minnich
Production: Linda Jupiter, Jupiter Productions

To David, my children, my grandchildren,

and children everywhere

Contents

Reasons to Care

Much of my life has been a quest. This quest started in my childhood, when my parents and I fled my native Vienna from the Nazis. It continued in the slums of Havana, where we found refuge, and later in the United States, where I grew up. It was a quest for answers to a basic question: Why, when we humans have such a great capacity for caring, consciousness, and creativity, has our world seen so much cruelty, insensitivity, and destructiveness?

In the course of my quest I looked for answers in many areas, from psychology, history, and anthropology to education, economics, and politics. And again and again I came back to economics because I saw that we have to change present economic systems if we, our children, and future generations are to survive and thrive.

As time went on, and I had children and then grandchildren, the passion animating my quest intensified. So also did my focus on economics.

As I looked at my grandchildren, I couldn't help thinking of the millions of children in our world, all born with a hunger for life, love, and joy, condemned to untimely deaths or lives of unnecessary suffering. As I reflected on the pristine beauty of our oceans and the grandeur of the coastal cities where so many of us live, I thought of the threats from climate changes caused by current economic rules and practices. As I took in the reality around me every day, I saw the stress of families vainly trying to find time for one another, and the pain of people displaced by new technologies that should have been used to improve our lives instead. And again I came back to economics.

I saw that in our inextricably interconnected world none of us has a secure future so long as hunger, extreme poverty, and violence continue unabated. I saw that present economic systems are despoiling and depleting our beautiful Earth. I saw that there is something fundamentally wrong with economic rules and practices that fail to adequately value the most essential human work: the work of caring for ourselves, others, and our Mother Earth.

Gradually, I began to explore economics from a new perspective. I saw the need for an economics that, while preserving the best elements of current economic models, takes us beyond them to a way of living, and making a living, that truly meets human needs. I also saw that we need a much broader approach to economics: one that takes into account its larger social and natural context.

I invite you to join me in exploring this new perspective on economics. I ask that you leave behind assumptions that have constricted our view, because what we will look at goes beyond what is usually considered the domain of economics. I also ask that, as you read on, you keep in mind what you most value and want in your own life.

In the pages that follow, we will look at economics through a wider lens that reveals the exciting possibilities of what I call *caring economics*. I realize that even putting economics and caring in the same sentence is alien to conventional thought. But this is no time for conventional thought. As expressed in popular clichés such as "thinking outside the box," it is a time that urgently calls for *unconventional* thought.

With the accelerating speed of economic globalization—when corporations that control international financial and technological flows still play by uncaring rules—the need for a caring economics is more urgent than ever before. This book offers a new vision of what economics is and can be. It provides a starting point from which to rebuild economic structures, practices, and policies in ways that maximize our positive potentials and minimize our negative ones.

I have called this book *The Real Wealth of Nations* because it shows that our most important economic assets are not financial—that the real wealth of nations consists of the contributions of people and our natural environment. In my choice of this title, I don't mean to imply that I have set out to write a technical treatise on economics such as Adam Smith's classic *The Wealth of Nations*. To address the needs of our world today, we have to bring together knowledge from many areas. I therefore draw from many fields in addition to economics, including advances in both the social and natural sciences. I also propose practical steps for moving both economic and social systems in a positive direction.

The new perspective on economics I am introducing in this book grows out of my research over the past thirty years applying evolutionary systems science to social systems. During this time, I became involved with pioneers in chaos and complexity theory,[1] and contributed to many books applying these revolutionary new approaches to the real-world problems of our time.[2] In my own books, beginning with *The Chalice and The Blade: Our History, Our Future*, I introduced a new lens for understanding social systems and determining how we can build foundations for a more equitable and sustainable world.

This lens is the analytical framework running through all my books and journal papers: the *partnership* or mutual respect system and the *domination* or top-down control system. These social categories are integral to the cultural transformation theory I introduced in earlier books.[3] They are also integral to understanding, and changing, dysfunctional economic structures, rules, and practices—which is the focus of this book.

When Adam Smith wrote *The Wealth of Nations*, his focus was on the market, or as he put it, on "the invisible hand of the market" as the best mechanism for producing and distributing the necessities of life.[4] This book goes beyond the market to reexamine economics from a larger perspective that includes the life-supporting activities of households, communities, and nature.

Moreover, and this is one of its central themes, this book shows that to construct an economic system that can help us meet the enormous challenges we face, we must give visibility and value to the socially and economically essential work of caring for people and nature. Indeed, if we really think about it, it's unrealistic to expect changes in uncaring economic policies and practices unless caring and caregiving are given greater value.

In the chapters that follow, we will see that moving to a more equitable and sustainable economic system requires attention to the interaction of economic and social systems. We will also see that for this movement to succeed we have to broaden the scope of what has traditionally been considered the domain of economics.

We start from the basic premise that economic systems should pro-mote human welfare and human happiness, a premise that seems to have been forgotten in much of today's economic discourse. Drawing from the work of advanced thinkers in economics and many other fields, we then explore exciting new frontiers for work, values, and life.

Chapter 1 takes us beyond the narrow band of economic relations taken into account by conventional models—whether capitalist, socialist, communist, or anarchist. It introduces the first of five foun-dations for a caring economics: a full-spectrum economic map that includes the life-supporting activities of households, communities, and nature.

Chapter 2 widens the lens through which we look at economics to include its larger cultural context. It takes us to the second founda-tion for a caring economics: cultural beliefs and institutions that value caring and caregiving. This chapter introduces the socio-eco-nomic categories of the partnership system and the domination sys-tem, revealing connections not previously considered. It proposes new standards and rules for what is or is not economically valuable. And it shows how all this directly affects our lives and the future of our children and our planet.

The next three chapters introduce three more foundations for a caring economic system: caring economic rules, policies, and prac-tices; inclusive and accurate economic indicators; and economic and social structures that support partnership rather than domination.

These chapters continue to connect the dots between our daily lives, economics, and cultural values and norms. They show how problem-solving, creativity, and entrepreneurship are supported by caring poli-cies and practices, and how this greatly benefits business, people, and our natural environment. They provide a redefinition of productive work appropriate for the postindustrial economy, where the most important capital is what economists like to call human capital. They describe new measurements of productivity that take into account the life-sustaining activities of both households and nature. And they pro-pose ways to protect what economists today call natural capital.

These chapters also take us on a journey into our past. They reassess unhealthy myths and values we inherited. They expose the hidden gender double standard that is our heritage from earlier, more unjust and economically inefficient times. They show that this has led to an economic double standard that lies behind unsustainable ways of living and working. And they explore how we can develop healthier alternatives.

Then, in chapter 6, we see the enormous personal, social, financial, and environmental costs of old economic and political systems and their inability to adapt to the challenges we face. In chapter 7, we look at how we can develop a caring economics. This chapter briefly traces the development of modern economic theories in the context of the times out of which they came, and proposes basic principles for the construction of a new conceptual framework that includes the best elements of both capitalism and socialism but goes beyond both.

Chapter 8 looks at postmodern technological breakthroughs such as robotics, biotechnology, and nanotechnology and how they affect both work and life. It introduces a new way of looking at technology that no longer throws everything, from can openers to nuclear bombs, into the same technological basket. It shows that rapid technological change makes a caring economics even more essential in the epochal transition to the postindustrial age.

Chapter 9 then takes us to where we are and where we can go from here. Drawing from arresting new findings from neuroscience, it shows that a caring economics supports the capacities that in the course of evolution made us uniquely human. Finally, chapter 10 proposes practical steps each of us can take to accelerate the move to a more humane, environmentally sustainable, and economically effective future.

I have written this book to invite discussion and action. It is a book for everyone who wants a better life and a better world, and is looking for practical tools to realize these goals. I am confident that together we can build a new economic system that promotes creativity and generosity rather than greed and destructiveness. Indeed, I am convinced that this is the only viable option at this critical juncture in our cultural and planetary evolution.

Riane Eisler
January 2007

CHAPTER ONE

We Need a New Economics

Jim Cross graduated at the top of his applied computer science class. But he hasn't found a job in California's prosperous Silicon Valley, once the golden Mecca for high-wage technology jobs. While sales and profits in the region have been skyrocketing again—an average of more than 500 percent over three years—employment has actually declined.

In Nigeria, Marian Mfunde has just buried her second baby. Like her first son—and millions of African children every year—her five-month-old daughter died of hunger. Marian herself is sick with HIV, which she contracted from her husband before he left to seek work in the capital, and was never heard from again.

In Rio de Janeiro, nine-year-old Rosario Menen sleeps on the street. She lives in terror of rats, rapists, and the police squads that periodically evict and brutalize street children. Like thousands of Brazilian girls and boys, Rosario has no place to go and no one to care for her.

In Riyadh, eighteen-year-old Ahmad Haman just joined a fundamentalist terrorist cell. In his native Saudi Arabia, his financial prospects are dim.[1] Population in the Middle East has tripled in the last fifty years, to 380 million in 2000 from 100 million in 1950—and today close to two-thirds of those 380 million Middle Easterners are under age twenty-five, and jobs are scarce.[2] Even in his oil-rich nation, Ahmad finds the promise of a heavenly afterlife with seventy virgins if he blows himself up in a suicide bombing more promising than his earthly future.[3]

In the midst of all this runaway dislocation, misery, and insanity, economists argue endlessly about free markets versus government regulations, privatization versus central economic planning. They talk about corporate profits, international trade agreements, job outsourcing, employment figures, interest rates, inflation, and gross national product. That's what's discussed in the news, in business schools, and in thousands of economic treatises—usually in a jargon most people find frustratingly out of touch with their real needs.

Of course, it's not that economists are unaware of people's real-life needs. Some, like Nobel laureates Amartya Sen and Joseph Stiglitz, vigorously criticize practices that cause hunger, ill health, and environmental destruction and pollution.[4] A few, like MacArthur fellows Nancy Folbre and Heidi Hartmann, also note that even in the rich United States working parents are stressed because they have too little time to care for their children, and even well-to-do people find it hard to juggle work and family.[5] But even now, when globalization is creating increasing stress for many families, most mainstream economic writings don't pay much attention to how economic models impact our day-to-day lives.[6]

Generally, economists don't write about people's daily lives—except as employers, employees, and consumers. And when they address our environmental and social problems, they're usually still caught in the free markets/privatization versus central planning/government regulation debate that framed the conflict between capitalism and communism.

These discussions ignore the fact that neither capitalist nor communist systems have been able to solve chronic problems such as environmental degradation, poverty, and the violence of war and terrorism that diverts and destroys economic resources and blights so many lives. Indeed, many of these problems have been the result of *both* capitalist and communist economic policies.

To effectively address our problems, we need a different way of looking at economics. In our time of rapidly changing technological and social conditions, we have to go much deeper, to matters that conventional economic analyses and theories have ignored.

There's a common denominator underlying our mounting personal, social, and environmental problems: lack of caring.[7] We need an economic system that takes us beyond communism, capitalism, and other old *isms*. We need economic models, rules, and policies that support caring for ourselves, others, and our Mother Earth.[8]

An economics based on caring may seem unrealistic to some people. Actually, it's much more realistic than the old economic models. Our old models strangely ignore some of the most basic facts about human existence—beginning with the crucial importance of caring and caregiving for all economic activities.

Consider that without caring and caregiving none of us would be here. There would be no households, no workforce, no economy, nothing. Yet most current economic discussions don't even mention caring and caregiving. This too is odd, since *economics* comes from *oikonomia*, which is the Greek word for managing the household— and a core component of households is caring and caregiving.[9]

This book proposes that a radical reformulation of economics is needed for us not only to survive, but to thrive. It shows that the exclusion of caring and caregiving from mainstream economic theory and practice has had, and continues to have, terrible effects on people's quality of life, on our natural life-support systems, and on economic productivity, innovativeness, and adaptability to new conditions. Failing to include caring and caregiving in economic models is totally inappropriate for the postindustrial economy, where the most important capital is what economists like to call *human capital*: people. Moreover, it's not realistic to expect changes in uncaring economic policies and practices unless caring and caregiving are given greater value.

It's not realistic to expect changes in uncaring economic policies and practices unless caring and caregiving are given greater value.

As Einstein remarked, we cannot solve problems with the same thinking that created them. We are at a critical juncture where a new way of thinking about economics is needed.

Giving greater value to caring and caregiving won't cure all our problems. But it is impossible to solve our current global crises, much less advance our personal, economic, and global development, unless we do. If we are to change dysfunctional government policies and business practices, we need a new approach to economics in which supporting caring—or even talking about caring—is no longer taboo.

WHAT *IS* ECONOMICS?

In the fall of 2004, I was invited by the Dag Hammarskjöld Foundation to a meeting to explore the future of economics. The site was the home of my long-time friend and colleague Hazel Henderson, a leading light in the movement toward a new economics. The twenty-five other participants came from Latin America, Europe, Asia, Africa, Australia, and the United States. They included academicians, social activists, and former government officials.

The departure point for our discussions was a critique of the so-called neoclassical economics that is today the dominant, often only, economic analysis taught in Western universities. Deriving from the earlier classical economics developed by Adam Smith, David Ricardo, and other "fathers" of modern capitalist theory, neoclassical economics is primarily concerned with analyzing and predicting how markets function. It relies heavily on mathematical modeling, and this modeling is something of a closed loop, as it is founded on some basic, indeed hallowed, assumptions.

One of these assumptions is that "rational economic man" makes informed economic choices based on rational self-interest. Another assumption is that competition then regulates these self-interested choices in a self-organizing dynamic that ultimately works for the common good. Still another assumption is that governments should keep a hands-off policy when it comes to the operation of markets. This last assumption is a centerpiece of the most recent offshoot of neoclassical theory: the so-called neoliberalism espoused by neoconservatives in the United States and elsewhere, who claim that privatization, market deregulation, and trade unhampered by national borders or interests will cure all our ills.

For a while, the Hammarskjöld Foundation meeting focused on the shortcomings of neoclassical and neoliberal economic theories and models. Some participants argued that these models are out of sync with scientific advancements. They cited the new work of physicists debunking the math of orthodox economic models, pointed out errors in computerized analysis methodology, and argued that these "reductionist" methods produce false pictures of reality. Some pointed to how markets are today heavily manipulated by sophisticated advertising campaigns that create artificial tastes, even artificial needs. Others critiqued the premise that competition regulates the market, pointing out how, all around us, huge corporations gobble up smaller firms through acquisitions and takeovers, or put them out of business by cutting prices until competitors are out of the picture.

The discussion then turned from economic theory to what is actually happening in the world today. Many participants criticized the trend toward privatizing water and other essentials of life and the consolidation of ever more wealth and power in multinational corporations. Others deplored the lack of accountability of globalization agencies such as the International Monetary Fund and the disastrous lack of regard for the destruction of our natural habitat. Still others advocated innovations such as new quality-of-life indicators like the Kingdom of Bhutan's "happiness index," international tribunals on product liability, and new textbooks and classes that would propagate alternative economic perspectives.

But as our discussions progressed, something else gradually became apparent. Despite many common concerns and critiques, there was one area of strong disagreement. This disagreement focused on what the domain of economics is and should be.

Some of the participants were only interested in the narrow band of economic relations in the market economy—just like the conventional economists they critiqued. They were adamantly opposed to economic models that take into account the nonmarket work of caring and caregiving performed primarily in the household and other parts

☐ Two Meanings of Economics

The term economics has both a scholarly and a popular meaning. The academic meaning of economics is as a social science: for example, the branch of social science that deals with the production, distribution, and consumption of goods and services and their management. When used in this sense, the term describes economic theories and economic models. The popular meaning of economics is much broader. It is often used as a shorthand for describing economic systems, policies, and practices: for example, in common phrases such as "U.S. economics and politics." I use the term economics in both its academic and popular sense, depending on the context. ■

of the nonmonetized economy.[10] They began by arguing that this work could not be quantified. When it was pointed out that it can, and actually has been, quantified, they were unified in holding that it shouldn't be.[11] While they noted that flawed economic models make for flawed economic policies, they made it clear that they were not interested in expanding, much less redefining, the domain of economics.

Nonetheless, this expansion and redefinition of economic models is already in progress. Thousands of women and men worldwide have for some time noted the irony of not including the most foundational human work in economic measures and policies. A few years ago, Marilyn Waring wrote a groundbreaking book on the subject.[12] More recently Barbara Brandt, Ann Crittenden, Marianne Ferber, Nancy Folbre, Janet Gornick, Heidi Hartmann, Hazel Henderson, Marcia Meyers, Julie Nelson, Hilkka Pietila, Genevieve Vaughan, and other economic thinkers have focused on the need to make caring visible in economic theory and practice.[13] Nirmala Banerjee, Edgar Cahn, Herman Daly, Devaki Jain, David Korten, Paul Krugman, Amartya Sen, and other pioneering thinkers have also started to insist that we look at economic relations from a broader perspective.[14] Their work, particularly that of Pietila and Henderson, provides the basis for the expanded economic model needed for a caring economics.

THE NEW ECONOMIC MAP

The new economic map includes all six economic sectors:

Core sector: Household economy
Second sector: Unpaid community economy
Third sector: Market economy
Fourth sector: Illegal economy
Fifth sector: Government economy
Sixth sector: Natural economy

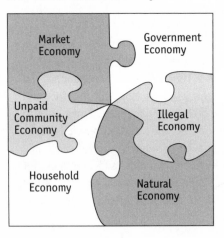

Market Economy

Government Economy

Unpaid Community Economy

Illegal Economy

Household Economy

Natural Economy

A NEW ECONOMIC MAP

To build a new economic model, we must include the *full spectrum* of economic relations—all the way from how humans relate to our natural habitat to intrahousehold economic interactions. This requires a complete and accurate map that includes all economic sectors.

THE OLD ECONOMIC MAP

In the old economic models, the foundational economic sectors—household, unpaid community, and natural—are omitted, which leads to distorted views and policies.

Our challenge is to develop a caring economics where human needs and capacities are nurtured, our natural habitat is conserved, and our great potential for caring and creativity is supported.

This new economic map begins with the household as the *core inner sector.* This sector is the real heart of economic productivity, as it supports and makes possible economic activity in all the other sectors. The household is not, as most economics texts have it, just a unit of consumption. It is, and has always also been, a unit of production. Its most important product is, and always has been, people—and this product is of paramount importance in the postindustrial economy where "high-quality human capital" has become a business mantra.

But no attention is given in conventional economic analyses to what is needed to produce this high-quality human capital: caring and caregiving. (See "The New Economic Map" and "The Old Economic Map").

The *second sector* is the unpaid community economy. This includes volunteers working for charitable and social justice groups in what is today often called civil society, as well as some aspects of the barter and community currency economy (which is growing). Here too caring and caregiving are important activities.

The *third sector* is the market economy. This sector is the focus of conventional economic analyses and indicators. The market is fueled by the first two economic sectors, but its measurements and rules accord them no value. As presently structured, the market economy often tends to discourage rather than encourage caring—even though studies show that when employees feel cared for they are much more creative and productive.

The *fourth sector* is the illegal economy, which includes the drug trade, the sex trade, some of the arms trade, and other economic activities that are in the hands of crime syndicates and gangs. The illegal sector's defining characteristic is lack of caring—not to speak of the killings and other horrors that are its hallmarks.

The *fifth sector* is the government economy: the sector that makes the policies, laws, and rules governing the market economy and provides public services, either directly or by contracting them out to private enterprises. Some of these services entail caring activities; for example, services provided by public health agencies. But in most nations, government policies give little support to the caring and caregiving activities of the household and unpaid community economy on which all economic sectors depend. Present government policies are often also uncaring of the mass of people, channeling funds to the wealthy. And in many nations, including the United States, government policies fail to protect nature from reckless exploitation and pollution.

The *sixth sector* is the natural economy, which like the household, is basic. Our natural environment, too, produces resources out of which the market economy maintains itself. But again, conventional economic models give little value to nature. Consequently, nature is exploited, with increasingly disastrous results as we move to ever more powerful technologies. Caring for Mother Earth is viewed as a liability in the conventional cost-benefit analysis, and until recently was not even an issue in economic theories.

These six economic sectors are in constant interaction. Only by taking all of them into account can we make the changes we need in our world today.

The challenge is to develop economic models, measures, and rules where the first, second, and sixth sectors are recognized and highly valued. This is foundational to a caring economic system where human needs and capacities are nurtured rather than exploited, our natural habitat is conserved rather than destroyed, and our great potential for caring and creativity is supported rather than inhibited.

CULTURE, ECONOMICS, AND VALUES

Economic systems are human creations. They can, and do, change.

During the last five hundred years of Western history, different technological phases gave rise to different economic systems. Gradually, as we shifted from mainly agricultural to primarily industrial technologies, feudalism was replaced by capitalism and in some areas, socialism. Today, we are in the throes of another major technological shift. But the shift taking us from industrial to postindustrial society is different from earlier ones.

Unlike earlier shifts, the shift to postindustrial/nuclear/electronic/ biochemical technologies is not happening over several centuries but over a few decades. Unlike earlier shifts, it is the subject of intense analyses *while* it is happening. Moreover, it is happening globally and is accompanied by growing consciousness that we cannot go on with business as usual, that we face a very uncertain future unless we make fundamental changes.

Historically, the introduction of new technologies has brought some changes in valuations. For example, in a primarily agricultural economy, land was considered the most valuable asset. With the technological shift to a primarily industrial economy, machinery and other capital assets gradually acquired greater value.

But valuations based on technological factors are only a small part of the values side of the economic equation. Much more important, and more resistant to change, are the underlying cultural values and social structures of which economic systems are a part.

Our beliefs about what is or is not valuable are largely unconscious. As we will see, they have been profoundly affected by assumptions we inherited from earlier times when anything associated with the female half of humanity—such as caring and caregiving—was devalued. In our Western world today, the ideal is equality between women and men, and men are increasingly embracing "feminine" activities, like the many fathers now caring for babies and young children in ways once considered inappropriate for "real men." But the failure of most current economic systems to give real value to caring and caregiving, whether in families or in the larger society, continues to lie behind massive economic inequities and dysfunctions.

Indeed, this systemic devaluation of the activities that contribute the most to human welfare and development lies behind a kind of economic insanity. For example, the bulk of caring work is not even included in indicators of economic productivity such as GDP (gross domestic product) and GNP (gross national product).[15]

Nor is that all. Not only is the work of caregiving—without which there would be no workforce—given little support in economic policy when it's done in the home. Work that entails caregiving is paid substandard wages in the market economy.

So in the United States, people think nothing of paying plumbers, the people to whom we entrust our pipes, $50 to $60 per hour. But child care workers, the people to whom we entrust our children, are paid an average of $10 an hour according to the U.S. Department of Labor.[16] And we demand that plumbers have some training, but not that all child care workers have training.

This is not logical. It's pathological. But to change it, we have to look beyond areas traditionally taken into account in economic analyses.

THE VALUE OF CARING

As current economic theory has it, what is valued is a matter of supply and demand, with scarce goods and services more valued than abundant ones. But this ignores two key points. The first, as I will develop in later chapters, is that current economic policies and practices often artificially create scarcities. The second point, to which I will also return, is that demand is largely determined by cultural beliefs about what is and is not valuable.

A much more sensible, and realistic, standard for what is given economic value is what supports and advances human survival and human development. By this standard, a caring orientation—that is, concern for the welfare and development of ourselves, others, and our natural environment—is highly valued. So also is the work of caregiving and the creation of caring environments, whether in homes, businesses, communities, or governments.

This does not mean that all caring and caregiving should be paid in money. As we will see, there are many other ways in which this work can, and must, be recognized and rewarded—from informal community networks where caregiving is exchanged to business and government policies that support and encourage caring and caregiving.

We will look more closely at caring economics in later chapters. Here, I want to clarify that by *caring work* I mean actions based on empathy, responsibility, and concern for human welfare and optimal human development. Moreover, as detailed in "Caring, Caregiving, and a Caring Orientation" below, a caring orientation gives visibility and value to caring and caregiving in all areas of life—from households and communities to businesses and governments.

As we will see in chapter 3, a caring business orientation can actually be more profitable in simple dollars and cents than the old uncaring one. For example, the highly successful software company SAS Institute has been extremely profitable precisely because its policies make

❏ *Caring, Caregiving, and a Caring Orientation*

When I speak of caring and caregiving, I mean activities guided by a caring orientation. A caring orientation not only fulfills human needs and aspirations. It also offers a wholly different approach to business and government policies that is both financially and socially profitable. A caring orientation is not solely a matter of giving visibility and value to the work of caring for children, the sick, and the elderly in households, as essential as this is. It is not only about giving more value to caring work in the market economy, such as child care, teaching, nursing, and caring for people in retirement homes. Nor is it only about being ethical in business and government.

A caring orientation spans the gamut, from caring for children, the sick, and the elderly, to caring for employees, customers, and other business stakeholders, to what Edgar Cahn calls the civic labor of building healthy communities, the social justice labor of progressive social movements, and the environmental labor needed to preserve a healthy natural environment for ourselves and future generations.[17]

A caring orientation is also distinguished by a longer time horizon. In other words, a caring orientation takes into account not only short-term but also long-term considerations. For instance, it takes into account the long-term costs of uncaring environmental policies as compared to the short-term profits they may yield. Or to come back to the example of the plumber and the child care worker, a caring orientation recognizes that the long-term economic impact of properly caring for a child is infinitely greater than that of fixing a pipe—and that this difference must be factored into the economic valuation of these two activities. ■

the welfare of employees a top priority. The same is true of the successful East Coast supermarket chain, Wegmans. Ranked Number 1 on *Fortune's* list of "100 Best Companies to Work For" in 2005, Wegmans states on its website that it offers "a welcoming, caring, diverse workplace that gives all people the opportunity to grow and succeed." Some companies have even incorporated caring into their management training programs, for example, the successful kitchen and bath cabinets manufacturer American Woodmark.

These companies are finding that concern for the welfare of employees and their families translates into increased competence and collaboration, encourages creativity and innovation, contributes to the organization's collective capacity, and transfers into better business relations, internally as well as externally. In short, they are seeing that a caring rather than uncaring orientation is good both for people and for business.

A caring orientation also offers a more effective approach to economic policy—not only in human terms but also in purely financial terms. For example, crime rates and attendant costs would be lowered. And the high-quality human capital needed for a healthy future economy would be assured because child care and education would be fully supported.

To provide just one illustration, in the United States alone, a single measure of caring work in the economy—early childhood development programs—has been proven to provide a 12 percent return on public investment. The North Carolina Abecedarian Project of the National Institute for Early Education found that participants in high-quality early child development programs can expect to earn approximately $143,000 more over their lifetimes than children who did not receive these benefits.[18]

Similarly, the Canadian Healthy Babies, Healthy Children program has been shown to enable children to score higher on most infant development measures. This includes self-help, gross motor skills, fine motor skills, and language development—all important indicators of a higher level of human capacity development. And of course, such programs directly lead to prospects for a brighter future for these children.[19]

Nordic nations such as Finland, Norway, and Sweden have found that investing in caring policies and programs—from universal health care and child care to generous paid parental leave—is an investment in a higher general quality of life, a happier population, and a more efficient, innovative economy. In 2003–04 and 2005–06, Finland was even ahead of the much richer and powerful United States in the World Economic Forum's Global Competitiveness ratings.[20]

These examples illustrate the enormous personal, social, and economic benefits of giving more value to caring and caregiving. They also show that we don't have to start from square one. There is already movement in this direction: policies and programs offer models that can be replicated and adapted worldwide as we move into the postindustrial economy.

◻ *Trends Showing Recognition of the Economic Value of Caring and Caregiving*

- A number of nations have already quantified the value of the unpaid work of caring and caregiving performed in households, and found that its monetary value is very high.

- The U.S. company Salary.com estimated that a fair wage for a typical stay-at-home parent would be $134,471 a year.[21]

- The U.N. Human Development Reports measure the health of communities by looking at maternal and infant mortality, education, the environment, and other factors that were not previously quantified.

- Most industrialized countries provide universal health care as an investment in their human capital.

- Many businesses recognize that valuing and rewarding caring leads to greater competence, effective communication, and successful collaboration.

- Social policies in New Zealand, Canada, and most West European nations recognize the value of caring work through government subsidies for child care (not just tax credits) and paid parental leave.

- Chilean President Michelle Bachelet announced shortly after taking office that a monthly payment of $40, as well as training courses, would be provided to caregivers of bedridden relatives in low-income families.[22] ■

BUILDING A CARING ECONOMICS

We stand at what a 2006 *Time* magazine article on global warming called a tipping point, a juncture in our planet's history when nothing less than fundamental change is needed.[23] As we use the economic measurements detailed in the pages that follow, we see that our global economy is running at a gigantic loss. It becomes evident that we can't continue to exploit and pollute our natural environment. It also becomes evident that to live more fulfilling and less stressful lives, we must adequately value caring and caregiving not only in the market but in all economic sectors, from the household to nature.

We delude ourselves if we think that we can solve our environmental problems by just trying to introduce less polluting technologies or changing consumption patterns. Even if we were successful in these efforts, which is doubtful without going deeper, new crises will erupt unless we make more fundamental changes.

We can make these changes once we become aware that a society's economic structures and rules, its system of values, and its other social institutions are in a continually interactive feedback loop. During periods of social equilibrium, this loop remains relatively stable, and the guiding system of values is so taken for granted that it's largely invisible. But during periods of great instability or disequilibrium such as ours, it is possible to more clearly see the system's underlying organizational structure and operant values. Hence, today, fundamental changes—changes that transform the system rather than simply modify it to some degree—are possible.

To construct a caring economics—and here I use the term economics in its popular sense as a shorthand for describing economic systems—we must focus not only on economic theory and practice but also on cultural values and social institutions. We can begin with three basic questions:

- First, to what kinds of qualities, activities, services, and goods do we want to give high or low economic value?

- Second, can we realistically expect the advantages of more socially and environmentally caring government policies and business practices as long as caring is not valued and rewarded?

- Third, what kinds of economic inventions do we need for the construction of a more caring, effective, innovative, and sustainable economic system?

All economic institutions are economic inventions—from banks, stock exchanges, Social Security, and health care programs to colonialism, sweatshops, and child labor. Unemployment insurance and parental leave are economic inventions designed to better care for the welfare of all members of the group. Slavery and forced labor camps are also economic interventions. But like sweatshops, colonialism, and child labor, these are economic inventions designed to more effectively exploit certain members of the group, even, if "necessary," to kill them.

In other words, an economic invention is a way of utilizing and allocating natural, human, and human-made resources. But the shape it takes—and the consequences it has—depend on the governing system of values and the social institutions it supports.

In our time, when high technology guided by values such as conquest, exploitation, and domination threaten our very survival, we need economic inventions driven by an ethos of caring. We need a caring revolution.

It's up to us to determine which existing economic inventions we want to retain, and which we want to discard. We must also develop new economic indicators, rules, policies, and practices guided by values appropriate for the more equitable and sustainable future we want and need. Above all, we must change the imbalanced cultural foundations on which both capitalist and communist economic systems were built, and move toward an economic system where the most essential human work—the work of caring and caregiving—is given real value.

A caring economics supports caring and caregiving on the individual, organizational, social, and environmental levels. It takes into account the full range of human needs, not only our material needs for food and shelter but also our needs for meaningful work and meaningful lives.

THE SIX FOUNDATIONS
FOR A CARING ECONOMICS

As detailed in the sidebar on pages 22–23, a caring economics has six foundations: a full-spectrum economic map; cultural beliefs and institutions that value caring and caregiving; caring economic rules, policies, and practices; inclusive and accurate economic indicators; partnership economic and social structures; and an economic theory I call *partnerism* because it incorporates the partnership elements of both capitalism and socialism but goes beyond them to recognize the essential economic value of caring for ourselves, others, and nature.

The shift to a caring economics will take time, and it won't happen all at once. It will move in increments, with advances in any one area setting in motion ripples of change in all the others. Changes in beliefs about what is or is not economically productive will lead to new ways of thinking about economics, and from this to more accurate economic indicators. These changes in beliefs and indicators will spur move-

⬛ What We Can Do: Building Six Foundations for a Caring Economic System

Progress in building any one of these foundations will set in motion progress in all the others in an interactive dynamic of change.

- *Foundation 1: A Full-Spectrum Economic Map:* A full-spectrum economic map includes the household economy, the unpaid community economy, the market economy, the illegal economy, the government economy, and the natural economy. This more accurate and inclusive map for economics is introduced in this chapter.

- *Foundation 2: Cultural Beliefs and Institutions That Value Caring and Caregiving:* Beliefs and institutions orient to the partnership system rather than the domination system, and include a shift from dominator to partnership relations in the formative parent-child and gender relations. The configurations of the Partnership System and the Domination System are introduced in chapter 2.

- *Foundation 3: Caring Economic Rules, Policies, and Practices:* Government and business rules, policies, and practices encourage and reward caring and caregiving; meet basic human needs, both material needs and needs for human development; direct technological breakthroughs to life-sustaining applications; and consider effects on future generations. Chapter 3 describes these rules, policies, and practices, showing their enormous business and social benefits.

- *Foundation 4: Inclusive and Accurate Economic Indicators:* Indicators include the life-sustaining activities traditionally performed by women in households and other parts of the nonmonetized economy, as well as the life-sustaining processes of nature, and do not include activities that harm us and our natural environment. Chapter 4

ment toward more caring policies and practices, which in turn will lead to more partnership-oriented economic and social structures. And all this will support further movement to a full-spectrum economic map, more inclusive economic theories and indicators, and cultural beliefs and institutions that value caring andcaregiving.

In other words, progress in any one area drives progress in others. So the more we do to advance change in any one area, the sooner we will see a shift in the whole economic system.

---

describes new economic indicators that include the life-sustaining activities of households, communities, and nature.

- *Foundation 5: Partnership Economic and Social Structures:* More equitable and participatory structures support relations of mutual benefit, responsibility, and accountability rather than the concentration of economic assets and power at the top. Chapter 5 contrasts partnership and domination economic and social structures, showing how these affect all aspects of our lives.

- *Foundation 6: An Evolving Economic Theory of Partnerism:* Economic theory incorporates the partnership elements of both capitalism and socialism, but goes beyond them to recognize the essential economic value of caring for ourselves, others, and nature. Chapter 7 introduces the concept of partnerism. ■

CARING ECONOMICS

MAP	CULTURE	RULES	INDICATORS	STRUCTURE	THEORY
MAP full spectrum economic map	CULTURE cultural beliefs and institutions that value and support caring and caregiving	RULES caring economic rules, policies, and practices	INDICATORS inclusive and accurate economic indicators	STRUCTURE partnership economic and social structures	THEORY an evolving economic theory of partnerism

The first step is changing the conversation about economics to include the term *caring* and raising awareness of the economic importance of caregiving. This is something every one of us can do.

The failure of present economic theories and policies to recognize that caring and caregiving are integral to personal, economic, ecological, and social health directly affects our lives and our children's future. It has saddled us with dysfunctional economic models and measures, which in turn have led to dysfunctional policies and practices. These policies and practices are major factors behind seemingly insoluble global problems such as poverty, overpopulation, and environmental devastation. They are obstacles to success in the postindustrial economy, where, more than money, markets, or super-computerized office equipment, human capital is the most important capital. And they have perpetuated an imbalanced and unhealthy system of values.

> *In our time, when high technology guided by values such as conquest, exploitation, and domination threaten our very survival, we need economic inventions driven by an ethos of caring.* We need a caring revolution.

The alternative seems obvious once we step aside from what we've been taught to focus on in economics and look at what we value most in our own homes and lives. It then is evident that without bringing equity and value to the work of caring and caregiving, we can't realistically expect more caring, peaceful, environmentally healthy, and just societies in which people live meaningful, creative, and fulfilling lives.

This isn't a matter of theory. It's a matter of immense practical, day-to-day impact on everything—from our families and the education of our children, to our work and business lives, and ultimately to our species' survival.

Globalization and the shift to the postindustrial age are bringing great economic and social dislocation. This dislocation is a source of fear for many people. But it also offers an unprecedented opening for new and better ways of thinking and living. It offers us the opportunity to use our vision and ingenuity to help create the social and economic conditions that support our evolution as individuals, as a species, and as a planet.

The chapters that follow point the way to a way of living and making a living that meets human needs and aspirations and preserves the beauty and bounty of our planet.

CHAPTER 2

Economics Through a Wider Lens

Today, millions of people no longer accept suffering and injustice as just God's will or the result of mysterious, unalterable, economic laws. All over the world, people are alarmed about the health and environmental effects of industrialization seemingly run amok. They're concerned about trade globalization rules that are lowering wages and worker protections earlier taken for granted in the West. They're aware that half the world still lives in poverty and hunger, and that even in the wealthy United States the gap between rich and poor is growing. They recognize that there's something very wrong with cutting funds for school lunches for millions of poor children while corporations get million-dollar subsidies and the super-rich get big tax refunds. They demand an end to accounting practices that enable corporate officers to enrich themselves at the expense of employee benefit plans and shareholder investments. In short, they decry uncaring economic policies and business practices, and want more caring ones.

The bad news is that efforts to move economic systems in a more caring direction have only succeeded in a few places and utterly failed in many others. Despite rhetoric about "compassionate conservatism," in the United States, economic policies have been moving backward rather than forward. Economic elites in both developed and developing nations still control the bulk of the world's resources, children still go hungry even in wealthy nations, and unprecedented threats to our natural habitat such as global warming are still often ignored.

The good news is that a multitude of nongovernmental organizations are somewhat softening the hardships caused by present policies, and there are some attempts to bring about structural change. A socially responsible business movement is working to institute new rules for corporations that require social and ecological accountability. There are attempts to replace economic indicators such as gross domestic product (GDP) with Quality of Life (QL) measurements that more accurately reflect what activities contribute to human well-being and environmental sustainability. There is movement to protect our natural environment, combat sweatshop labor, and develop standards for international treaties that protect workers worldwide.

All these are important efforts to remedy specific defects in present economic policies and practices. But we need more. We need a systemic approach that takes into account the larger system of which economics is a part.[1]

THE SOCIAL FOUNDATIONS OF ECONOMICS

Economic systems don't spring up in a vacuum. They emerge out of a larger social, cultural, and technological context. Only by understanding, and changing, this larger context can we build the foundations for a new economic system that accomplishes what an effective economic system should: supporting human well-being, advancing human development, and protecting nature's life-support systems for our children and future generations.

Strange as it may sound, we can't just focus on economics to change economic systems. We have to go deeper and further.

We *can* move beyond inefficient, inequitable, environmentally destructive economic practices. But to do this we have to look at the social factors that shape economics, and are in turned shaped by economics. In other words, we cannot understand, much less improve, economic systems without also looking at their larger context: the psychological and social dynamics of relations in all spheres of life.

Economic systems are about a form of human relations. It isn't the goods that relate, it's the people. Therefore, people, and the activities that support and enhance human life and human relationships, need to be the focus of economic analyses.

Relationships define our lives. They are the foundation for all social institutions, from the family and education to politics and economics.

As I mentioned in the Introduction, the new analysis of economics introduced in this book grows out of my multidisciplinary research applying the perspective of evolutionary systems science, chaos theory, complexity theory, and other new approaches to the study of social systems. This was the research that led to my book *The Chalice and The Blade: Our History, Our Future,* which introduced a nonlinear approach to the study of human history to get at the heart of what drives us forward or backward in cultural evolution.[2] It also led to other books, where I analyzed sex and power from this perspective.[3] And with this book, I have set out to apply this research to economics, completing the cycle of reexamining sex, power, and money—which are said to make our world go round.

> *Strange as it may sound, we can't just focus on economics to change economic systems.*

In examining economics from the new perspective of evolutionary systems science, I am drawing on what seems to me the best work in the field of economics. I am not an economist by training, as my formal schooling has been in sociology, anthropology, and law. This makes me an outsider, a fact that has both advantages and disadvantages. The advantage is that it makes it possible to look at economics with fewer preconceived ideas—which is why many advances in different fields have come from outsiders.

What I bring is an approach that draws on several disciplinary streams, a research method that is gaining currency because to effectively address the real needs of our complex world we have to bring together knowledge from many areas. This broader analysis examines matters not considered by most mainstream economists, including cultural beliefs and social institutions that on the surface seem unrelated to economics. It pays special attention to beliefs about what is and is not valuable. It looks at relationships, at women and men, families and work, technology, politics, and all the many other threads that together form the living economy of our interconnected and increasingly threatened planet. Indeed, it takes into account areas completely alien to conventional economic analyses: the early parent-child relations and the relations between the female and male halves of humanity that profoundly affect people's values and interactions, including economic ones. And it looks at all these areas through the new lens of the *partnership*, or mutual respect, system and the *domination*, or top-down control, system as two basic social categories.

The analytical lenses of earlier social categories—right versus left, religious versus secular, Eastern versus Western, industrial versus pre- or postindustrial—only focus on particular aspects of social systems, such as technological development, location, or ideology. This makes a truly systemic analysis impossible.

By contrast, the partnership system and the domination system describe the *totality* of a society's beliefs and institutions—from the family, education, and religion to politics and economics. In other words, they describe larger social configurations that cannot be seen through the narrow lenses of older categories.

As psychologist Robert Ornstein writes in *The Psychology of Consciousness*, if we don't have categories for phenomena, it's hard to perceive them. "Language," he writes, "provides an almost unconsciously agreed on set of categories for experience, and allows the speakers of that language to ignore experiences excluded by the common category system."[4]

To bring about systemic change, we need categories that don't leave out critical parts of society. The partnership and domination systems provide these categories. They describe a society's core values and institutions, both in the so-called private sphere of our family and other intimate relations and in the public sphere of local, national, and international communities. Most important, these social categories identify what values and institutions support or inhibit two very different kinds of relations in all spheres of life—including the sphere of economics.

THE DOMINATION SYSTEM
AND THE PARTNERSHIP SYSTEM

In the *domination system*, there are only two alternatives for relations: dominating or being dominated. Those on top control those below them—be it in families, workplaces, or society at large. Economic policies and practices in this system are designed to benefit those on top at the expense of those on the bottom. Trust is scarce and tension is high, as the whole system is largely held together by fear and force.

To maintain rankings of domination, caring and empathy have to be suppressed and devalued, beginning in families and from there to economics and politics. This is why one of the foundations for a caring economics consists of beliefs and institutions that orient more to the partnership system.

The *partnership system* supports mutually respectful and caring relations. There are still hierarchies, as there must be to get things done. But in these hierarchies, which I call *hierarchies of actualization* rather than *hierarchies of domination*, accountability and respect flow both ways rather than just from the bottom up, and social and economic structures are set up so that there is input from all levels. Leaders and managers facilitate, inspire, and empower rather than control and disempower. Economic policies and practices in this system are designed to support our basic survival needs and our needs for community, creativity, meaning, and caring—in other words, the realization of our highest human potentials.

No society is a pure partnership or domination system. It is always a matter of degree. But as we will see, in the Nordic nations, which orient more closely to the partnership system, the general quality of life is far higher than in nations that orient more to the domination side of the continuum.[5] And not coincidentally, Nordic nations are noted for policies that give caring and caregiving visibility and value.

There are partnership elements in existing economic models. But many of our global problems are due to the fact that to a large extent the orientation of both capitalist and communist economies has been to the domination system.[6]

Although there are major differences between capitalist and communist economies, in both cases natural resources and the means of production have largely been controlled by those on top. In Soviet-style communism, top-down control was exercised through fear and force by the political establishment as well as through large state-owned corporations controlled by the government. In present U.S.–style capitalism, large corporations and the government also work in tandem. Through campaign contributions, powerful lobbies, and other means, corporations wield enormous influence over the government, and hence over economic policies and practices.

This top-down control was also characteristic of earlier feudal and monarchic times when the domination system was even more firmly in place. Indeed, many basic assumptions behind present economic policies and practices are our legacy from times when kings ruled over "subjects" and talk of freedom and equality would have been a sure ticket to the most horrible public torture and execution.[7] These were times we only left behind relatively recently, and then not completely, and certainly not everywhere: times when autocratic fathers ruled in the family and autocratic nobles and kings ruled city-states, fiefdoms, and nations.

One assumption we inherited from these more rigid dominator societies, with their large underclass of slaves, serfs, and later almost

---

⊡ The Problems of Capitalism and Socialism

Neither capitalism nor socialism has succeeded in conserving and protecting nature's life-support systems, largely because both are still caught up in the dominator "conquest of nature" and have given little value to environmental housekeeping. Capitalism spawned massive environmental pollution and deterioration, and even now giant corporations fight environmental regulations as unwarranted interference with free markets. Socialism, as implemented in the former Soviet Union and communist China, also led to environmental pollution and deterioration, as exemplified in the destruction of Lake Aral and the Chernobyl nuclear disaster in the Soviet Union, and the fact that 70 percent of China's rivers and lakes are polluted.[8]

Both capitalism and communism have promoted rather than prevented wars, a form of conflict resolution inherent in domination systems. The conflict between nations with these two economic systems led to the Korean and Vietnam Wars, and even after the end of the Cold War, both capitalist and communist nations have manufactured, used, and exported ever more destructive and expensive weaponry, fueling violence worldwide.

Communism did alleviate extreme poverty, but at the cost of severely curtailed civil rights and freedoms. While capitalism raised the standard of living for many people and adopted some "economic safety nets," such as unemployment insurance and Social Security, it hasn't solved the problem of global poverty. Indeed, it has sometimes exacerbated it—with report after report showing that the globalization of capitalism is actually widening the gap between haves and have-nots in both the developed and developing worlds.[9] ∎

destitute factory workers, is that the main motivations for work are fear of pain and scarcity. Indeed, a still popular definition of economics is that it is the social science that studies the allocation of scarce resources to satisfy unlimited wants.[10]

This definition is based on two assumptions: that scarcity is inevitable and that human beings are inherently greedy and hence have unlimited wants and demands. However, what this definition describes is not economics per se, but economics in a domination system.

Although sometimes scarcity is caused by natural conditions, as we will see, dominator economic systems artificially create and perpetuate scarcity—and with this, pain and fear. They do this through misdistribution of resources to those on top, heavy investment in armaments, lack of investment in meeting human needs, ruthless exploitation of nature, and waste of natural and human resources from wars and other forms of violence—all of which are inherent in the domination system.

Moreover, because domination systems make it hard to meet basic human needs—including our needs to be valued, to be cared for, to be loved, to be recognized, and to feel that our lives have meaning and purpose—it's hard for people to feel satisfied. So greed and a sense of needing ever more material goods and status are also artificially produced by the domination system. And this sense of never having enough is today further fueled by advertising campaigns that create artificial, even harmful, needs and demands.

So when we consider the impact of artificial scarcities and artificial needs and demands, we get a very different picture of supply and demand than the one presented in conventional economic analyses. We see that what is or is not valued in the market is often distorted by dominator dynamics that get in the way of meeting authentic human needs.

An enemy mentality and mistrust of others, except those in positions of dominance who are to be unconditionally respected and obeyed, is also basic to domination systems, and hence to dominator economics. The belief that human beings are essentially evil and selfish—and hence the necessity for their strict control through hierarchies of domination—is a cornerstone of dominator mythology. It's embedded in religious ideas of "original sin" and sociobiological theories about "selfish genes."

This view of human nature is integral to popular free market capitalist theories, which are based on the premise that if each person acts only in their own selfish interest the result will be an economic system that benefits all. Of course, nobody would think of telling a child that if we're all selfish everything will turn out fine. Yet this notion continues to be propagated—maintaining *not* a free market (which cannot exist under such circumstances) but the idealization of greed that helps fuel dominator economic systems.

> *When we consider the impact of artificial scarcities and artificial needs and demands, we get a very different picture of supply and demand than the one presented in conventional economic analyses.*

Still another basic premise we've inherited is that "soft" qualities and activities such as nonviolence and nurturing are inappropriate for social and economic governance. Part of this legacy is the belief that caring and caregiving are impediments to productivity, or at best irrelevant to economics. In other words, rather than inheriting cultural beliefs and institutions that support caring and caregiving, we have inherited the opposite. And this has led to many unrealistic, and increasingly dangerous, economic theories, rules, measures, and practices.

◻ *Dominator Economic Assumptions*

- The main motivations for work are fear of pain and scarcity.
- People cannot be trusted.
- "Soft" qualities and activities are inappropriate for social and economic governance.
- Caring and caregiving are impediments to productivity, or at best irrelevant to economics.
- Selfishness will lead to the greater good of all. ∎

THE HIDDEN VALUATIONS

We would all be dead if it weren't for the work of caring for children, the elderly, and the sick. We would be in very bad shape if our day-to-day needs for food, clean clothes, and a habitable place to live weren't cared for. There wouldn't even be a labor force to go to their jobs or businesses if it weren't for the work of caregiving.

So why has the essential work of caring and caregiving been given so little economic value? Why has caring in business been systematically discouraged, as in the old commercial motto of *caveat emptor* (buyer beware)? Why are people who work tirelessly for a more caring and just society often disparaged as do-gooders and bleeding hearts? And why are the women, and increasingly men, who work long hours caring for children, the sick, and the elderly in the non-monetized economy of households and communities still labeled "economically inactive?"

The devaluation of the caring work without which we could not survive—and with it, the devaluation of caring itself—has nothing to do with logic. It has everything to do with our inheritance from a time when our society oriented far more closely to the domination system: a social and economic organization based on rigid top-down rankings of domination ultimately backed up by fear and force.

As we will see in chapter 4, a mainstay of this top-down system is the ranking of the male half of humanity over the female half. This ranking has led to the automatic valuing of men and the stereotypically "masculine" over women and the stereotypically "feminine." In other words, with the subordination of women to men, anything associated with "real masculinity" was given higher value than anything stereotypically associated with women and femininity, including the so-called women's work of caring and caregiving. This system of valuations is reflected in economic systems—tribal, feudal, capitalist, communist—that give little or no value to the work of caring and caregiving.

Stereotypes of masculinity and femininity should not be confused with anything to do with innate male or female traits. Women can do "men's work," be it as welders, politicians, or priests, and sometimes do it better than men. Men can do the "women's work" of caring for children, and sometimes do it better than women. That so many men and women are today rejecting old stereotypes is a testimony to their wish, and capacity, for less constricted gender roles.

But according to the belief system we inherited, caring and caregiving are unfit for "real men." This work is supposed to be done by women for free in male-controlled households. It is "soft" work that has no visibility and is given no real economic value. And this profoundly affects not only the roles and relations of individual women and men, but our economic system.

Some people may find it strange to speak of economics and gender in the same breath. Indeed, some people think that any questioning of traditional gender roles and relations violates what's natural for women and men—and is thus beyond the pale of discussion. Yet this very avoidance of gender issues should give us pause.

As the sociologist Louis Wirth pointed out, the most important things about a society are those that are seldom talked about. Not long ago, racial superiority was so taken for granted it was rarely talked about. Even now, some people don't like to talk about racial inequality, much less acknowledge that it's not "natural." So the fact that talking about gender inequality feels uncomfortable, and that its existence is often denied or considered "natural," is a signal that we're dealing with something very important.

The devaluing of traits and activities stereotypically associated with women is a hidden system of valuations that is integral to domination systems. It is deeply embedded in the economic rules and models that came out of earlier times that oriented more closely to such systems. And current economic indicators reflect and perpetuate this devaluation.

What is or is not included in economic indicators directly affects what policymakers consider or don't consider. So our hidden system of gendered values has shaped economic policies.

This unrecognized system of values is like the invisible mass of an iceberg. It is a massive obstacle to a saner, more effective, and more humane economics.

THE IMPERATIVE FOR SYSTEMIC CHANGE

Most conventional economic policies and measures still bear a strong dominator stamp. They are based on an incomplete model of economics that only takes into account three of the six sectors that form

❑ *What Do Mainstream Economic Indicators Leave Out?*

Mainstream economic indicators such as the GNP (gross national product) and GDP (gross domestic product) leave out all activities that are not monetized and/or not reported for official records—a huge segment of every nation's economic activity. GNP and GDP also provide no information about how goods and services (including such basics as food, health care, and education) are distributed and how this impacts people's lives. Not only that, most mainstream productivity indicators include activities that actually worsen, rather than improve, the quality of life, because they fail to take into account environmental, health, and other costs of market activities.

So unrealistic are these measures that instead of providing a full-cost accounting that shows the environmental and economic costs of uncaring economic habits, measures like GDP and GNP make these costs look like economic profits. For example, the costs of cleaning up the damage from toxic industrial spills are included in indicators of economic productivity, rather than subtracted from them.

Recognition of these problems led to a search for new economic measurements. One of the earliest results of this search was the Physical Quality of Life Index, or PQLI, developed in the 1960s by the Society for International Development.[11] More recently, the United Nations began to issue Human Development Reports, which were over the years expanded to monitor human rights violations, environmental problems, and, particularly in 1995, the status of women.[12]

The newest trend in economic measurements addresses another major inadequacy of the GDP and GNP approach: their failure to include as "economically productive" the socially essential work of caring and caregiving still primarily performed by women in homes and as volunteers.[13]

For example, there is now a satellite account in the U.N. System of National Accounts, or SNA (an international standard for national income accounting), that includes statistical data on household and other unpaid work. In addition, a growing number of nations have been quantifying the economic contribution of this work. A 2004 Swiss government survey reported the value of unpaid work at 162 billion Euros or $190 billion—70 percent of the reported Swiss GDP.[14] ▪

the total economy—and then, only the three in which caring and caregiving are given little or no value. They largely focus on the formal market economy, and fail to take into account in their measurements and policies the three sectors that constitute our basic life-support systems: the household economy, the unpaid community economy, and the natural economy, all of which are essential for human survival and welfare.

By contrast, an economy embedded in the partnership system rests on the six foundations we looked at in chapter 1. It is based on a full-spectrum economic map that takes into account all six economic sectors, including the household economy, the unpaid community economy, and the natural economy. It is supported by cultural beliefs and institutions that value caring and caregiving. Its economic theories, policies, and practices encourage rather than discourage these essential activities; its economic indicators are more accurate and inclusive; and its structures are more equitable.

The problem, and it is a huge problem, is that conventional economic policies and practices are not sustainable. They have led to massive global problems that cannot be solved within the system that created them.

Scientists warn us that unless we make radical changes in practices and policies that are accelerating global warming, by the end of this century floods will engulf the world's coastal cities—including New York, Miami, and London. They also warn that the economic costs of these disasters could bankrupt the world economy.[15] Yet to date there have only been minor changes in the old economic policies and practices based on the not-so-long-ago idealized "conquest of nature."

Trends in hunger and poverty also show that fundamental change is essential. Even for eleven of fifteen industrialized nations—including the United States—the percentage of children living in low-income households has risen during the last decade.[16] In the United States in 2004, this was nearly fourteen million children.[17] As reported by the U.S. National Council on the Aging, the number of seniors who suffer from hunger in the United States is also growing.[18] All this in the world's most bountiful food-producing country. According to the report *Household Food Security in the United States, 2004*, 38.2 million Americans now live in households that suffer from hunger and food insecurity—an increase of 43 percent since 1999.[19] Yet because caring policies are still often associated with what is disparagingly called a "nanny state," during this same period the U.S. government radically cut social services for the most vulnerable: children, women, and the elderly.

In the developing world, millions of people have even less access to essentials such as food, health care, and water. Yet due to structural adjustment and privatization programs required by the International Monetary Fund and other international agencies, here too services that ensure people are cared for have been slashed. In developing nations to which corporations have been exporting jobs, working conditions in sweatshops are often even more miserable than they were in the "developed" world during the days of nineteenth- and early twentieth-century robber-baron capitalism. And as is characteristic of the domination system, elites in these nations continue to sock away fortunes at the same time that their people barely manage to survive, and all too often don't.

Even in the United States, real wages as adjusted for inflation have been falling rather than rising for the majority of workers over the last decade, while pay for corporate executives has skyrocketed to astronomical sums.[20]

The exponential growth of world population is also aggravated by existing policies. The already immense present world population of 6.5 billion will grow to more than 9 billion in less than fifty years— with over 90 percent of this growth in the poorest world regions where every day thousands of children (as well as women and men) die of starvation and violence. This, plus a huge surplus of unemployed young people, makes a more equitable, peaceful, and sustainable future impossible unless there are radical changes in economic policies.

Yet in keeping with the dominator requirement that women be denied reproductive freedom, U.S. funding for international family planning has been severely retrenched. This has been done on the pretext of reducing abortions, when in fact abortions cannot be reduced without family planning.[21] All this makes a significant decrease in population growth extremely problematic.

Equally problematic is the future of work itself. Many people in the United States have lost well-paying jobs because of the export of manufacturing and high-technology jobs to poorer regions. There has also been increasing polarization of jobs. On one end are the high-paying and high-status positions of corporate executive, technocrat, and upper-echelon service professions such as law, medicine, and higher education. On the other end are the low-paying, often menial, jobs for the rest of the population—if these are available at all.

Even beyond this, looming ever more closely, is the structural unemployment due to increasing automation. In wealthier nations, employment formerly provided by industrial technologies—from the jobs of factory assembly workers, receptionists, and telephone opera-

□ Who Owns America?

In the United States, the top 1 percent of the population owns 40 percent of the nation's financial wealth. The top 10 percent owns 85 to 90 percent of stocks, bonds, trust funds, and business equities, and over 75 percent of non-home real estate. As University of California Professor

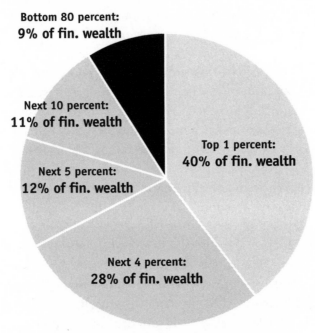

FINANCIAL WEALTH DISTRIBUTION, 2001[23]

tors to those of middle managers—are being phased out. And lying ahead is what will happen to jobs in both the developed and developing world when we move more to robotics, artificial intelligence, and other forms of technologically sophisticated automation.

For some time now, we've been seeing symptoms of massive unrest in both the developing and developed worlds as the young enter a severely constricted job market in a rapidly changing, unstable world. In developing countries, leaders of so-called fundamentalist religious groups preach the old dominator in-group-versus-out-group hatred,

G. William Domhoff notes, "Since financial wealth is what counts as far as the control of income-producing assets, we can say that just 10 percent of the people own the United States of America." By comparison, the bottom 80 percent own only 9 percent of financial wealth, and a large number of Americans have zero assets or even negative wealth due to debt.[22] ▪

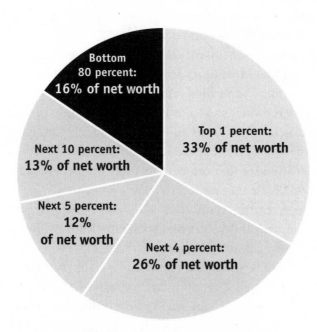

NET WORTH DISTRIBUTION, 2001[24]

using terror to achieve their ends. In the United States, fundamentalism is also on the rise, and blue-collar hate groups blame immigrants,
Jews, blacks, gays, and sometimes women for all their ills. In Europe,
their skinhead ideological relatives plant bombs and likewise scape-
goat those perceived as most powerless. In short, as part of the current dominator regression, demagogic leaders are increasingly
directing people's fear and frustration into scapegoating and violence,
causing untold misery and creating ever more unstable conditions for
business worldwide.[25]

To effectively address these problems requires a systemic
approach that takes into account not only economic policies but
also social institutions and cultural traditions. It requires an
approach that recognizes, and changes, the distorted system of values, and hence economic priorities, that is our invisible legacy from
earlier, more rigid dominator societies.

PRACTICAL STEPS TO A CARING ECONOMICS

If we look at our current fiscal priorities, we see that policymakers
always seem to find money for control and domination—for prisons,
weapons, wars. But we're told there's no money for caring and caregiving—for "feminine" activities, such as caring for children and people's health, for nonviolence and peace.

This imbalanced system of values is deeply entrenched in our
unconscious minds. Most of us aren't even aware that much of what
we value or devalue—and thus our economic system—is based on a
system of gendered values. As a result, the devaluation of caring—and
its real-life consequences for us all—remains largely unrecognized.

What we need isn't more tinkering with old economic models. We
need a new economics that can help us meet the personal, social, and
environmental challenges we face: a *caring economics*.

Shifting to a caring economics will take time. It will require
changes in both cultural values and social institutions. But if enough
of us become engaged, it will happen.

Changes in beliefs, practices, and policies happen through human
agency. Some of us can directly influence what happens in our own
communities. Most of us can wield some influence through civic,
professional, and political organizations by urging them to include
caring economics in their resolutions and agendas. A few of us can

directly influence national and international policies. And all of us can spread awareness of the dysfunctional values embedded in current economic models, and use the proposals in this book and our own ingenuity and initiative to talk or write about what needs to be done.

An essential step toward a caring economics is developing a more accurate system of economic bookkeeping. We need economic indicators that include in assessments of economic productivity the value of caring and caregiving as well as the costs of not valuing them.[26] These indicators would naturally flow from the first principle of a caring economics: a full-spectrum economic map that includes the household, unpaid community, and natural economic sectors.

◘ Seven Steps Toward a Caring Economics

Effectively dealing with our mounting global problems calls for fundamental changes, including key changes in economic measurements, institutions, and rules. This will take time, but every action, no matter how small, sets in motion ripples of change. Here are seven examples of steps we can promote, if only by talking or writing about them:

1. *Recognize how the cultural devaluation of caring and caregiving has negatively affected economic theories, policies, and practices.*

2. *Support the shift from dominator to partnership cultural values and economic and social structures.*

3. *Change economic indicators to give value to caring and caregiving.*

4. *Create economic inventions that support and reward caring and caregiving.*

5. *Expand the economic vocabulary to include caring, teach caring economics in business and economics schools, and conduct gender-specific economic research.*

6. *Educate children and adults about the importance of caring and caregiving.*

7. *Show government and business leaders the benefits of policies that support caring and caregiving, and work for their adoption.* ▪

Changing our economic models and measurements paves the way for another important step: developing economic inventions that adequately value caring and caregiving. This, as we have been examining, in turn requires attention to the second foundation for a caring economic system: shifting cultural beliefs and social institutions so that they value, rather than devalue, caring and caregiving.

Many of our values and social and economic structures are our inheritance from times that oriented more closely to the domination system. This legacy is a major obstacle to a more equitable and sustainable economic system. Once we become aware of this problem, we can work for government and business policies that support partnership rather than dominator values and structures.

We need a market economy that gives greater value to the caring professions such as nursing, child care, and elder care, which are essential for a healthy society and economy. The devaluation of these professions is not, as is sometimes argued, just a function of supply and demand. It is primarily a function of the cultural devaluation of anything stereotypically associated with women and femininity, and, as we will see in succeeding chapters, adversely affects all of us.

Due to less rigid gender stereotypes, many men are today also interested in doing caring work, but they're discouraged by the low wages and status it's accorded. A key example here is work in child care centers. There is also the work of counselors; nursery school, kindergarten, and primary school teachers; and others dealing with both children and their parents. We also need a battery of economic inventions that recognize the value of the socially indispensable work of caring and caregiving in the nonmarket economy. We need fiscal policies that invest in these essential activities—an investment that should be amortized like other investments, rather than added to national budgets as an expense. We must also change business rules so they encourage, rather than impede, caring and caregiving.

We need government programs to ensure that women and men train and prepare themselves to effectively care for children. This training, drawing from what we today know about the kind of child care that supports or inhibits healthy development, is essential, if only in light of all the scientific evidence showing how critical the early years are in the production of high-quality human capital.

In a time when many U.S. jobs are being phased out by both automation and outsourcing to other nations, what makes sense is not just paying people for doing nothing, as has been proposed by some economists.[27] What makes sense are government stipends that not only support caring and caregiving but also training for caring and caregiving. These essential life skills are now becoming even more necessary to adequately care for our growing aging population.

Expanding the economic vocabulary to include caring is still another important step toward a caring economics. Also important is teaching caring economics in business and economics schools and conducting gender-specific economic research.

In addition, the importance of caring and caregiving should be communicated through education, starting early on. Early training in the caring arts also needs to be a central focus of schooling.[28] This will serve multiple purposes—from helping to prevent teen delinquency and pregnancy to promoting teamwork, mutual support, and equity.

One of the Nordic nations, Finland, is a good example, demonstrating the benefits of partnership education. It ranks way ahead of the United States in international ratings of high school literacy and math. But the Finns don't just invest in the old ways of educating children; they are developing a new quality of education. At the heart of this concept is individual attention to children—caring for the young—and the early development of self-learning. Older schoolmates care for younger ones, students can pursue their own interests, teachers facilitate rather than control. All this means moving toward a new partnership structure for the national educational system.

There is consensus that our educational system must change to ensure we have the quality of human capital needed for the postindustrial economy. But only with greater value placed on caring and caregiving can the high-quality human capital needed for the postindustrial economy be assured, because only then will effective caregiving and education be fully supported.

We can, and must, show government and business leaders the benefits of policies that support caring and caregiving. And we all can, and must, join in building a more caring economic and social system.

In human terms, the benefits of recognizing the value of caring and caregiving are incalculable. But not only will a caring economics help us meet human needs and enhance our lives; as the next chapter details, a caring economics is more effective in purely monetary terms.

⬛ *Meeting Human Needs: Caring versus Uncaring Economics*

A caring economics can meet the following basic human needs:

Individual. Need for material sustenance and meaningful work and lives

Organizational. Need for competent and creative people

Social. Need for caring values and policies

Environmental. Need for natural resources protection

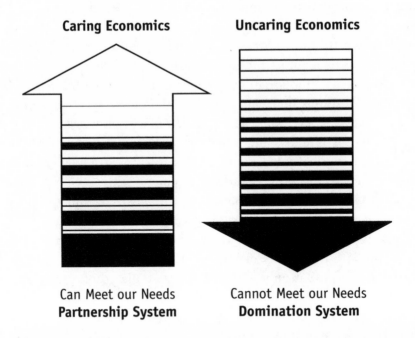

Caring Economics	Uncaring Economics
Can Meet our Needs	Cannot Meet our Needs
Partnership System	**Domination System**

In the old economic models, caring is considered irrelevant to a well functioning economy, or even an obstacle to economic success. In reality, the opposite is true. ■

CHAPTER 3

It Pays to Care—in Dollars and Cents

▙ The SAS Institute, the world's largest privately held software company, is a highly successful business. It's also a business that demonstrates the benefits of caring policies and practices in dollars and cents.

SAS is a leader in family-friendly policies. It has the largest on-site daycare operation in North Carolina. Its cafeteria has high chairs and booster seats for children so they can eat with their parents. The company pays the entire cost of health benefits for employees and their domestic partners. Workers are only required to work a seven-hour day, and employees get unlimited sick days, which may be used to care for sick family members.

SAS's corporate headquarters in Carey, North Carolina, has a swimming pool, track, medical facilities, counseling services, and live music at lunch. Employees enjoy a thirty-six thousand square foot company gym with workout rooms and classes, an area for yoga, and two full-length basketball courts. Outside are fields for softball and soccer. A masseuse comes in several times a week, and employees can discuss their workouts with the company's wellness coordinator. The company even washes employees' gym clothes.

All this sounds more like a combination health spa, child care center, and social welfare agency than a successful business. But SAS has had nearly twenty consecutive years of double-digit growth.[1]

What SAS does is create a work environment that supports employees' well-being on all levels. It leaves them time and energy to have a healthy family life, offers them preventative health and wellness care (as opposed to just sick care), provides education and caregiving for everyone in their families, and helps them with housing. It further offers them stability of employment, an ergonomically safe work environment, and respect for the work they do.[2]

Not surprisingly, SAS regularly scores in the top ten of *Fortune* magazine's "100 Best Companies to Work For," and job applications come in by the thousands. Also not surprisingly, SAS workers are committed to making the company successful—and to staying with SAS to enjoy this success.

Hundreds of studies show the cost-effectiveness of supporting and rewarding caring. And that's not all. The costs of uncaring business and government rules, policies, and practices are also quantifiable—and immense.

Because the company offers so many benefits to workers and their families, SAS's employee turnover rate is just 4 percent, far below the industry average of 20 percent. Employees also like the company's more participatory management style, which encourages communication and is yet another factor in SAS's success.

SAS is just one example of how a growing number of companies are making more money by replacing hierarchies of domination with hierarchies of actualization and giving real value to caring and caregiving. In 2004, the Winning Workplaces' *Fortune Small Business* award went to Carolyn Gable, CEO of New Age Transportation. Gable, a former waitress and single mother of five children, started New Age Transportation out of her home. Thanks to her innovative leadership in creating a tightly knit workplace of intensely loyal workers, it is now a $25 million company.

Gable fosters an environment where employees, particularly those with children, can focus on their jobs while still maintaining a healthy work/life balance. The company's offices include an on-site playroom where working parents can bring their children, a "quiet room" where employees can take a break and recharge, and a deck with a grill where the staff can get together for barbecues on warm days. Gable also encourages her staff to take care of themselves outside of the office by paying for health club memberships and offering them $250 per quarter for up to a year to quit smoking. Rather than being a drag on profits, these policies led to an average 37 percent yearly growth.[3]

Other companies, from successful publishing houses such as Berrett-Koehler and New World Library to the giant health-care products manufacturer Johnson & Johnson, which has been on the *Working Mothers* Best Companies list for over twenty years, also illustrate the benefits of caring policies and practices for both large and small businesses. They show that caring is not a luxury good of booming companies but a major factor in making companies more successful.

But do we just have anecdotal evidence that caring economic rules, policies, and practices are good for both people and the bottom line? Can we calculate the benefits of valuing caring and caregiving through quantified statistical methods?

The answer is a resounding yes. Hundreds of studies show the cost-effectiveness of supporting and rewarding caring. And that's not all. The costs of uncaring business and government rules, policies, and practices are also quantifiable—and immense.

THE STATISTICAL EVIDENCE

I am in this book arguing that business activities must be socially as well as financially profitable. But the two are far from mutually exclusive.

Caring business policies sharply reduce employee turnover, saving companies millions of dollars. The cost of replacing hourly employees is about six months of their earnings. The cost of replacing salaried employees can be as high as eighteen months of their salary. Job turnover can cost employers as much as 40 percent of annual profits. And this doesn't even take into account what a recent study found: between 30 and 40 percent of employees planning to leave have already checked out mentally and emotionally, focusing on their next job rather than their current one.[4]

There are also high business costs from absenteeism, which is often the direct result of workers' family responsibilities. For instance, Chemical Bank discovered that 52 percent of employee absences were caused by family-related issues.[5]

Businesses that have more caring policies radically cut turnover and absentee-related losses. Intermedics, Inc. decreased its turnover rate by 37 percent with on-site child care, saving fifteen thousand work hours and $2 million. Virginia Mason Medical Center in Seattle reported 0 percent turnover among employees using its on-site child care center, compared to about 23 percent turnover among other workers. Johnson & Johnson found that absenteeism among employees who used flexible work options and family leave policies was an average of 50 percent less than for the workforce as a whole.[6]

Difficulties securing child care are a particularly important factor in the high rates of absenteeism, turnover, and as a consequence, overtime costs, in companies with extended-hours operations. A 2003 report by Circadian Technologies, Inc. found that extended-hours child care reduces the absenteeism rate by an average of 20 percent. This study, "Cost Benefits of Child Care for Extended-Hours Operations," found that turnover rates among extended-hour employees also decreased substantially when child care services were available—from 9.3 percent to 7.7 percent. Since on average it costs companies $25,000 to recruit and train each new extended-hour employee, this too was a big savings.[7]

Of course, these savings don't show the enormous benefits of child care services to the approximately 28 percent of American women who regularly work nights, evenings, or weekends. Nor do they show the benefits to society at a time when latchkey children are a major U.S. concern.

This is one reason that, as emphasized by Professor Joan C. Williams, director of the Center for WorkLife Law at the UC Hastings College of the Law, support for caregivers in the formal workforce is not just a business issue but a public policy issue. Legislation against what Williams calls family discrimination is urgently needed, especially for workers on the lowest economic rungs, who have the least bargaining power.[8]

Today, 37 percent of the workforce has children under age eighteen. Small wonder that in a Radcliffe survey, 83 percent of women and 82 percent of men ages twenty-one to twenty-nine put having time to spend with their families at the top of their priority list, way ahead of a high salary and a prestigious job.[9]

The number of caregivers in the workforce will rise even more dramatically as Americans age. By 2020 the U.S. over-fifty population will increase 74 percent compared to 1 percent for those under fifty.[10] Polls show that 54 percent of U.S. workers anticipate caring for an elderly parent or relative in the next ten years.

Reports from the Families and Work Institute (FWI)[11] and scores of other organizations, as well as books such as Sandra Burud and Marie Tumolo's *Leveraging the New Human Capital*, show that factoring these realities into workplace policies is not only socially essential; it makes good business sense.[12]

Many studies show that the costs of pretending that when people go to work they leave all else behind are huge. And so are the benefits from business policies that take workers' lives into account.

A study of clients of the KPMG emergency back-up child care program, for example, showed that offering employees child care yielded a 125 percent ROI (return on investment) within six months of

---

⊡ The Business Return on Investment in Caring

In *Leveraging the New Human Capital* Sandra Burud and Marie Tumolo showcase a large number of studies showing that child care, flexible work hours, and paid family leave all have a very high return on investment (ROI).

- Chase Manhattan's investment in backup child care services for employees yielded a 115 percent ROI, saving the company sixty-nine hundred workdays in just one year.

- American Express had $40 million in increased sales productivity when it introduced telecommuting; Aetna had a 30 percent increase in claims processed after employees began working from home.

- A 2001 study showed that firms offering paid parental leave had 2.5 percent higher profits than firms that did not.

- Companies on *Working Mothers'* list, "100 Best Companies for Working Mothers" (which have child care benefits, flexible scheduling, telecommuting, and other caring policies) had high customer satisfaction ratings—and this translated into a 3 to 11 percent market value increase, or $22,000 per employee.

- Companies rated by *Fortune* as the best places to work also yielded shareholder returns on investment of 27.5 percent, much higher than the Russell 3000 stocks, which only had average returns of 17.3 percent.

Source: Sandra Burud and Marie Tumolo, *Leveraging the New Human Capital* (Mountain View, Calif.: Davies-Black, 2004). ▪

implementation. By the fourth year, the ROI was a whopping 521 percent. A General Services Administration Child Care study found that 55 percent of workers who were offered a child care subsidy were better able to concentrate at work and 48 percent were more likely to stay on the job.[13] A study of users of Bristol-Myers Squibb's child care centers showed that they had a deeper commitment to the company and felt more positive about their relationship with their supervisors. And a Bright Horizons Child Care survey showed that even many employees without children feel worksite child care will have a positive impact on the organization for which they work.[14]

UPS found that flexible work schedules reduced employee turnover from 50 percent to 6 percent.[15] Aetna's retention rate rose from 77 percent to 88 percent when it initiated a six-month maternity leave with flexible return-to-work possibilities, for a savings of $1 million per year. A survey of nine employers in Silicon Valley found telecommuters to be 25 percent more productive on the days they worked at home and 20 percent more productive overall.[16] Illinois Bell found that telecommuting increased productivity by 40 percent.[17]

❏ Savings from Wellness and Fitness Programs

- Pepsi's fitness program produced a return on investment of $3 for every $1 invested (a stunning 300 percent ROI).[18]

- Johnson & Johnson's Corporate Wellness Program saved the company an average of $225 per employee per year in reduced hospital admissions, mental health visits, and outpatient services, even after deducting the cost of paying employees to participate.

- Steelcase benefited from 55 percent lower medical claims for participants in its wellness program over six years.[19]

- Applied Materials' Fitness Center participants had medical payments that were one-fifth lower and accident-related disability costs that were a third lower than nonparticipants. In addition, its workers compensation costs per claim were 79 percent lower for program participants. ∎

According to the Watson Wyatt Human Capital Index, companies that support flexible work arrangements have a 3.5 percent higher market value than companies that do not offer this flexibility to employees with caregiving responsibilities.[20]

While these statistics focus on particular policies and practices, I want to emphasize that what matters is not just instituting one or two caring policies. What really produces results is creating a caring company.

First Tennessee National Corporation is a shining example of how businesses are beginning to see the organizational savvy of doing more than simply creating a series of caring activities, terrific as those may be. This financial institution found that by transforming its corporate culture into a truly caring one—really putting the interests of employees first—it became the most profitable in its class, by a factor of two. It was consistently the most profitable bank, according to *Forbes*. It discovered that measurable profits flowed from this caring, as the bank retains 97 percent of customers, who are better served by long-term employees who feel valued. That incredible customer retention rate along with the retention of good employees were key factors in the bank's profits and shareholder value.[21]

In short, many companies have found that the long-term benefits of caring policies far exceed their cost.[22] Caring policies make for happier, more productive workers, stronger families, and more fulfilling lives. They lead to higher financial profits. And in the bargain, they make for a stronger, more productive economy. (See "Small Businesses That Care" on the following page.)

SCIENCE AND THE REAL BOTTOM LINE

Businesspeople often say they need dollars-and-cents information before they try anything new. The case histories and statistics we just looked at offer this information. They demonstrate the dollars-and-cents benefits of investing in the real bottom line: the health and welfare of people.[23]

The benefits from this investment are also confirmed by a growing body of scientific research examining the conditions that promote positive behavior in organizations. Known as *positive organizational scholarship*, or POS for short, this research shows that positive connections with others are fundamental to better organizational performance.[24]

As University of Michigan researchers Jane E. Dutton and Emily D. Heaphy write in "The Power of High-Quality Connections at Work," POS takes into account findings that human growth is enabled through mutually empathic and mutually empowering connections.[25] As Dutton puts it, when people feel cared for, they become fully alive.[26]

Just like the statistics we looked at, POS shows that caring connections have a beneficial effect on profits. For instance, studies by Dutton, Jacoba Lilius, and Jason Kanov show how compassion creates relational resources that promote trust, felt connection, and positive emotions—all of which lead to streams of action that greatly benefit organizations. Their studies even document that compassion in organizations generates positive relational resources not only in those directly involved but in third-party organizational members who witness or are made aware of compassionate interactions.[27]

☐ Small Businesses That Care

In *Values-Driven Business: How to Change the World, Make Money, and Have Fun*, Ben Cohen and Mal Warwick show how even small businesses with limited resources can derive enormous benefits from caring policies. Drawing from their own business experiences in Ben & Jerry's Ice Cream and Mal Warwick and Associates, as well as from those of hundreds of other small companies, they focus on five basic relationships:

1. Relations with employees
2. Relations with suppliers
3. Relations with customers
4. Relations with the community
5. Relations with the natural environment

In addition to good employee benefits, Ben and Mal emphasize the importance of participatory management styles and profit-sharing plans that further ensure that employees feel they have a real stake in the company's success.

Source: Ben Cohen and Mal Warwick, *Values-Driven Business: How to Change the World, Make Money, and Have Fun* (San Francisco: Berrett-Koehler, 2006). ■

Emotional intelligence expert Daniel Goleman, Case Western School of Management professor Richard Boyatzis, and Teleos Leadership Institute director Annie McKee show how empathic listening and caring make for more effective leadership. David Cooperrider and his associates at the Organizational Behavior Department at Case Western show how a new approach to organizational development called *appreciative inquiry* builds enduring collaborations that transform organizations in positive directions.[28]

The experiments of psychologist Alice Isen and her colleagues show that when people feel good—which they do when they feel cared for—they are more productive and innovative. They are better negotiators, get along better with others, and are much more creative.[29]

These findings are readily available in books such as *Positive Organizational Scholarship* and *Appreciative Inquiry and Organizational*

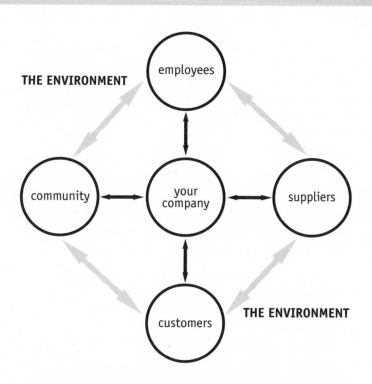

THE FIVE DIMENSIONS OF VALUES-DRIVEN BUSINESS

Transformation. They demonstrate something that would seem obvious: the energy produced in caring organizational contexts drives productivity, with all this implies for business success and a more prosperous economy.[30]

Yet many people still believe the only possibility is a dog-eat-dog, uncaring economics. They think of caring as soft or feminine, and either consciously or unconsciously dismiss it as counterproductive, or at best as irrelevant to business success and economic development. These assumptions, and the flawed economic indicators that support them, lead to a tunnel vision that makes it impossible to see, much less act on, anything that contradicts them. And many business and government leaders cling to these assumptions, despite all the empirical data showing they're just plain wrong.

THE COST-EFFECTIVENESS OF CARING

A striking example of just how wrong these old assumptions are is the enormous economic cost of failing to support good care for children. From a purely financial cost-benefit perspective, investing in high-quality care for children is one of the best investments a nation can make.

An extensive cost-benefit analysis of the return on investment for supporting good caregiving in Canada led to Ontario's Healthy Babies, Healthy Children program. When government leaders were shown the financial benefits of investing in caring for children—and the costs of failing to do so—the Ministry of Health and Long-Term Care (MOHLTC) launched a program focusing on children's critical early years, from before birth to age six.

I should note that the Healthy Babies, Healthy Children program was launched by a fiscally conservative government. This government saw the cost-effectiveness of supporting good parenting. Premier Mike Harris committed $44 million in annual funding for the program's initial operation, as well as $27 million for hospitals to provide new mothers with the option of sixty hours of care after childbirth and $17 million for the Healthy Babies home visit program. Harris also approved funding for additional neonatal intensive care beds and for encouraging better communication among community services to make it easier for all families with young children to get the services they want and need.[31]

Delivered by the province's thirty-seven public health units, Healthy Babies, Healthy Children offers screening and assessment for all pregnant women through prenatal programs or by their doctors. It provides needs assessments for all new mothers by nurses in the hospital or by midwives. It offers all families with new babies information on parenting and child development. It delivers extra help, including home visits by a public health nurse or lay home visitor, to families who can benefit from this support.[32] In addition, the program provides referrals to breastfeeding, nutrition, and health services, as well as to play and parenting programs and child care services.

In 2003, almost all families in Ontario with very young children had some contact with Healthy Babies, Healthy Children. Families requiring extended home visits received a 1–2 hour home visit every eighteen days. There were also many referrals to other agencies, and this coordination led to less overlap in services, with substantial savings in service delivery.[33]

Preliminary assessments of Healthy Babies, Healthy Children have shown that, in addition to its immediate benefits for children and their families, the program is a highly cost-effective investment in the future Canadian workforce. Children in the home-visited families score higher on most infant development measures than children in similar families who do not receive home visits. These measures include self-help, gross motor skills, fine motor skills, and language development, all indicators of a higher level of human capital development, not to speak of prospects for a brighter future for the children involved in the program.[34]

Another benefit has been better child and family health among home-visited families. This too is a predictor of higher-quality human capital, as well as of future savings in family and state medical expenses, business expenses from absenteeism, and other health-related costs.

Rates of family violence have also been reduced. Because family violence is often a predictor of later crimes, this too translates into substantial savings for both business and society at large. According to the United Nations World Health Organization (WHO), above and beyond the physical and emotional devastation it causes, child abuse costs the United States economy as much as $94 billion a year.[35]

In addition to community support for good parenting, another extremely cost-effective national investment is funding for high-quality child care and preschool programs. Again, this was the subject of a Canadian policy study, *The Benefits and Costs of Good Child Care: The Economic Rationale for Public Investment in Young Children*.[36]

The authors of this 1998 study were two University of Toronto economists. They calculated that the net additional cost for all Canadian children to participate in high-quality child care and preschool programs would be about $5.3 billion per year. But the economic value of the additional benefits to children and parents would be double: about $10.6 billion per year—a 200 percent return on investment.[37]

The authors urged the Canadian government to make high-quality child care and preschool education a top priority, even though the costs of providing it to all children would be high. They pointed out that the collective benefits to society and the workforce of the future would be immense. "If Canada is to maintain and improve its competitive position internationally," they wrote, "it must invest in the human capital of today's children. Dollars spent on education for young children are far more effective than dollars spent at any other time in a person's life. . . . any reasonable industrial and educational strategy requires high-quality child care."[38]

The Canadian report counseled the government to take a long view. "Canada depends for its economic well-being on its ability to function well socially and economically," it concluded. "Its competitiveness rests above all on the talents and efficiency of its workforce."

THE REAL WEALTH OF NATIONS

Ultimately, the real wealth of a nation lies in the quality of its human and natural capital. I should here add that an investment in human capital is an investment in human beings. It is the enhancement of the quality of life of human beings, of human happiness and fulfillment, not just of the ability to earn income in the market.[39] This is fundamental to the holistic concept of caring economics. I should also add that by natural capital I don't just mean a nation's natural resources but also our planet's ecological health, since without this we risk losing everything, including our lives. This too is fundamental to caring economics.

Financial profits should not be the be-all and end-all of business and economic policy. The welfare of people and the health of the planet must be overriding goals of sound business and economic policies.

However, investment in human beings is the best way of enhancing their productive capacities—and hence ensuring business profits and economic effectiveness. And this investment has to start at birth. In fact, it should start before birth, with prenatal care for mothers and health care, high-quality child care, and education for children. Moreover, it is a particularly urgent investment today, when knowledge and service work represent the vast majority of jobs (85 percent according to business expert Peter Drucker), and even the remaining jobs (15 percent in manufacturing and agriculture) are becoming more knowledge-intensive and interactive.[40]

Yet the United States has no coherent policy for investing in human capital. On the contrary, at this writing budgets for health, education, and welfare are being slashed.[41]

Not only that, the Structural Adjustment policies of international organizations such as the International Monetary Fund (IMF) have imposed budget-cutting requirements on developing nations. And as

☐ Investing in Human Capital and Social Security

British economist Richard Layard points out that the U.S. discussion about Social Security should refocus from privatizing the program (which has been a disaster for many British families who chose private investment options) to how to promote a more skilled and educated future workforce that can sustain government funding that protects the elderly. He notes that today one-fifth of U.S. workers are functionally illiterate (they can't even understand a simple instruction on a medicine bottle), as compared to one-tenth of workers in nations such as Germany, Sweden, and the Netherlands. Not coincidentally, these are all nations where parental leave, early childhood education, and other policies that support caring and caregiving have contributed to a more skilled workforce that commands higher wages, and hence can add more to the tax base for Social Security and other such programs.[42] ■

these cuts have been made primarily in human services such as health, education, and welfare, the result has been less, rather than more, investment in human capital.[43]

Fortunately, many industrialized nations are not so shortsighted. Despite pressure for similar human services cuts, most European nations continue to invest heavily in caring for their people through government funding for health care, child care, and paid parental leave.

Among the most generous programs are those of the Nordic nations. In Sweden, either parent has the right to be absent from work until a child is eighteen months old, and the government pays an allowance for the first 390 days based on a sliding scale according to the salary of the parent taking the leave. To encourage more men to take parental leave, sixty of the total allowance days must be used by the other parent. When a child is ill, a parent has the right to a temporary parental allowance that enables her or him to stay home and take care of the child. Norway too has a paid parental leave program, providing from forty-two to fifty-two weeks of parental leave (100 percent of earnings for forty-two weeks, 80 percent for fifty-two weeks). Denmark allows eighteen weeks of maternity leave (at 100 percent of earnings) and ten weeks for each parent as parental leave (paid full-time).[44]

Nordic nations have found that investing in caring policies and programs—from universal health care and child care to generous paid parental leave—is an investment in both a higher general quality of life and a more efficient economy. These countries regularly come out high in the United Nations Human Development Reports' measures of national quality of life. Because of their investment in children— starting with child care allowances for all families and high-quality child care and preschool education for all children—their high school students rank high on international math and reading scores. These nations also do well on international economic competitiveness ratings, with high scores on both the 2003–04 and 2005–06 World Economic Forum's Global Competitiveness ratings.

These are not ideal, problem-free, nations. But their government and business leaders, as well as the vast majority of their people, recognize that how much one earns is not the only measure of wealth.

While on average U.S. workers earn more than European ones, Americans have much higher expenses for essential services such as health care. In addition, a full quarter of the population has no health care protection. And even though U.S. health care is the most expensive in the industrialized world, largely because of the high administrative costs of its market-based system, a 2005 survey shows that the quality of care is no better, and actually worse, than that of the other nations studied: Canada, Australia, New Zealand, Britain, and Germany.[45] Most U.S. workers also have to pay for child care out of their own pockets unless their employers offer it, because the U.S. government does not subsidize child care except for some very low-income families. Consequently, most American workers do not have access to the high-quality child care and preschool education necessary if children are to receive the attention and care they need to develop their full capacities.

U.S. workers also spend more time at their jobs than their West European counterparts. As political science professor Janet Gornick and public policy professor Marcia Meyers note, while dual-earner couples with children in many European nations average between sixty-five and seventy-eight hours a week, U.S. couples jointly spend over eighty hours a week at work.[46]

All this, some argue, leads to greater U.S. productivity. But in fact, from 1995 to 2004, the United States ranked only eighth in GDP annual compound growth per worker-hour among the thirty nations that belong to the Organization for Economic Cooperation and Development (OECD).[47]

Tragically, the situation of American children is also much worse than in nations with a lower GDP than the United States. American children are more likely to be poor, to perform poorly on international math and science tests during their adolescent years, and to have babies as teenagers than children in other rich Western countries.

American children are even more likely to die than children in nations with lower GDP. According to the U.S. Department of Health and Human Services 2004 report, the infant mortality rate in the United States was twenty-seventh among industrialized nations in 2000, behind Greece and just ahead of the far less wealthy Cuba.[48] By 2006, according to the latest CIA *World Factbook*, Cuba had moved

◻ *Work, Values, and How We Live*

A survey conducted by the Families and Work Institute found that over half of American employees report that they experience conflict in balancing jobs, personal life, and family life. By contrast, in European Union countries, 80 percent of parents report that their work hours and private commitments fit "very well" or "fairly well."[49]

People in the United States also get much less for their taxes in human services such as health care, child care, and education than do citizens of most West European nations. U.S. law requires only a short, unpaid parental leave (people employed in small enterprises don't even get that), and only a few states fund any wage replacement through public disability insurance for mothers after childbirth or adoption.[50] Waiting lists for public child care are long, and most American workers can't afford to pay for high-quality child care. Add to this the longer working hours and lack of benefits for part-time workers (many of whom are also caregivers), as well as the absence of the family allowances for children that are standard in many West European nations, and the result is a highly stressed population.[51]

Of course, Americans are hardly the most stressed people on Earth. The billions of people who are poor and hungry in our world have much more stressful lives. As U.N. Secretary-General Kofi Annan noted, "Almost half the world's population lives on less than two dollars a day, yet even this statistic fails to capture the humiliation, powerlessness, and brutal hardship that is the daily lot of the world's poor."[52] Nor does this statistic show that the mass of the poor and hungry worldwide are women and children, and that this is largely due to an economic system that fails to give visibility and value to the most essential human work: the work of caring and caregiving.

None of this is inevitable. As Carol Bellamy, former UNICEF director, writes: "The quality of a child's life depends on decisions made every day in households, communities, and in the halls of government. We must make those choices wisely, and with children's best interests in mind. If we fail to secure childhood, we will fail to reach our larger, global goals for human rights and economic development. As children go, so go nations. It's that simple."[53] ▪

ahead of the United States, which as number forty-two lagged behind
not only every major industrialized nation but also Malta, Andorra,
Macau, Aruba, and other much less wealthy countries.[54] The 2005
Human Development Report actually showed that infant death rates
are higher in Washington, D.C., than in Kerala, India. (I should add
that Kerala is the Indian province where the status of women is higher than anywhere else in India, a fact that, as we will see in the next
chapter, plays a major role in a higher quality of life for all.)

Clearly, the United States has not been allocating its enormous
resources to ensure the welfare of its children. It may be the wealthiest nation in the world in dollars and cents. But its policies fail to care
for its most important asset: its future human capital. If the United
States does not change this false economizing, our national economy
will pay dearly for it in the next generation, and millions of American
children will continue to unnecessarily suffer and die.

HIDING THE COSTS OF UNCARING ECONOMICS

The failure to care for people and nature is costly to children and families, to businesses and communities, to nations and the planet. These
costs, however, are not visible in current measurements of economic
health such as GDP and GNP.

As we saw earlier, these economic indicators put many of the costs
of uncaring business practices on the plus, rather than minus, side of
productivity calculations. For example, rather than listing the
cleanup costs from negligent oil spills as an economic liability, GNP
and GDP include them as part of national productivity. So the billion-
dollar cost of the 1989 Exxon-Valdez spill was included in U.S. GNP.[55]

This catastrophic spill—from a thin-walled old tanker that had no
business carrying eleven million gallons of crude oil—polluted the
ocean for miles. It killed fish and other sea life, and endangered millions of migratory shorebirds and waterfowl, hundreds of sea otters,
harbor porpoises, sea lions, and whales. It ruined the livelihood of
local people for years and damaged their health.

But instead of coming forward to pay for the damage, Exxon spent
millions of dollars on lawyers—expenses that were included in U.S.
GNP since they were market transactions. Also included in GNP were

the costs of the lawyers hired by property owners, indigenous people, and commercial fishers who lost their livelihood and all too often health due to the spill. So were the court costs of the long appeals Exxon lawyers mounted, the costs of all the expert witnesses they hired, and the costs of the fourteen million documents they filed (including one claiming that the crude oil onboard the Exxon Valdez was not a waste but a commodity, and that therefore its spill did not violate the federal Clean Water Act).

The immediate financial expenses stemming from cleaning up the oil spill that were included in GNP were actually only a small part of its real economic cost. Four years after the spill, the journal *Science* reported that significant amounts of crude oil remained on the beaches and seabeds, harming salmon eggs and poisoning mussels and clams, and by extension, the otters, ducks, and other animals that feed on these creatures. Even now, the contaminated area, and the people and animals in it, continue to suffer from the spill.[56]

Yet none of the damage from the Exxon oil spill was reflected in measurements of economic productivity. Nor can this damage be reflected in existing economic indicators and rules, since they do not take into account the value of the life-supporting activities of nature any more than they do the life-supporting activities that take place in households.

The enormous economic costs of wars are another example of how the real costs of uncaring economic policies and practices are hidden by current measurements. These costs, too, are often put on the plus rather than minus side of GNP. For example, the billions of tax dollars the U.S. government paid to contractors, soldiers, and others involved in the Iraq War have been included in GNP, along with the medical costs for all the soldiers maimed in the war and the funeral costs for the thousands killed in it. On top of this, the expenses of trying to reconstruct Iraq after the damage caused by the U.S. invasion—including fees to large U.S. corporations—are also on the plus side of U.S. GNP.

U.S. GNP also failed to accurately reflect the billion-dollar damage to New Orleans when levies were breached by Hurricane Katrina after the federal government ignored calls for reinforcing them. Instead, the costs of post-hurricane reconstruction, including the colossal wastefulness of building trailers for Katrina refugees when thousands of vacant apartments could have been used, are again on the plus side of GNP.

In the same way, the enormous costs from air pollution caused by irresponsible uses of industrial technology are on the plus side of GNP. This, too, fails to provide an accurate cost and benefit analysis, even though these costs are readily measurable in dollars and cents— that is, in billions of dollars and trillions of cents.

In the Canadian province of Ontario, for example, which has a population of 11.9 million, air pollution costs citizens at least $1 billion annually in hospital admissions, emergency room visits, and worker absenteeism.[57] In more environmentally polluted areas, the monetary expenses related to air pollution–induced illness are even higher. According to the World Bank, the medical and other costs of exposure to airborne dust and lead in Jakarta, Bangkok, and Manila approached 10 percent of average incomes in the early 1990s.[58]

In China, which has some of the world's worst urban air pollution, the World Bank estimates that this pollution costs the Chinese economy $25 billion in health care costs and lost working hours per year.[59] Another study estimated that the illnesses and deaths of urban residents due to air pollution cost China 5 percent of its gross domestic product.

These financial costs do not include the death toll from air pollution, even though the World Health Organization reports that three million people die each year from the effects of outdoor air pollution, three times as many as in traffic accidents.[60] Of course, the medical and funeral bills for these deaths are still reported on the plus side of GDP and GNP.

There are scores of other hidden costs misreported as "productivity" in current economic indicators. For example, the profits from the growing U.S. prison industry are presented as economic pluses, when in fact investment in incarceration as compared to rehabilitation is wasteful and inefficient.

To illustrate, the recidivism rate in Missouri is far lower than in California. The difference is that Missouri has replaced the traditional approach to young criminals—large lockups with an emphasis on punishment and isolation—with small group settings that blend highly trained staff with constant therapy and positive peer pressure. This more caring approach also gives importance to family connections, taking pains to house children within fifty miles of their homes and even sending vans to enable parents to visit.[61]

Because a more caring and participatory approach doesn't just warehouse kids, which generally leads to more violence and gang involvement, Missouri has an outstanding record on rehabilitation. A 2003 study found that of the fourteen hundred teenagers released in 1999, only 8 percent wound up in adult prisons. By contrast, in California, where the privatization of prisons has become a highly profitable business, about half of those released from juvenile prisons are back behind bars within two years.

Missouri's system also delivers when it comes to another important measurement: cost per juvenile. It spends about $43,000 a year per child. California's per-capita tab is nearly twice that: $80,000.[62]

Yet in terms of GNP, the California system comes out on top. The cost of building prisons is on the plus side of productivity calculations, while the savings of dollars—not to speak of lives—from a system that costs less and requires fewer prisons is invisible.

TAKING OFF OUR BLINDFOLDS

Why do people, even bright and generally well-meaning people, fail to see how unrealistic present economic cost and benefit analyses are? How is it that they don't see the ineffectiveness and wastefulness of economic rules, policies, and practices that give little or no value to caring and caregiving?

It certainly isn't that we lack studies proving that we need more accurate economic indicators. Nor do we lack studies showing the high costs of not supporting caring and caregiving.

For instance, there is no lack of data on the human and financial costs of child abuse and neglect, and of their frequent corollary, juvenile and, later, adult crime.[63] The majority of people in prison for violent crimes have a history of abuse or neglect. Costs stemming from child abuse include huge tax-dollar expenses for court proceedings, incarceration, probation, and other crime-related expenditures, not to speak of loss of worker productivity and other financial and human costs of not investing in good care for children.

Studies also show that when children receive high-quality care they do better financially as adults, with all this means for economic development as well as government tax revenue. One of the best-known of these studies is the Perry Preschool Project. This was a long-term study of what happened to 123 African-American children born in poverty and at high risk of failing in school. From 1962 to 1967, at ages three and four, the subjects were randomly divided into two groups. One group was put in a high-quality preschool care program and the comparison group was not. The study found that at age forty the subjects in the high-quality preschool program had lower crime rates, were more likely to have graduated from high school and hold a job, and had substantially higher earnings than those not in the program.[64]

Nonetheless, government leaders invest millions in prisons, even though warehousing people clearly does not solve the problem of crime. They, and many of their constituents, view investment in caring for children so they don't become criminals as a waste of tax money. Not only that, when wars, such as the invasion of Iraq, and misdistribution of resources, such as big tax rebates for the wealthy, cause budget deficits, the first thing that's cut is funding for caring: child care, health care, education, and welfare.

A major factor underlying these twisted priorities is an economic double standard we inherited from times that oriented more closely to the domination system. This economic double standard, in which caring and caregiving is associated with women and "femininity" and seen as inferior to anything stereotypically associated with men and "masculinity," is reflected in and perpetuated by economic measurements that falsify the costs of uncaring policies. These measurements blind people to these costs, as well as to the enormous benefits society derives from the essential work of caring and caregiving, be it in families, businesses, or society at large.

We must change these distorted ways of measuring economic productivity. However, we cannot realistically expect fundamental changes in either economic indicators or policies unless there is greater awareness of the hidden assumptions and values that keep us locked into a dysfunctional economic paradigm.

Because they've learned to accept and value the dominator "masculine" archetype of the punitive father, many people see spending government money for punishing rather than rehabilitating as only natural and right. Allocating money for weapons and wars rather than for health, education, and welfare is in their unconscious minds also justified by the high valuing of another dominator "masculine" arche-type: the hero as warrior.

These are some further reasons that to move away from dominator economics, not only must economics change, but beliefs, values, and institutions must also change. We will look more closely at these beliefs, values, and institutions—and how they affect, and are in turn affected by, economics—in the next chapters.

CHAPTER 4

The Economic Double Standard

Sometimes we don't see what is in plain sight. This is particularly true when it comes to beliefs and values we've inherited.

In the Bible, we're told that when King David had his famous affair with Bathsheba, he had her husband sent to the front lines, where his rival was conveniently killed. But instead of being punished for adultery and murder, David continued to reign.[1] On the other hand, under biblical law a girl accused of not being a virgin would be taken by her father to the city gates and slowly stoned to death.[2]

The Bible also tells us that men could sell their daughters into slavery as servants or concubines and that marriage itself was a sales transaction. In Genesis, we read that Jacob worked seven years to get Laban's daughter Rachel for his wife, and when Laban gave him her older sister Leah instead, he had to work another seven years to finally get the woman he'd bargained for. Another famous biblical story tells of how Lot offered his little daughters to a mob to be gang-raped—and instead of being punished, was chosen by God as the only moral man in the sinful cities of Sodom and Gomorrah![3]

All this went along with the belief that women are male property. So if a man raped a girl, he had to marry her and pay her father for having destroyed his marketable goods.[4] And since fathers had absolute control over their daughter's sexuality, the girl had no say whatsoever in this.

Many of us now consider these kinds of laws and practices barbaric. We recognize that we've inherited a brutal gender double standard for sex in which those who held power (men) were judged by very different rules than those who did not (women).

But what's still not generally recognized is that we've inherited this same double standard for economics—and that this has distorted our economic systems, beginning with the economic indicators that purportedly measure what is economically valuable.

THE INVISIBILITY OF THE OBVIOUS

Beliefs that glaring inequalities are inevitable, even moral, are by no means confined to gender. These beliefs have been used to justify every kind of oppression. The belief that the subordination of one group over another is inevitable, even moral, has served to justify the subjugation of different races, religions, and ethnic groups. It has served to justify slavery, serfdom, and other forms of economic exploitation. It has justified every kind of social and economic injustice. It has justified pogroms, lynchings, terrorism, and religious and ethnic wars.

In-group versus out-group rankings are inherent in domination systems. They can be based on race, gender, religion, ethnicity, or other differences. All these rankings mutually reinforce one another. They also reinforce two assumptions basic to domination systems. One is that there are only two alternatives: dominating or being dominated. The other is that beginning with the most fundamental difference in our species—between female and male—difference should be equated with superiority or inferiority.

This male-superior/female-inferior model of our species is a template that children in dominator families learn early on for viewing relations of domination and submission as normal and moral. It serves as a basic model for ranking one kind of person over another. It is therefore foundational to the imposition and maintenance of a system structured to perpetuate inequity and inequality.

Not so long ago, inequality was so taken for granted that the idea of equality was a heresy. Saint Augustine (who, not coincidentally, in his famous theory of original sin blamed Eve for all human ills) declared that no one should try to change his or her station any more than a finger should wish to be the body's eye.[5]

Rebellion against authority was considered immoral. But the oppression of subordinate groups, and even the violence used to maintain this oppression, were moral. So effectively were people indoctrinated to accept different rules for those on top and those on the bottom that the soldiers and police meting out this violence were often recruited from these subordinate groups. Women themselves became agents for the subordination of their own sex, as well as for the elevation of anything associated with men over anything associated with women, including the "women's work" of caring and caregiving.

For the last several centuries, movements for social and economic justice have chipped away at the double standard for those who hold power and those who do not. But these movements primarily focused on the public spheres of politics and economics, which were, until recently, exclusive male preserves.

Indeed, instead of challenging the gender double standard, the most eminent "fathers" of modern egalitarianism adamantly supported it. Their "rights of man" ideal explicitly excluded women—a fact largely ignored in history and political science.

John Locke, the leading seventeenth-century philosopher of political democracy, proposed that freely chosen representative governments replace autocratic monarchs. Locke attacked the then-prevalent notion of the patriarchal family as the natural foundation for absolute monarchy. Nonetheless, he vigorously asserted that there is "a Foundation in Nature" for the legal and customary subjection of women to their husbands.[6]

Jean-Jacques Rousseau, the eighteenth-century philosopher famous for his advocacy of freedom and equality for men, also upheld this double standard. Rousseau actually asserted that girls "should be restricted from a young age" because "docility" is something women will need all their lives. In his view, women will, and should, "always be in subjection to a man or to men's judgments."[7]

Movements for social and economic justice have chipped away at the double standard for those who hold power and those who do not. But instead of challenging the gender double standard, the most eminent "fathers" of modern egalitarianism supported it.

Both these leaders in the modern movement toward democracy and equality were blind to an absurdity. How can one seriously speak of a free and democratic society with equality and justice for all as long as the domination of one half of humanity over the other half continues?

The two leading nineteenth-century philosophers on economic equality were also prisoners of this male-centered view of society. Karl Marx and Friedrich Engels recognized the subordination of women when they wrote that the first class oppression was that of male over female. But for them, as for many socialists to this day, this "woman question" was a secondary matter.

Robert Owen, William Thompson, Anna Wheeler, August Bebel, and a number of other nineteenth-century socialists had argued that the unequal distribution of wealth between men and women is a

☐ Early Challengers of the Gender Double Standard

Not all Western philosophers accepted the gender double standard that devalues women and the "feminine." Particularly during the European Renaissance, there were vigorous challenges to the subordination of women. In her 1405 *The Book of the City of Ladies*, Christine de Pizan wrote that the derogation of women is founded on irrational prejudice, and pointed to important contributions to civilization made by women.[8] In his famous 1516 book *Utopia*, Sir Thomas More advocated education for women. In 1790 the Marquis de Condorcet caused a sensation by asserting women should have the same political rights as men.[9]

The best-known eighteenth-century advocate for women's equality was the British philosopher Mary Wollstonecraft. During her short life (1759 to 1797), she wrote a number of works arguing passionately against the subordination of women, including *A Vindication of the Rights of Women* (1792), which became a classic feminist text. Wollstonecraft defied many conventions, including that of marriage, which in her time gave men absolute control over their wives. She founded a school to educate girls and joined a radical group that included poets William Blake and Henry Wordsworth as well as Thomas Paine. Her first child, Fanny, was born out of wedlock in 1795, the daughter of an American businessman. After discovering his infidelity, she lived with activist William Godwin, a long-time friend whom she married in 1797. She died a few days after the birth of their daughter, Mary Wollstonecraft Shelley (who wrote *Frankenstein* and other novels and married the famous poet Percy Bysshe Shelley).

Over the following century, feminist challenges to male dominance escalated. But even as late as 1869, when the famous philosopher John Stuart

major factor in economic inequity.[10] But Marx and Engels dismissed these matters as secondary to the oppression of the working class.

In 1848, the year Marx and Engels proclaimed their communist manifesto, a feminist manifesto was also proclaimed by the American philosopher and activist Elizabeth Cady Stanton. But Marx and Engels ignored her documentation of the economic oppression of women. In the 1860s, when another American feminist, Victoria Woodhall, spoke against the emerging labor movement's discrimination against women workers, Marx recommended that the unions

---

Mill (influenced by his wife Harriet Taylor) published his essay *The Subjection of Women*, the idea of equality for women was thought radical. In fact, Mill delayed its publication until shortly before his death to avoid controversies that he feared would lessen the impact of his other work.

Probably the best known nineteenth-century American advocate for women's rights was Elizabeth Cady Stanton (1815 to 1902). Stanton was born into a blue-blooded New York family, but was drawn to helping the oppressed. She began her social activism in the abolitionist movement to free slaves, where she met her future husband Henry Stanton, as well as other women who were to become her colleagues in the struggle for women's rights. Even though Stanton bore seven children, and devoted a good deal of her time to caring for them, she spent every spare moment thinking, reading, and writing about women's rights. Her famous 1848 Seneca Falls feminist manifesto begins with a revised version of the American Declaration of Independence: "We hold these truths to be self-evident, that all men *and women* are created equal."

Stanton was ridiculed, calumnied, and denounced for subverting the moral order. One of her works, *The Women's Bible*,[11] is still considered scandalous by many people today for its scathing attack on the role of Judeo-Christian religion in the oppression of women. But Stanton remained undaunted. Her goal was to bring about a fundamental shift in beliefs and institutions, and she saw the liberation of women as integral to the struggle for freedom and equality for all. In her manifesto, she wrote: "The world has never yet seen a truly great and virtuous nation, because in the degradation of women the very fountains of life are poisoned at the source."[12] ■

expel the faction that "gave precedence to the woman question to the question of labor."[13]

For Marx and Engels, what mattered was class. So instead of taking a systemic approach that includes the whole of humanity, they focused only on the male half of our species: the working-class men they passionately wrote about in their revolutionary tracts. What they called the "woman question" would just have to wait until the capitalist system had been destroyed.

Since caring and caregiving are stereotypically associated with women, and Marx and Engels saw anything associated with women as secondary, they paid little attention to this work. As a consequence, they failed to see how the devaluation of caring and caregiving dehumanizes the economics they so wanted to humanize. Despite their commitment to economic equity, they were blind to how the double standard for men and women not only impacts women but the whole social and economic system.

But these men were hardly unique in their blindness to the gender double standard. So powerful is this affliction that it's infected, and continues to infect, how most of us look at the world.

STORIES WE LIVE AND DIE BY

We humans live by stories. Our stories tell us what's natural or unnatural, possible or impossible, valuable or not valuable. We learn these stories early, before our critical faculties are developed, long before our brains are fully formed. So we tend to accept their messages as immutable truths. And a major theme in the stories we've inherited is the devaluation of one half of humanity and everything associated with it.

I grew up in a time when the belief that females are inferior to males was still firmly entrenched even in the United States. As late as the 1950s, people would say "Hope next time it's a boy" when a girl baby was born.

Traditions of valuing males more than females are so strong that even people who pride themselves on their egalitarian principles still often think of anything affecting the female half of humanity as "just a women's issue." Of course, they would never think of matters affecting the male half of humanity as "just men's issues."

I remember vividly a conversation with an eminent human rights activist whom I was trying to convince that women's rights are human rights. After politely nodding in agreement with my passionate arguments, he informed me that he couldn't include women's rights in his activities. He already had his hands full working on life-and-death issues such as political torture and assassination. When I pointed out that women's rights *are* life-and-death issues—that violence against women takes hundreds of thousands of lives each year, far, far more than the number affected by political torture and assassination—for him these were still "just women's issues" to be dealt with after more "important issues" had been addressed.

I hasten to add that not only many men but also many women subscribe to this male/female double standard. For example, in the United States many women prefer male to female political candidates. And in other world regions, this gender bias has far more extreme consequences.

The laws, customs, and policies of many nations still blatantly discriminate against women and girls. In many African, Southeast Asian, and Middle Eastern nations, women are not permitted to own land, go into business for themselves, or even move around freely. In some of these nations, parents often deny girls access to education, give them less health care, and feed girls less than boys.[14]

This nutritional double standard—often perpetrated by mothers on their own daughters—directly contributes to skewed ratios of female mortality. According to the Nobel Prize winning economist Amartya Sen, one quarter of Indian girls died before they reached the age of fifteen in 1990.[15] Annual death rates for girls are also significantly higher than for boys in other nations around the world. According to a special U.N. report on women released in 1991, in Pakistan deaths per year per thousand population age two to five years were 54.4 for girls and 36.9 for boys, in Haiti the ratio was 61.2 for girls as compared to 47.8 for boys, in Thailand it was 26.8 versus 17.3, and in Syria it was 14.6 as compared to 9.3.[16]

Classifying such matters as "just women's issues" effectively blinds us to what otherwise would seem obvious. Giving less food to girls and women profoundly affects the development of *both* boys and girls. It is well-known that children of malnourished women are often born in poor health and with below-par brain development. Nutritional and health care discrimination against girls and women robs *all* children, male or female, of their birthright: their potential for optimal development.

This sexual discrimination not only causes enormous unhappiness and suffering but also impedes human and economic development. It directly affects a nation's workforce capacity. It affects children's, and later, adults' abilities to adapt to new conditions, tolerance of frustration, and propensity to use violence. And this in turn impedes solutions to chronic hunger, poverty, and armed conflict, and with this, chances for a more humane, prosperous, and peaceful world for us all.

In most nations, there is also little or no support for the work of caring and caregiving traditionally performed by women. For example, only a few nations provide government allowances for families with children. Nor is caring work generally considered worthy of good pay in the workplace, or of any remuneration if done in the home.

Add this to traditions of educational, health care, economic, and even nutritional discrimination against girls and women, and the result is predictable. Globally, women and children are the mass of the poor and the poorest of the poor.

It's not realistic to expect real changes in world poverty rates unless we address the gender economic double standard. As long as the devaluation of women and anything associated with women remains unchanged, women and their children will continue to swell the ranks of the world's poor.[17]

This is not to say that economic inequities based on gender are more important than those based on class, race, or other factors. But as noted earlier, a basic template for the division of humanity into "superiors" and "inferiors" that children in dominator families internalize early on is a male-superior/female-inferior model of our species. And as long as people internalize this mental map for relations, it's not realistic to expect changes in the in-group versus out-group patterns of thinking that lie behind so much injustice and suffering.

Nor can we realistically expect more generally caring social and economic policies unless the life-sustaining work of caring and caregiving is no longer devalued as "just women's work" by both men and women. If caring is not socially valued, it will not be valued in economic policies and practices.

In this connection, I want to say that when I speak of caring and caregiving as "women's work" I am only echoing conventional beliefs we inherited from times when gender roles were much more rigid. The goal is not a society in which only women do the caregiving but a society in which women have equal job opportunities and both men and women share caregiving responsibilities at home. In other words, the goal is an economic and social system that no longer bars women from areas traditionally reserved for men and no longer views caring and caregiving as fit only for women or despised "effeminate" men.

I also again want to say that giving visibility and value to caring won't in itself solve our global problems. As we will see, the process of shifting from a domination to a partnership system is much more complex. But leaving behind the gender double standard is essential, as the shift from domination to partnership cannot take place unless we do.

In short, what I'm reporting about the devaluation of women and the "feminine" is not intended to blame men for our world's social and economic ills. What we're dealing with are traditions that have adversely affected not only women but also men. They've obviously had very negative impacts on women. But they have negatively affected us all.

THE ALIENATION OF CARING LABOR

In proposing socialism as an alternative to capitalism, Marx and Engels wrote of the *alienation of labor*.[18] They argued that the devaluation and exploitation of industrial and farm workers is at the root of economic inequity. In proposing that we need an economics that goes beyond both capitalism and socialism, I write of the *alienation of caring and caregiving labor*, and argue that the devaluation and exploitation of this foundational work is a core factor behind economic inequity.[19]

The devaluation and exploitation of caring and caregiving is our inheritance from times in which women's bodies and women's work were male property.[20] As a consequence, women and anything associated with women were basically invisible in economic thinking, which focused on transactions between men.

When Adam Smith, and later Marx, mentioned the caregiving work done by women in households, they relegated it to the secondary realm of "reproduction" rather than "production," and gave minimal space to this "women's work" in their voluminous writings. And to this day, the failure to give visibility and value to the stereotypically feminine work of caring and caregiving in economic theories and models still directly affects economic measurements, practices, and policies.

As we saw earlier, professions that involve caregiving are less valued than those that do not. In the former Soviet Union, factory workers (predominantly male) were paid more than schoolteachers and even more than doctors (largely women), in contrast to the United States where physicians were mainly male and among the highest paid professionals.[21] Even now in the United States, child care work and elementary school teaching (professions where women predominate) are typically lower paid than occupations where caring and caregiving are not integral to the work, such as plumbing and engineering (jobs in which men predominate). And this is only part of the story.

As we also saw, caregiving work is even more devalued when it's performed outside the labor market. It's not counted in measures of economic productivity such as gross domestic product (GDP)—measures that instead include building and using weapons, making and selling cigarettes, and other activities that destroy rather than nurture life.[22]

This invisibility of caring and caregiving work in economic indicators perpetuates the economic double standard that assigns less value to work stereotypically considered feminine rather than masculine—whether it is done by men or women. And this economic double standard, in turn, lies behind many of our world's seemingly insoluble problems.

Politicians give us catchy slogans like "a more gentle, caring world" and "compassionate conservatism." But when it comes to caring for children, the sick, the elderly, and the homeless, their policies are often far from caring. And why would policies be caring when the devaluation of the "feminine" work of caring and caregiving is deeply embedded not only in our unconscious minds but in the economic rules and models most politicians accept?

Some people will argue that we do give value to caregiving. There's Mother's Day, when we're supposed to give mothers candy and flowers. There's the rhetoric about how mothers are treasured, as in the mantra that "motherhood and apple pie" are core American values.

But in reality, we don't value mothering. If we did, the poverty rate of elderly women in the United States—the majority of whom are mothers—would not be almost twice that of elderly men.[23] Nor would women and children worldwide be the majority of the poor.

Even our environmental crisis is largely a symptom of the distorted values that stem from the gender double standard. It's commonly

---

⧠ Little-Noted Effects of the Economic Double Standard: As Percentage of Women Supervised Increases, Pay of Both Male and Female Managers Drops

How pervasive the gender economic double standard is was dramatically shown by a recent study of the differences in pay rates of 2,178 male and female managers working in 512 different companies across a wide variety of industries and areas. Published in the American Psychological Association's *Journal of Applied Psychology*, this study reported:

- When females become the majority in a workgroup, both male and female manager pay decreases sharply

- A male or female manager whose supervised group is comprised of 80 percent females receives approximately $7,000 less in pay annually than a manager whose supervised group is 80 percent male.

- A manager who supervises a group made up of only women receives approximately $9,000 less annually than one who supervises a group comprised of 50 percent women.

- A manager whose supervisor is female receives approximately $2,000 less pay annually than one whose supervisor is male.

Source: Cheri Ostroff and Leanne E. Atwater, "Does Whom You Work with Matter? Effects of Referent Group Gender and Age Composition on Managers' Compensation," *Journal of Applied Psychology*, 2003, 88(4). The results of this study are congruent with many others. Also well documented is that professions where females predominate are paid less than those where males predominate, and that women on average earn less than men in the same fields. A major factor in this often unconscious discrimination is that men and the "masculine" are given higher value than women and the "feminine." This devaluation is so powerful that studies have found that when the same work of art is attributed to a male rather than female artist it is evaluated more favorably.[24] ■

believed that the scientific/industrial revolution that gained momentum in the eighteenth century is to blame for the havoc we're wreak-
ing on our natural life-support systems. But the "conquest of nature"
worldview goes back much further.

We've inherited an economics based on the premise that man is
entitled to control both woman's and nature's life-sustaining activities. In Genesis 1:28, we read that man is to "subdue" the earth and
have "dominion . . . over every living thing that moveth upon the
earth." In Genesis 3:16 we read that man is to rule over woman, who
is to be his subordinate.

I want to add that this notion of male control over nature and
woman was *not* introduced in the Bible. We already find its appear-
ance millennia earlier.

For example, the Babylonian *Enuma Elish* tells us that the war god
Marduk created the world by dismembering the body of the Mother
Goddess Tiamat. This creation myth is a clue to a radical cultural
shift: a change from earlier myths about a Great Mother, who created
nature and humans as part of nature, to a story where the world is
created by the violence of a male deity. This new myth not only
replaced older ones in which creation comes from woman's life-giving
powers; it signals the beginning of a period when female deities,
along with women and anything associated with the feminine, were
subordinated.[25]

Certainly, the mechanistic scientific paradigm that gained currency
in the eighteenth century needs to be left behind. And it is true that
modern science led to powerful technologies that in service of the
"conquest of nature" have created severe environmental problems. But
to lay our environmental problems at the feet of Newtonian science
and Cartesian rationalism flies in the face of thousands of years of history. When Sir Frances Bacon made his much-quoted remark that man
must "torture nature's secrets from her" to bring about a more rational
order,[26] he was simply echoing a much earlier worldview.

ECONOMIC INDICATORS THAT
INCLUDE CARING AND CAREGIVING

Science and technology aren't the problem. The problem is the deep-
seated culture of domination we've inherited, and with it, the economic double standard that gives little or no value to caring and

caregiving, whether it's for people or for our natural habitat. (See "Budgets and Values" on the following pages.)

Some people argue that an economic system that gives value to the work of caring and caregiving in households and other parts of the nonmonetized economy just isn't feasible. Since this work is done outside the market, they tell us, its value can't be quantified. But while it's true that we can't assign a dollar value to all the benefits flowing from caring and caregiving, to say that the economic value of this work cannot be measured ignores the facts.

Back in the 1930s, the economist Margaret Reid already showed that it's possible to statistically measure the unpaid work performed in households.[27] By the 1980s, as Marilyn Waring details in her ground-breaking book *If Women Counted*, several quantitative methods for measuring work performed outside the market had been proposed.[28]

In the early 1990s, the Organization for Economic Cooperation and Development (OECD) examined three methods for measuring nonmarket household work and production.[29] One is the opportunity cost method, based on the wage opportunity lost by a woman who cares for her children or parents, does subsistence farming, or performs other unpaid work instead of having a paid job. The second is the global substitute method, where the market wages of a housekeeper are used. (I should add that this is a poor method, since the value given to housework is still so low in the market.) The third is the specialist substitute or "replacement cost" method, which values household work by using a combination of the market salaries of cooks, nurses, gardeners, and others.

In addition to these "input-based" methods, so called because they measure the value of household work in terms of inputs such as working hours, the U.N. International Research and Training Institute for the Advancement of Women (INSTRAW) has proposed another method: output-based evaluation. This approach measures household productivity in terms of the market value of the products and services produced; for example, meals served in a restaurant, child tutoring done by a professional, and so forth.

Developing, honing, and applying the best methods for quantifying unpaid economic contributions and integrating these measurements into mainstream indicators is not a simple task. But more and more economists and statisticians recognize that it is an essential task.

A host of economists, among them Lourdes Beneria, Nancy Folbre, and Duncan Ironmonger, have written extensively about these issues. Ironmonger, for example, proposes that the value added to the economy from unpaid household work be called gross household product (GHP) and the value added by the market economy be called gross market product (GMP). The sum of GHP and GMP would then be a more accurate economic measure, which he suggests calling gross economic product (GEP).[30]

Like Beneria, Folbre, Scott Burns, Julie Nelson, and other economists, Ironmonger points out that unless statistical measures of productivity include the caregiving in the home that maintains and

⊡ Budgets and Values

Over half of U.S. discretionary spending goes to the military, whereas only a fraction is reserved for education, health, and human services.

President's Budget FY 2005

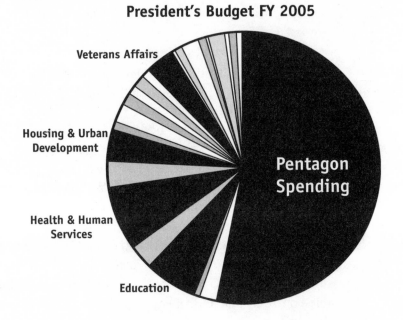

FEDERAL DISCRETIONARY SPENDING

develops human capital, we get an inaccurate, indeed bizarre, picture of economics. As Hilkka Pietila and Ann Chadeau observe, had household production been included in the system of macroeconomic accounts, governments would have quite a different picture of economic development, and may have implemented quite different economic and social policies.[31]

A growing number of nations, from Australia, Canada, and New Zealand to Switzerland and South Africa, have by now conducted surveys of nonmarket housework. The pioneers were the Nordic nations, with the first Norwegian survey dating back to 1912 and continuing since then. As Julie Aslaksen and Charlotte Koren note in their analy-

---

In March 2006, Congresswomen Lynn Woolsey and Barbara Lee introduced H.R. 4898 (the Common Sense Budget Act) to reassign $60 billion of unnecessary Pentagon spending to underfunded domestic priorities. Among the cuts: $7 billion from the National Missile Defense Program and $13 billion to reduce the American nuclear arsenal to one thousand warheads. According to defense scholar Lawrence Korb, formerly President Reagan's Assistant Secretary of Defense for Manpower, Installation, and Logistics, this $60 billion can easily be cut without endangering U.S. security.[32] The $60 billion would be reallocated as follows, without a single tax increase or one additional dime in federal spending: *Children's health care:* $10 billion annually to provide health care coverage for the millions of uninsured American children. *School reconstruction:* $10 billion over twelve years to rebuild and modernize every K–12 public school in the country. *Medical research:* $2 billion a year to restore recent cuts to the National Institutes of Health budget. *Job training:* $5 billion per year to retrain 250,000 Americans who have lost their jobs because of foreign trade. *Global hunger:* $13 billion a year in humanitarian assistance to allow poor nations to feed six million children who are at risk of dying from starvation every year. *Energy independence:* $10 billion each year to kick the imported oil habit by investing in efficient, renewable energy sources. *Homeland security:* $5 billion a year to make up for funding shortfalls in emergency preparedness, infrastructure upgrades, and grants for first responders. *Deficit reduction:* $5 billion devoted to putting a dent, if small, in the $8.2 trillion national debt.

Source: Figure and data reprinted with permission from Business Leaders for Sensible Priorities; www.sensiblepriorities.org/. ∎

sis of the Norwegian experience, these surveys were important in shaping Norwegian economic policies, which like those of other Nordic countries, are more supportive of caring and caregiving than the policies of any other nation.[33]

The 1995 United Nations Human Development Report estimated that the value of women's unpaid work is a whopping $11 trillion per year, and noted that "if national statistics fully reflect the 'invisible' contribution of women, it will become impossible for policymakers to ignore them in national decisions."

Such national surveys have uniformly shown that the monetary value of unpaid work is very high. For instance, a 2004 Swiss government survey based on 2000 census data showed that the value of unpaid work was 250 billion Swiss francs (162 billion Euros or $190 billion). This amount was 70 percent of the reported Swiss GDP. The Swiss data also showed that by far the largest part of the unpaid work was the work of women in the household, with women contributing almost two-thirds of the total value of all unpaid work.[34]

These surveys further show that the time spent in unpaid labor is on average as much, or more, than that spent in the paid workforce. Moreover, they confirm that the majority of that time is the time women spend in households caring for children, the elderly, the sick, and ensuring there is a clean home environment.

In 1985, the United Nations International Women's Conference in Nairobi called for the unremunerated contributions of women to be recorded in all national accounts. The 1995 U.N. Women's Conference in Beijing reiterated and strengthened that call. The 1995 United Nations Human Development Report, which focused heavily on women because of the U.N. Women's Conference that year, also urged that women's unpaid work be counted as part of national income.

This U.N. report estimated that the value of women's unpaid work is a whopping $11 trillion per year, and noted that "if national statistics fully reflect the 'invisible' contribution of women, it will become impossible for policymakers to ignore them in national decisions." The report also noted: "If women's unpaid work were properly valued, it is quite possible that women would emerge in most societies as the major breadwinners—or at least equal breadwinners—since they put in longer hours of work than men."[35]

In response to pressure from women's organizations and U.N. World Conferences on Women, the United Nations in 1993 recommended a significant accounting change: a new System of National Accounts that includes household work in a "satellite" account. More recently, Eurostat (the statistical office of the European Commission) has put out a manual for a satellite account of household production.

While satellite accounts are still separate from GDP or GNP, they are an important step toward more realistic international economic measures. They also show that whether or not the value of the unpaid caregiving work done in households is recognized is basically a matter of politics rather than statistical constraints.

A growing number of nations, from Australia, Canada, and New Zealand to Switzerland and South Africa, have conducted surveys of nonmarket housework. These national surveys have uniformly shown that the monetary value of unpaid work is very high.

BEYOND THE ECONOMIC DOUBLE STANDARD

There is, of course, no way of quantifying how the human spirit soars when it is enfolded in a sense that we are valued and valuable, that we are worthy of care, and that we can enrich the lives of others by caring for them.

How do we put a dollar value on the physical, emotional, mental, and spiritual benefits of caring and nurturance, of feeling safe and cherished? How can we quantify the value of being seen for who we truly are, of the lift to our hearts from relations where our essential humanity and that of others shines through?

There is no way of quantifying the happiness we humans obtain from being loved and cared for. Nor can we quantify the happiness we derive from caring for others, even though there's no lack of substantiation of this happiness—from poetry and philosophy to psychological and sociological studies.[36]

At the same time, as we saw in chapter 3, we *can* quantify many of the economic benefits of caring and nurturance. Findings from neuroscience show that good caregiving is foundational for children to grow into productive, creative adults, and that there is a strong connection between poor child care and later health, social, and employment problems.[37] Studies also show that good child care programs have long-term economic benefits—for instance, children in high-quality early child development programs earned substantially more over their lifetimes than those who did not receive these benefits.[38] Moreover, adults who feel cared for are healthier and live longer, which translates into substantial dollars-and-cents savings, including large savings in the medical costs that are today a major economic drain for businesses and governments.

Economic indicators must take into account the benefits to society of the work of caring and caregiving. In addition, we must find ways of rewarding this work in tangible ways that help put food on the table and a roof over people's heads.

Of course, the idea that caring and caregiving in families should be socially supported in tangible ways runs straight into the argument that this work should not be sullied by crass material considerations, that it should be done solely out of love. Certainly the intrinsic motivation of love plays a major factor in these activities. And so it should. But this does not change the fact that society derives enormous benefits from these activities, so much so that it could not function at all without them. Nor does it change the fact that the people who primarily perform these activities—women—have been condemned to be the mass of the world's poor, so that even in affluent nations like the United States older women are nearly twice as poor as older men.

Neither does it change the fact that the failure to recognize the economic value of this work has distorted economic policies so that funding for caring activities is a lower priority than funding for prisons and wars. As I have emphasized throughout this book, it is simply not realistic to expect caring policies as long as caring is systematically devalued.

Certainly we don't want wages for caring paid by the person—usually a man—where there are two parents. But we don't have to continue to penalize those who do the caring work for families, as we do today, by denying them Social Security and other public benefits in their own right.

We can give more visibility and value to caring work in families through a variety of approaches. These range from social investment in good training for caregivers, caregiver tax credits, and Social Security for caregivers. Moreover, through flex time, child care stipends, universal health care, paid parental leave, and other family-friendly workplace policies supported by governments and employers, both women and men can balance work inside and outside the home. This will give more men the opportunity to be closer to their children and give more women the opportunity to express and develop other aspects of their human potential, and at the same time also derive income from employment.

We also need higher wages and better benefits for caring professions. This takes us to a common argument used to justify low pay for caregiving: that caregiving is not "skilled" work. In reality, good caregiving requires a great deal of knowledge and skill. For example, good child care requires knowledge of stages of child development (including brain development) and of what children are capable of understanding and doing at different ages—an understanding that is tragically absent in "traditional" punitive childrearing approaches.

There will be those who argue that the motivation of workers in caring professions should be intrinsic rather than extrinsic, that good pay would "cheapen" the work. But, as Julie Nelson and other economists document, if money payments are perceived as acknowledging and supporting workers' goals and desires, they actually reinforce and magnify, rather than replace, interior motivations and satisfactions. In other words, as with other rewards to reinforce positive behaviors, higher pay for caring work would tend to encourage, rather than discourage, caring.[39]

WOMEN, MEN, AND THE QUALITY OF LIFE

All this takes us back to the hidden system of valuations in which women, and the work of caring and caregiving stereotypically associated with women, is devalued. It also leads to yet another set of studies showing that changing this gendered values system will benefit us all.

A statistical study I conducted together with social psychologist David Loye and sociologist Kari Norgaard under the auspices of the Center for Partnership Studies (CPS) found just that. This study, reported in *Women, Men, and the Global Quality of Life*, compared measures of the status of women with quality-of-life measures using statistics collected by international agencies from eighty-nine nations. It showed that the status of women can actually be a better predictor of general quality of life than GDP or gross domestic product.[40]

For example, Kuwait and France had almost identical levels of per capita GDP. But their rates of infant mortality, one of the most basic indicators of quality of life, were very different. In France, the infant mortality rate was eight infants per one thousand live births. In Kuwait, where the status of women is much lower than in France, it was nineteen infants per one thousand live births, more than double the rate of France.[41]

It is of course difficult to show causal relations when looking at interactive systems dynamics. But the fact that we see such differences in basic quality-of-life indicators in nations with the same GDP but different levels of gender equity shows that gender equity or inequity are integral to a generally higher or lower quality of life.

The CPS study found that higher GDP tends to go along with movement toward gender equality. But it also found that societies with the same GDP can have great variations in gender relations—and that the nature of these relations correlates strongly with a higher or lower general quality of life.[42]

There are many reasons for this correlation, but one factor is that in nations where women have higher status, caring and caregiving is given more value, whether it is performed by women or men. For example, in nations such as Sweden, Norway, and Finland, caregiving professions such as child care, nursing, and teaching have higher status. Caring for people and nature is also given more priority in national budgets and other policies. All this contributes to a higher quality of life for all.

This relationship between the status of women and a society's general quality of life has been confirmed by other studies, including the World Values Surveys, the largest international surveys of attitudes and how they correlate with economic development and political structure.[43] For the first time in 2000, the World Values Survey focused attention on attitudes toward gender equity. And based on data from sixty-five societies representing 80 percent of the world's population, it found that the relationship between support for gender equality in politics and the society's level of political rights and civil liberties is "remarkably strong."[44] It also found that greater power for women is important for success in the postindustrial economy.[45]

As Ronald Inglehart, Pippa Norris, and Christian Weizel write in "Gender Equality and Democracy," "In advanced industrial societies authority patterns seem to be shifting from the traditional hierarchical style toward a more collegial style that parallels the differences between stereotypically 'male' and 'female' styles of social interaction."[46] They further note that, along with other cultural changes associated with higher status for women, this "feminization of leadership styles" is closely linked with the spread of democratic institutions.[47]

☐ Women, Men, and the General Quality of Life

In its study *Women, Men, and the Global Quality of Life*, the Center for Partnership Studies found that measures of the status of women can be an even better predictor of quality of life than conventional indicators such as GNP or GDP.[48]

For example, gender equity variables correlated more highly with overall literacy rates than GDP. A higher literacy gap between females and males correlated strongly with lower life expectancy and higher infant mortality. Of particular interest was that the prevalence of contraception had a stronger relation to basic quality-of-life indicators such as infant mortality and life expectancy than GDP.[49]

This is not to say there's no relationship between a low GDP and such basic quality-of-life indicators as rates of infant and maternal mortality, lack of drinkable water, lack of adequate health care, lack of contraceptive availability, and low literacy rates. There obviously is, as countries with a low GDP have fewer economic resources for these purposes. However, a higher general quality of life does not necessarily follow a higher GDP.

For more information on *Women, Men, and the Global Quality of Life*, see www.partnershipway.org. ■

The 2000 World Values Survey found that the belief that women and men should be equal goes along with a shift from traditional authoritarian styles of child rearing to increasing emphasis on imagination and tolerance as important values to teach a child. And these shifts in attitudes about gender and child rearing, in turn, are linked with greater interpersonal trust, a lessening of reliance on outside authority, a rising sense of subjective well-being, a higher living standard, and other aspects of what Inglehart, Norris, and Weizel call postmodern "self-expression" rather than traditional "survival" values.[50]

In nations where women have higher status, caring and caregiving are given more value, whether they are performed by women or men, and this contributes to a higher quality of life for all.

These studies show that economic systems cannot be understood, or effectively changed, without attention to other core cultural components—and that a central cultural component is the construction of the roles and relations of the female and male halves of humanity. They show the benefits that societies reap when women and activities stereotypically associated with women have higher status.

When caring and caregiving are devalued because they are associated with the "inferior" female half of our species, policies and practices are generally also less caring. Not only is there less support for the "women's work" of caring for children, the sick, and the elderly; there is also less support for caring for our natural environment and for policies and practices that make for greater social and economic equity.

This lack of caring is economically costly. The costs include huge outlays for the criminal justice system and police, as well as the enormous costs to business of lost productivity. On top of this are the costs that cannot be quantified: the economic and human costs of devastated lives.

The economic double standard we've been examining has led to unrealistic assessments of economic well-being. It has led to economic indicators that obscure the enormous benefits society derives from the essential work of caring and caregiving, whether it is performed by women or men. Without understanding these benefits, policymakers get a distorted picture of what are economically productive activities, and the results are distorted and uncaring economic policies and practices.

Of course, we really don't need statistics to show that caring and caregiving is the most valuable, and essential, human work. Without it we die, and with it we not only survive but thrive. But given that policy-makers rely so heavily on quantifications, the inclusion of the benefits of caring and caregiving in statistics on what constitutes productive work is essential.

Giving real value to caring and caregiving won't solve all the world's ills. But it will greatly add to human happiness and fulfillment, and is essential for a more prosperous, equitable, and sustainable future.

CHAPTER 5

Connecting the Dots

There's an old parable about three blind men and an elephant. The first blind man felt the animal's trunk and said it's a leathery snake. The second blind man felt its leg and said it's a tree. The third blind man felt its tail and said it's a rope. It's such an old parable that it's become a cliché. But it graphically describes a basic obstacle to fundamental economic and social change.

Today, thousands of experts are analyzing our economic, social, and ecological problems from their particular perspectives, disagreeing on what lies behind them. But just as an elephant can't be understood by only describing some of its parts, it's not possible to understand what lies behind our global problems unless we take into account the whole system.

As noted in chapter 2, we can't change economic systems by just focusing on economics. Economic systems are embedded in larger social systems. To effectively change dysfunctional economic policies and practices, we need an understanding of their larger social matrix.

Reexamining social dynamics through the analytical lens of the partnership/domination continuum helps us connect the dots. It makes it possible to see what scientists call *systems self-organization*: the interactions of the core components of a system that maintain its basic character.[1] This chapter describes these interactions. It examines the contrasting structures of the partnership system and the domination system. It gives real-life examples of societies that orient to either end of the partnership/domination continuum. And it shows how each of these systems directly impacts economics.

A NEW SOCIAL AND ECONOMIC FRAMEWORK

I was born in Europe at a time of massive regression to a rigid domination system: the rise to power of the Nazis first in Germany and then in my native Austria. I was too small to understand what happened, but when the Nazis took over Austria, my life radically changed. Fear became our constant companion. On November 10, 1938—the infamous Crystal Night, so-named because of all the glass shattered in Jewish homes, shops, and synagogues—a gang of Nazis came to our home and dragged my father away. By a miracle, my mother obtained his release, and we fled Vienna. Had we not, we would have been killed in the Holocaust, as was the fate of six million European Jews, including my grandparents and most of my aunts, uncles, and cousins, as I found out to my horror after World War II ended.

These early life experiences profoundly affected me. They led to my lifelong quest to understand how such a thing could happen, and what we can do so it never happens again. They eventually led to my years of multidisciplinary, cross-cultural, and historical research, which, in turn, led to the discovery of the new social categories of the partnership system and the domination system.

Older social categories, such as capitalist versus socialist, Western versus Eastern, and industrial versus pre- or postindustrial, came out of times when the gender double standard we've been examining was generally accepted. Consequently, they fail to factor in how the construction of gender roles and relations affects the structure of the entire social system. Not only that, these categories ignore early childhood relations—even though these relations profoundly affect what kinds of societies people grow up to accept and perpetuate.[2]

By contrast, the categories of the partnership system and the domination system take into account the *whole* of humanity—both its male and female halves—and the *whole* of our lives—both the public sphere that was not long ago called the "men's world," and the private sphere of family and other intimate relations to which women and children were traditionally confined.

Looking at this larger picture makes it possible to see patterns that had not been identified before. These patterns, which are only visible if we look at the full spectrum of roles and relations that comprise a society, are the configurations of the partnership system and the domination system.

The degree to which a particular society orients to one or the other of these systems profoundly affects which of our large repertoire of human traits and behaviors are reinforced or inhibited. The partnership system brings out our capacities for consciousness, caring, and creativity. The domination system tends to inhibit these capacities. It brings out—indeed, requires—insensitivity, cruelty, and destructiveness.

Human beings have the biological potential for all these traits and behaviors. Some people may be born with a genetic tendency for one kind or for another.[3] But psychology and neuroscience show that people's life experiences, and particularly their early relationships, profoundly affect whether these tendencies are inhibited or expressed. And anthropology and sociology show that people's life experiences and relationships are largely shaped by their cultures.

The degree to which a culture or subculture orients to either end of the partnership/domination continuum produces different life experiences and supports different kinds of relationships. The domination system's configuration supports relations based on rigid rankings of domination ultimately backed up by fear and force. The partnership system's configuration supports relationships based on mutual respect, mutual accountability, and mutual benefit. Therefore, understanding the configurations of the partnership system and the domination system is an important step toward positive changes in how we relate to ourselves, others, and Mother Earth.

THE DOMINATOR CONFIGURATION

Some of the most brutal, violent, and oppressive societies of the twentieth century were Hitler's Germany (a technologically advanced, Western, rightist society), Stalin's USSR (a secular, leftist society), Khomeini's Iran and the Taliban of Afghanistan (Eastern religious societies), and Idi Amin's Uganda (a tribalist society). There are obvious differences between them. But they all share one thing: they orient very closely to the configuration of the domination system, including top-down economic institutions and practices guided by uncaring rather than caring values.

The first core component of the dominator configuration is a structure of rigid top-down rankings maintained through physical, psychological, and economic control. This authoritarian structure is found in both the family and the state or tribe, and is the template or mold for all social institutions.

The second core component is a high level of abuse and violence, from child and wife beating to chronic warfare. Every society has some abuse and violence. But in the domination system we find the institutionalization and idealization of abuse and violence. This is needed to maintain rigid rankings of domination—man over woman, man over man, race over race, religion over religion, and nation over nation.

The third core component of the domination system is the rigid ranking of one half of humanity over the other half.[4] When Hitler came to power, a Nazi rallying cry was "get women back into their traditional place."[5] This was also the rallying cry for Khomeini in Iran and the Taliban in Afghanistan. Stalin's policies retreated from earlier attempts to equalize the status of women and men.[6] In Idi Amin's Uganda, women were so subordinate to men that as late as the 1980s women in rural areas were still expected to kneel when speaking to a man.[7]

This superior/inferior view of our species is a central component of inequitable, despotic, and violent cultures. It provides a mental map that children learn for equating all differences—whether based on race, religion, or ethnicity—with superiority or inferiority.

This ranked view of our species also manifests itself in a skewed system of values. Along with the ranking of male over female comes the ranking of qualities and behaviors classified as "hard" or "masculine" over those classified as "soft" or feminine. "Heroic" violence and "manly" conquest, as in funding for weapons and wars, are valued more than caring, nonviolence, and caregiving. These "feminine" values and activities are relegated to women and "effeminate" men, and given little policy support.

This in turn leads to the fourth core component of the domination system: beliefs and stories that justify domination and violence as inevitable, even moral. Cultures and subcultures that orient closely to this system teach that it's honorable and moral to kill people of neighboring nations or tribes, stone women to death, enslave "inferior" people, and beat children to impose one's will. War is "holy"—and this is true not only for religious dominator cultures but also for secular ones. For Nazi youth, going forth to kill the enemy and purify the race was a holy mission, just as terrorists today invoke God to justify their inhuman acts.

These four core components—a social structure of rigid top-down rankings, a high level of abuse and violence, a male-superior/female-inferior model of our species, and beliefs that justify domination and violence as inevitable and moral—shape all social and economic institutions of the domination system.

DOMINATION AND ECONOMICS

Dominator economics are based on rankings of "superiors" over "inferiors." Economic rules, policies, and practices advantage those on top, with little or no consideration for those on the bottom, who are seen as "naturally" inferior or as getting what they deserve for not working hard enough to change their situation.

The structure of economic institutions embedded in a domination system maintains top-down rankings by concentrating economic control in the hands of those on top. These structures are built and

---

◨ *Human Nature: Myths and Realities*

Our picture of human nature has been distorted by what happens to the human psyche in a dominator context. Freud, for example, brilliantly described the male dominator psyche with his *Oedipus complex*. He asserted that every son wants to kill and replace his father, in an endless struggle for domination. This theory was then accepted as a description of the male psyche, rather than of the distorted psychological dynamics of the more rigid dominator culture of Freud's time. Freud's theory that women suffer from "penis envy" was also accepted as a description of the female psyche, obscuring the fact that what women in dominator systems envy is not male anatomy but male privilege, autonomy, and opportunity for action. Although these Freudian theories have been discredited, many dominator beliefs and institutions are still prevalent worldwide. It's up to us to debunk these beliefs and change these institutions. ◼

maintained not only through the laws and rules specifically governing economics but through the larger social system of laws, rules, beliefs, habits, and norms.

As we have seen, institutions such as the family, education, religion, and governments all interact with economic institutions to maintain the basic character of a society. And, as we also saw, cultural norms for early childhood and gender relations are particularly important, since it is through these relations that people first learn what kinds of relations, social structures, and behaviors are considered normal and desirable.

Flowing from the double standard for "men's work" and "women's work," dominator economics rests on the devaluation and exploitation of the life-supporting activities of both women and Mother Earth. While men derive some advantages from the gender double standard, these advantages are outweighed by the disadvantages. The toll of the domination system on men is huge—from being maimed and injured in constant wars, to being controlled and oppressed by those above them.

When children are taught that half our species is put on earth to be served and the other half to serve, they acquire a mental map for economic inequity that is then generalized to other relations. They learn to unconsciously accept the subordination and economic exploitation of all "inferior" out-groups by "superior" in-groups.

This mutually reinforcing interconnection between the ranking of men over women and an unjust economic system was starkly clear in feudal and monarchic days. In those rigidly male-dominated times, kings, emperors, and nobles lived in luxury. But the men and women who worked for these "superiors" from dawn to dusk, supplying their tables and filling their coffers with gold, barely survived.

We also see this interconnection later, in times when dogmas of women's inferiority resurged. These too were characteristically times when the economic gulf between those on top and bottom widened. For instance, in the "robber baron" days of early industrial capitalism, when workers were often mercilessly exploited, Social Darwinists were countering feminism with the argument that women are naturally inferior to men. Currently, at the same time that sociobiologists maintain that the domination of male over female is an evolutionary imperative, economic stratification has also intensified:

multimillion-dollar corporate salaries contrast sharply with home-lessness and hunger.

I want to again emphasize that economic inequity is not only a characteristic of unregulated capitalism. It is a characteristic of domi-nator economics. Under the former Soviet Union's communist regime, those on top ate caviar and lived in comfortable flats and vil-las in the country, while most families lived in overcrowded apart-ments and women stood in long lines for hours to buy bare necessities.

Another characteristic of dominator economics is corruption. It is often said that power corrupts. Although this is by no means inevitable, corruption in the sense of gaining advantage for oneself or one's group without regard for others, particularly those lower in the pecking order, is built into the domination system. Traditions of dis-honesty in business and government go way back, and it's only with the move toward a partnership system that ideas such as business and government "transparency" have started to gain ground.[8]

In rigid dominator cultures, bribery at all levels of government, from the most petty local functionary to the highest official, is still often accepted practice. Even in the United States, big political donors often write legislation that profits them at the expense of tax-payers. It is common practice for scientific studies to be funded by pharmaceutical and other corporations that have a vested interest in their outcome. And as happened at Enron, WorldCom, and Tyco, cor-porate officials often enrich themselves by falsifying company books at the expense of employees and shareholders. All this is not, as we're sometimes told, due to an innately flawed "human nature." But it is also not just due to a few "bad apples" in the business and govern-ment barrels. It is deeply embedded in traditions of corruption inher-ent in hierarchies of domination where caring and empathy are systematically inhibited.

In these and other ways, dominator economics interfere with the operation of markets. Rather than being arbiters of supply and demand, to the extent that a society orients to the domination system, markets will be skewed to benefit those on top at the expense of those on bottom.

The outright appropriation of property from others is another hall-mark of many rigid dominator regimes. Stalin appropriated the holdings of millions of *kulaks*, the small landed peasants murdered by his regime. Khomeini confiscated the property of Kurds and Baha'i. His fundamentalist regime terrorized these out-groups until they fled, or simply killed them in the name of God and morality. The confiscated assets of Jews, another despised out-group, were used to finance the German economic recovery under the Nazis. The Nazi state forcibly took the homes, art, businesses, and bank accounts of Jewish families—including those of my parents. Nazi party members were rewarded with booty from these legalized armed robberies. Jewish women, men, and children were herded into concentration camps or, as my parents and I, forced to flee.

⬚ Free Markets: Myths and Realities

A tenet of neoclassical economic theory is that when markets are free of government regulation, they will efficiently allocate a society's resources through the interaction of supply and demand. As a consequence, "a free market" has become a slogan against government regulations.

But the reality is that in the context of a domination system, markets can hardly be "level playing fields." Rather than ensuring fair prices and wages through supply and demand, markets are distorted through misleading advertising, weak or no standards for working conditions, interference with labor's bargaining power, little or no consumer protection, and government policies that leave the rich and powerful free to do what they want.

In domination systems, monopolies flourish and smaller competitors are driven out of business. In addition, as detailed in chapter 6, domination systems create artificial scarcities as well as artificial needs. And all this is still further compounded by the domination system's devaluation of caring, caregiving, and anything else stereotypically considered "soft" or "feminine."

In short, to the extent that a society orients to the domination system, markets will be controlled by those who hold power—whether through governmental or private means. Indeed, freedom in a domination system is often a code word for those in control to use power without accountability. ∎

All this was done in the name of the purification of the race, God's will, combating the evils of private property, and other slogans justifying insensitivity, brutality, and greed. These slogans obscure a basic truth: that hurting and oppressing others is inhuman and immoral.

Indeed, the domination system maintains itself through denial. It constricts consciousness, making it difficult to see the harm one causes to others, even to oneself. This lack of consciousness is necessary if in-group versus out-group rankings are to be imposed and maintained.

Even in societies that are not as close to the domination end of the partnership/domination continuum as the ones just described, some of the same dynamics can be seen, albeit in less overt and brutal form. Over the last several decades, the United States has regressed toward the domination model, with a reconcentration of political and economic power at the top, attempts to return us to a "father-headship" family, and increasing use of violence in foreign relations. This regression has brought a retreat from earlier economic safety-net policies, and a return to rules, policies, and practices that advantage powerful in-groups with little or no concern for disempowered out-groups.

While U.S. government officials have certainly not confiscated the assets of "inferior" out-groups directly to reward their cronies, they have effectively accomplished this by diverting tax revenues to those on top, providing lucrative contracts to underperforming crony corporations, and cutting social programs that provide essential services to the poor. So during the years of regression to a domination system, funding to aid poor children and families was cut, tax revenues were used to reward large corporations and other major political donors with no-bid contracts, tax reductions, and repeal and/or nonenforcement of environmental and consumer protections, while government turned a blind eye to the most blatant antitrust law violations.[9]

These are not accidental developments. They are inherent in the domination system. A society that orients primarily to this system cannot have equitable economic policies. A caring and sustainable economic system can only flourish as society shifts more to the partnership end of the continuum.

THE PARTNERSHIP CONFIGURATION

Cultures that orient to the partnership end of the partnership/domination continuum also transcend conventional categories such as religious or secular, Eastern or Western, industrial, preindustrial or postindustrial. They can be tribal societies, such as the Teduray of the Phillippines, studied by the University of California anthropologist Stuart Schlegel, or agrarian societies, such as the Minangkabau of Sumatra, studied by the University of Pennsylvania anthropologist Peggy Reeves Sanday. They can be highly technologically developed societies such as Sweden, Norway, and Finland. In fact, we see movement toward the partnership system in many nations today.

The first core component of the partnership system is a democratic and egalitarian structure in *both* the family and society at large. However, orientation to the partnership system does *not* mean a flat, leaderless structure. In the partnership system, parents are still responsible for children, teachers for students, managers for workers. But there's a big difference. This is the difference between what I call *hierarchies of domination*, which are based on control and fear, and *hierarchies of actualization*, where parents, teachers, and managers inspire, support, and empower rather than disempower others—a subject I will return to.

The second core component of the partnership system is that abuse and violence are not culturally accepted, so there is more trust and mutual respect. This doesn't mean there is no abuse or violence. But because they're not needed to maintain rigid rankings of domination, they don't have to be institutionalized or idealized.

The third core component is equal partnership between women and men. With this comes a system of values in which qualities and behaviors such as nonviolence and caregiving, denigrated as feminine in the domination system, are highly valued in *both* women and men.

These values are foundational to an economic system that supports relations based on mutual benefit, mutual accountability, and mutual caring. Again, this does not mean that everyone has the same economic position as everyone else. But there are no huge gaps between haves and have-nots in partnership economies. And since caring and caregiving are not devalued, business practices and economic policies can be guided by an ethos of caring for self, others, and our natural habitat.

This leads to the fourth core component of the partnership system: beliefs and stories that offer a more balanced and positive view of human nature. In the partnership system, cruelty, violence, and oppression are recognized as human possibilities. But they're not considered inevitable, much less moral, and cultural values and beliefs support empathic and mutually respectful relations. Moreover, this system relies more heavily on positive rather than negative human motivations.

PARTNERSHIP AND DOMINATION SYSTEMS

Component	Domination System	Partnership System
1. Structure	Authoritarian and inequitable social and economic structure of rigid hierarchies of domination.	Democratic and economically equitable structure of linking and hierarchies of actualization.
2. Relations	High degree of fear, abuse, and violence, from child and wife beating to abuse by "superiors" in families, workplaces, and society.	Mutual respect and trust with low degree of fear and violence, since they are not required to maintain rigid rankings of domination.
3. Gender	Ranking of male half of humanity over female half, as well as of traits and activities viewed as "masculine" over those viewed as "feminine," such as caring and caregiving.	Equal valuing of male and female halves of humanity, as well as high valuing of empathy, caring, caregiving, and nonviolence in women, men, and social and economic policy.
4. Beliefs	Beliefs and stories justify and idealize domination and violence, which are presented as inevitable, moral, and desirable.	Beliefs and stories give high value to empathic, mutually beneficial, and caring relations, which are considered moral and desirable.

Societies that orient to the partnership side of the partnership/domination continuum are not ideal societies. But their beliefs and institutions—from the family and education to politics and economics—support respect for human rights and for our natural environment. They are democratic cultures where there aren't huge gaps between haves and have-nots and where nurturance and nonvio-

DYNAMICS OF THE PARTNERSHIP/DOMINATION CONTINUUM

The Partnership System

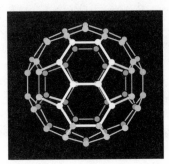

Democratic and economically equitable structure

Mutual respect and trust with low degree of violence

Equal valuing of males and females and high regard for stereotypical feminine values

Beliefs and stories that give high value to empathic and caring relations

The Domination System

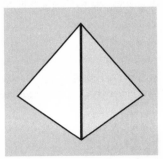

Authoritarian and inequitable social and economic structure

High degree of abuse and violence

Subordination of women and "femininity" to men and "masculinity"

Beliefs and stories that justify and idealize domination and violence

The relationship among the components of each of these two systems is interactive, with all four core components reinforcing one another. These interactions shape all social institutions and relations, including economic ones.

lence are considered appropriate for both men and women and are socially supported.

There are two basic human motivations. One is avoiding pain. The other is seeking pleasure. These motivations operate in both the partnership and domination systems, but the emphasis is different in each.

In the domination system, fear of pain is a major motivation. This can be fear of punishment from "superiors" or fear of losing power and status. Consequently, much of earlier thinking about effective workplaces was based on the belief that the more employees feel threatened, the harder they will work.

Today, most business experts recognize that people actually perform better when they are not afraid, when they feel safe and cared for rather than threatened and unsafe. They recognize that a workplace based on these principles not only fosters greater productivity and company loyalty but also the creativity, risk taking, and innovation that Gifford and Elizabeth Pinchot call "intrapreneurship."[10] Consequently, as we saw in chapter 3, many successful companies are recognizing that the pleasure of being valued and cared for motivates people to do the most consistently excellent work.

But this shift to relying primarily on motivations of pleasure rather than pain did not happen in a vacuum. It is part of a larger social movement: the movement to shift from the domination system to the partnership system, not only in business organization but in all institutions and relations.

PARTNERSHIP STRUCTURES, VALUES, AND RELATIONS

The four core components of the partnership system—a democratic and egalitarian family and social structure, a low level of abuse and violence, equal partnership between the male and female halves of humanity, and beliefs and stories that support relations based on mutual benefit, accountability, and caring—shape all social institutions and relations, including economic ones.

We can see the interaction of these components more clearly by looking at less complex societies, such as the Teduray. I first heard of this tribal society when I received a phone call from the anthropologist Stuart Schlegel. He told me that for many years he had studied a culture in the Philippines. "I described them as radically egalitarian," he said. "But now that I've read your work, I see that the forest Teduray were clearly a partnership society."

In his book, *Wisdom from a Rainforest*, Schlegel writes that among the Teduray "all human beings, whether men or women, whether adults or children, whether the finest shaman or the most ordinary basket weaver, were considered of equal worth and of equal standing in society."[11] This valuing of each individual carried over into all aspects of work and life.

As Schlegel writes:

Although women were specialists in childbearing, both men and women carried around young children, nurtured them, and helped raise them. Greater male strength was recognized, but it did not in any way suggest the supremacy of one gender over another. Nor did it provide the rationale for any form of social oppression, organized warfare, or concentration of private property. Weeding and felling trees, weaving baskets and hunting for wild pigs, giving birth and fathering children—all were really just different but equal specialties.

Family and social structure were egalitarian, and social relations unranked and peaceful. Decision-making was typically participatory; softer, stereotypically "feminine" virtues were valued; and community well-being was the principal motivation for work and other activities. Nature and the human body were given great respect. The emphasis on technology was on enhancing and sustaining life.[12]

Of course, the Teduray didn't always behave in caring ways. As Schlegel writes, "They occasionally turned to violence to settle their problems, even though their beliefs and institutions all said violence was never right."[13] But their culture had elaborate mechanisms to prevent feuding. Legal sages from both sides tried to work out a settlement, and this was a role played by both men and women.

The Minangkabau, an agrarian culture of over two million people, are another example of how the four core components of the partnership system are mutually reinforcing. The anthropologist Peggy Reeves Sanday, who lived in the Minangkabau village of Belubus on and off for over twenty years, reports that this culture's social and family structure is based on mutual respect and caring rather than rankings of domination and submission.[14] Because the Minangkabau orient to the partnership system, neither women nor men dominate. The family and social structure is more egalitarian. And violence is not institutionalized or idealized.

To begin with, as among the Teduray, violence is not part of Minangkabau childraising. "Child care is not authoritarian or punitive," Sanday writes. "Children aren't hit, I never heard mothers screaming at their children. . . . The idea is that they will learn sooner or later to behave as proper Minangkabau."[15]

Although women and men are valued equally, the Minangkabau trace descent through the mother. Biological paternity is not an issue in relation to passing on male property. Sociobiologists would argue that under these circumstances, fathers wouldn't play much of a role in their children's lives. But in fact, they do. However, the connection of father to child is not tied to the transmission of land and houses. It is an emotional rather than a material bond. As Minangkabau elder Nago Besar put it, "Concerns about biological fatherhood deflect attention from the more important emphasis on the child's wellbeing."[16]

The Minangkabau also contradict the famous dictum of anthropologist Claude Levi-Strauss that men exchange women to form social bonds between families or groups. Among the Minangkabau, social bonds between clans are fostered through the giving in marriage of sons by mothers to other clans. Unlike marital exchanges in dominator-oriented cultures, these bonds are not cemented by anything like bride-price or dowry. In line with the culture's partnership orientation, exchanges are reciprocal, with both the bride and the bridegroom's families contributing to the wedding feast.

Of course, as in other partnership-oriented cultures, life among the Minangkabau is not perfect. But both men and women are expected to be nurturing in this culture. As Sanday observes, nurture (not dominion) is the primary social lesson the Minangkabau take from nature. Consequently, social institutions protect the vulnerable and foster caring. In addition, like the Teduray, the Minangkabau use mediation to prevent violence and encourage a peaceful way of life.

PARTNERSHIP IN NORDIC NATIONS

Some people might say that these two examples show that partnership can work in technologically undeveloped cultures such as the

Teduray and Minangkabau, but that more complex industrialized cultures require a dominator organization. But the highly technologically developed, industrialized Nordic nations are extremely successful precisely because of their partnership orientation.

Nordic nations such as Sweden, Norway, and Finland created societies with both political and economic democracy. These nations don't have the huge gaps between haves and have-nots characteristic of dominator-oriented nations. While they're not ideal societies, they have succeeded in providing a generally good living standard for all, greater gender equity, and a low level of social violence. Studies also show that most workers in Nordic nations are more satisfied and happier than people in countries like the United States where GNP is higher.[17]

At the beginning of the twentieth century, Nordic countries were extremely poor, with a low standard of living and a very low life expectancy. There were even famines, leading to mass emigration to the United States and other nations. But today, these nations regularly rank high in the United Nations annual Human Development

Nature, Nurture, and Evolution

The Minangkabau view nurture as a core principle of nature. As anthropologist Peggy Sanday writes: "Unlike Darwin in the nineteenth century, the Minangkabau subordinate male dominion and competition, which we consider basic to human social ordering and evolution, to the work of maternal nurture, which they hold to be necessary for the common good and the healthy society. . . . Like the seedlings of nature, infants must be nurtured so that they will flower and grow to their fullness and strength as adults. This means that culture must focus on nurturing the weak and renounce brute strength."[18]

This focus on the life-sustaining powers of nature, characteristic of cultures orienting to the partnership system, is today integral to the environmental movement. It is in sharp contrast to the adversarial view of nature that animates the once hallowed "conquest of nature," which at our level of technological development could take us to an evolutionary dead end. ■

Reports in measures of quality of life. They are also in the top tiers of the World Economic Forum's annual Global Competitiveness Reports.[19]

The Nordic nations' economic success has sometimes been attributed to their relatively small and homogeneous populations. But in smaller, even more homogeneous societies such as some oil-rich Middle Eastern nations where absolute conformity to one religious sect and one tribal or royal head is demanded, we find large gaps between haves and have-nots and other inequities characteristic of the domination system. We have to look at other factors to understand why the Nordic nations moved out of poverty to develop a prosperous, more caring and equitable economic system.

What made the Nordic nations successful was their move to the partnership configuration. As we have seen, in addition to a more democratic and egalitarian family and social structure and lower levels of violence, a key element of this configuration is much greater equality between women and men.

⊡ *An Economist Explains Why Nordic Nations Prosper*

According to the chief economist and director of the Global Competitiveness Network, Augusto Lopez-Claros, "In many ways the Nordics have entered virtuous circles where various factors reinforce each other to make them among the most competitive economies in the world." In his September 28, 2005 interview on the occasion of the World Economic Forum's release of its *Global Competitiveness Report 2005–2006* (in which Finland came in first), Lopez-Claros noted that "there is no evidence that high taxes are adversely affecting the ability of Nordic countries to compete effectively in world markets, or to deliver to their respective populations extremely high living standards." On the contrary, he observed that "When high tax rates generate resources that are used to deliver world-class educational establishments, an effective social safety net, and a highly motivated and skilled labor force, then competitiveness is boosted, not undermined."

Source: www.weforum.org/site/homepublic.nsf/Content/Global+Competitiveness+Report+2005-2006%3A+Interview. ∎

In Sweden, Norway, Iceland, Denmark, and Finland, women can, and do, occupy positions of political leadership. Indeed, women have held the highest political offices in the Nordic world. And approximately 40 percent of national legislators are female, a larger number than anywhere else in the world.

As among the Teduray and Minangkabau, the higher status of Nordic women has important consequences for how men define masculinity. As the status of women rises, so does the status of caregiving, nonviolence, and other traits deemed inappropriate for men in dominator societies because they're associated with "inferior" femininity. In partnership-oriented cultures, men can value these traits and activities in themselves as well as in society because women are no longer subordinate.[20]

Along with the higher status of Nordic women come fiscal priorities that support more "feminine" values and activities. These more partnership-oriented nations pioneered caregiving policies such as government-supported child care, universal health care, and paid parental leave, making life easier and happier for families and contributing to a less stressed and more productive workforce.

As they moved toward the partnership configuration, Nordic nations also pioneered laws prohibiting violence against children in families. They pioneered nonviolent conflict resolution, establishing the first peace studies programs when the rest of the world only had war academies. They have strong men's movements working to stop male violence toward women.[21]

In addition, Nordic nations pioneered environmentally sound industrial approaches such as the Swedish "Natural Step." They recently pioneered laws that prohibit commercial advertising targeting children in an effort to prevent the rampant materialism that afflicts most industrialized nations. Not surprisingly, these nations also contribute a larger percentage of their gross domestic product than other developed nations to caring international programs: programs working for fair economic development, environmental protection, and human rights.

Not only that, the Nordic nations were among the first to use more partnership-oriented economic structures. Some of the first experiments in industrial democracy came from Sweden and Norway, as did studies showing that a more participatory structure where workers play a part in deciding such basic matters as how to organize tasks and what hours to work can be extremely effective.

Moreover, Nordic nations have a long history of business cooperatives, jointly owned and democratically controlled enterprises that have traditionally included as one of their guiding principles concern for the community in which they operate. These cooperatives are still a significant part of Nordic economic life. COPAC (the Committee for the Promotion and Advancement of Cooperatives, which works with the U.N. to promote and coordinate sustainable cooperative development) reported that in 1997 Finnish cooperatives were responsible for 79 percent of agricultural and 31 percent of forestry production. In the same year, Folksam, a Swedish insurance cooperative, held 48.9 percent of the household insurance market and 50 percent of group life and accident insurance.[22] Moreover, cooperatives have been heavily involved in renewable energy projects. For example, 75 percent of Denmark's extensive wind turbine installations are owned by local cooperatives, and many Swedish housing cooperatives are switching to alternative energy sources to help meet Sweden's goal of oil independence by 2015.[23]

THE CONSTRUCTION OF SOCIAL AND ECONOMIC INSTITUTIONS

What we have been examining are not coincidental, unconnected developments. They are all outcomes of the fact that the Nordic world orients more to the partnership system than the domination system.

The Teduray, Minangkabau, and Nordic nations are not "pure" partnership societies. There's no such thing as a pure domination system or partnership system in practice. The difference is always a matter of degree.

But in partnership-oriented systems, social institutions, from families to governments, are designed to promote mutual respect, accountability, and benefits, rather than to facilitate the concentration of control at the top. The legal framework supports these kinds of structures. And the cultural norms—that is, what is considered normal and desirable—are another part of the glue that holds more partnership-oriented structures together.

I here again want to say that partnership families are of particular importance in determining whether the institutions of a society are authoritarian and inequitable or democratic and equitable. Certainly, partnership families are not totally democratic structures in the sense that young children have an equal say in all family decisions. Parents have to make important decisions for children, guide children, and teach them limits and expectations—which children need. But from the start, children are respected in partnership family structures, and their caregivers are attuned to their needs and wants. As children grow older, they are encouraged to think for themselves and make their own choices, which are honored whenever possible. There is no use of physical force, and equitable and caring behaviors are modeled and rewarded. These partnership family structures also model equality between women and men rather than inequality and authoritarianism, as in the father-headship families of traditional dominator cultures. And these families model caring and caregiving—not as something "soft" or "feminine" but as integral to both male and female identity.

When the rules and norms governing family structures value and support participation, empathy, equity, and caring, people carry this model for structuring relations into other institutions. But while partnership family structures are foundational for the construction of a more equitable and democratic socio-economic structure, this is not a one-way process.

As I have emphasized, all social institutions—from the family, education, and religion to politics and economics—form a mutually supporting, interactive whole. That is, their interaction molds and maintains a society's basic character.

As I have also emphasized, a society's economic institutions, policies, and practices play a particularly important role in this process. In a system based on top-down rankings, economic institutions will ensure that control of resources is concentrated in the hands of those on top. These institutions will be designed to maintain and further consolidate economic power in the hands of a few. This power will be used to see that the legal framework, government policies, and business rules, as well as the organs of communication, support this concentration of power. This is why changing economic structures, rules, and values is key to accelerating the contemporary movement toward partnership.

I here want to return to one of the obstacles to the construction of partnership-oriented structures: the misconception that only dominator structures are economically efficient. As we glimpsed in chapter 3 when we looked at more partnership-oriented business policies and practices, in reality partnership structures are economically efficient while at the same time offering enormous human and environmental benefits.

For example, cooperatives are today a huge sector of the European Union's economy, and a growing sector of the global economy.[24] And part of their success is due to the fact that these partnership structures can combine social and environmental responsibility, benefits to local communities, and entrepreneurship with a sharing of profits and a participatory management style.[25]

However, cooperatives are not the only kind of economic structure that incorporates partnership principles. As we saw earlier, businesses of all kinds—both large and small—can be socially and environmentally responsible, have more participatory management styles, and be accountable to all stakeholders.

Moreover, contrary to some popular misconceptions, a well-functioning participatory structure is not completely flat. Certainly partnership social and economic structures are flatter than dominator ones, and have much more democracy and participation in decision making. But there are still leaders in governments, managers in businesses, parents in families, and teachers in schools. In fact, there are more leaders in partnership institutions, since power is not concentrated at the top, and the ideas of all group members are valued.

Therefore, partnership social and economic structures still have hierarchies. However, as I noted earlier, these are what I have called *hierarchies of actualization* rather than *hierarchies of domination*. Whereas leaders and managers in hierarchies of domination give orders that must be obeyed, leaders and managers in hierarchies of actualization seek and consider input from others. In some cases, decisions in partnership structures are made in a participatory manner. In other cases, they are made by the leaders or managers after consideration of all inputs. But in both cases the inputs and those offering them are valued and recognized.

Nor is the difference between partnership and dominator institutions that one is cooperative and the other competitive. As detailed in "The Social Construction of Cooperation, Competition, and Power," the difference is that power, cooperation, and competition are structured very differently depending on the degree of orientation to the partnership or domination model.

I should here add something about networks, which many of us (including me), hailed as an emerging partnership social structure because of their decentralized construction.[26] Certainly networks offer more opportunities for democracy since, unlike traditional dominator organizations, they link people in voluntary, reciprocal, and horizontal patterns of communication and exchange. But unfortunately time has shown that networks can also be effectively used to dominate and destroy.

☐ The Social Construction of Cooperation, Competition, and Power

When in 1985 I chose *partnership* to describe the more equitable and peaceful social configuration identified by my research, the term was still used mainly to describe a business partnership. It seemed a good choice to describe a system that supports relations of mutual benefit, respect, and accountability, since members of a business partnership stand on an equal footing, have a voice in decision making, and work for mutual benefit. Then, within a decade after *The Chalice and The Blade* came out, the term partnership acquired a much broader usage. It came to mean working together, particularly in strategic alliances and other cooperative ventures. As a result, for those not acquainted with my work, the term partnership is often associated with cooperation versus competition.

Certainly the partnership system is more conducive to cooperation since it does not sort people into superior-inferior rankings. But terrorists, invading armies, and monopolies all cooperate. In other words, there is also cooperation in the domination system. So unfortunately it's not true, as some people think, that all our problems will be solved if people would just cooperate. People in a domination system regularly cooperate to advance in-group interests while at the same time dominating, exploiting, and even killing out-groups, as was the case in the Austria of my childhood.

Moreover, there is competition in the partnership system. But it is achievement-oriented competition, spurred on by seeing another's excel-

Starting in the 1960s and continuing today, networks have often served as vehicles for activists working for environmental protection, women's and children's rights, economic justice, and other ways of advancing the movement to a more caring, less violent, partnership system. However, networks have also been used, and in fact are increasingly used, by terrorists, criminal drug cartels, and others pushing us back to a more violent, authoritarian, male-dominated way of life.

Indeed, fundamentalist terrorist networks such as Al-Qaeda have ushered in a new form of warfare that analysts today aptly call "net-

---

lence, rather than the brutal competition designed to humiliate, destroy, or put an opponent out of business encouraged by the domination system.

Power too is defined and exercised differently in the domination system and the partnership system. In terms of the title *The Chalice and The Blade*, in the domination system the metaphor for power is the blade: a symbol of the power to dominate, exploit, and take life. In the partnership system, the metaphor for power is the chalice: an ancient symbol of the power to give, nurture, and illuminate life. The shift to this more stereotypically feminine view of power goes with a shift from *hierarchies of domination* to *hierarchies of actualization* where accountability, respect, and benefit don't just flow from the bottom up but both ways.

That this view of power, stereotypically associated with the ideal of the caring mother, is gaining currency, is reflected in today's leadership and management literature, where we read that the good manager is not a cop or controller but someone who inspires and nurtures our highest potential. This higher valuing of stereotypically feminine qualities— whether they are embodied in women or men—is vital for the postindustrial economy. This economy requires a creative, flexible, innovative workforce—which in turn requires leaders and managers that empower rather than disempower others.

Sources: For a more detailed discussion of these issues, see Riane Eisler, *The Chalice and The Blade* (San Francisco: Harper & Row, 1987) and Riane Eisler, *The Power of Partnership* (Novato, California: New World Library, 2002). ▪

wars." Unlike traditional warfare, these netwars are not between states, although states often supply terrorist networks with their weapons, as in the case of Iran and Hezbollah. Rather than battles between soldiers, these netwars primarily target civilians. Moreover, since terrorist networks are dispersed in civilian communities, it is very difficult, indeed impossible, to combat them without also harming the civilians around them.

As David Ronfeldt and John Arquilla write in "Networks, Netwars, and the Fight for the Future," there is thus not only a bright but also a dark side to the network phenomenon. As they also write, there seems no question that in our complex world networks will continue to grow as an emerging organizational form, and that this trend is facilitated by new information technologies such as the Internet, which permit the expansion of networks with little financial investment.[27] But the real question is not whether the network is a viable social structure, which it clearly is, but whether it will be used to advance partnership or dominator goals.

This takes us back to the larger web of factors that determine the character of partnership or dominator structures. Unlike physical structures such as houses and other buildings, social and economic structures don't consist of material elements. The elements that give social and economic structures their particular character are the beliefs, habits, norms, laws, rules, and even language, of a particular culture.

For example, in dominator language there are only two terms to describe the structuring of relations between women and men: patriarchy or matriarchy. What these terms describe are two variations of a dominator structure. Our conventional language offers no partnership alternative for these relations.[28]

Given the importance of their larger cultural context, we cannot simply describe partnership or dominator economic and social structures by their form. We must also take into account their guiding values, which in turn are embedded in the culture or subculture of which they are a part.

We will look further at these interactive dynamics—and how they directly affect our happiness, quality of life, and natural environment—in the chapters that follow, as we continue our exploration of economics in its larger social matrix.

CHAPTER 6

The Economics of Domination

Some people see capitalism as an ogre that insatiably demands inequality and exploitation. They blame capitalism for all our ills, pointing to corporations that pollute our planet and disregard the welfare of employees, host communities, and even their shareholders. But it's not capitalism that's the ogre; it's the underlying dominator beliefs, structures, and habits we've inherited.

It's true that predatory capitalist practices cause great harm. But long before capitalist billionaires amassed huge fortunes, Egyptian pharaohs and Chinese emperors hoarded their nations' wealth. Indian potentates demanded tributes of silver and gold, while lower castes lived in abject poverty. Middle Eastern warlords pillaged, plundered, and terrorized their people. European feudal lords killed their neighbors and oppressed their subjects.

In all these precapitalist societies, the idea that "common people" could be equal to their "betters" was inconceivable. Economic exploitation was just a fact of life—as was the misery of the masses, whose only hope, they were told, was a better afterlife.

It was not always so. There were earlier more equitable cultures, such as the Minoan civilization that flourished on the Mediterranean isle of Crete until approximately 1400 B.C.E. It is from this technologically advanced prehistoric culture that the ancient Greeks derived much of their love of beauty, architecture, artistic bent, and other hallmarks of civilization. The Minoans were the great artisans and traders of their time. This led to a highly prosperous society with a generally high standard of living.

While Minoan Crete was not an ideal society, it oriented more to the partnership system. Unlike most later civilizations, Minoan Crete was not a slave society. There are no signs of warfare between the various city-states on the island. And a spirit of harmony between women and men as joyful and equal participants appears to have pervaded life.[1] We can still see evidence of women's high status in Minoan frescos. For example, the "procession fresco" in Knossos shows a high priestess being brought offerings of fruit and wine by both priestesses and priests. The Minoans' beautiful art also shows their love of nature. As the Greek archeologist Nicolas Platon writes, "The whole of life was pervaded by an ardent faith in the goddess Nature, the source of all creation and harmony."[2]

But the Minoans were displaced by the Mycaeneans we read about in Homer's epics. Although the Mycaeneans retained some of the Minoan heritage, theirs was already a warrior culture where wealth was largely acquired through conquest rather than trade. The Mycaenean ascendancy was then followed by a period of bloody strife and cultural decay—the centuries historians call the Greek Dark Ages. And when European civilization resumed in Athens and other ancient Greek city-states, it followed a very different direction than that of Minoan and other earlier, more partnership-oriented cultures.

OUR BRUTAL ECONOMIC INHERITANCE

We're taught to idealize our heritage from ancient Athens. There are certainly wonderful aspects of this old Western civilization that we should cherish. On the other hand, there was also a darker side of this much-extolled society that becomes evident once we look at Athenian economics.

The Athenian economy was largely household-based. And households were structured in rigid rankings of domination. Athenian children were the property of the male head of household. He decided if a newborn child should live or die. If it was a healthy boy, chances were he'd be kept. But if it was a baby girl, she could be wrenched from her mother's arms and condemned to death. Outright killing was not legal—although it might have been more merciful. The accepted practice was to "expose" unwanted babies. The child was abandoned to slowly starve, freeze to death, or perhaps replenish the Athenian army of young slave prostitutes.

Although this also isn't mentioned in most books about ancient Greece, the fabled Athenian democracy was a slaveholding society. Only free men with property could vote or hold office. The rest of the population, slaves and women who were not slaves, had no political rights and hardly any civil rights.

There are accounts of slaves who enjoyed a certain amount of freedom and respect. Yet the lot of most slaves was hard. According to the Greek writer Demosthenes, the Athenians maintained a public tor-

□ The Greek Mix of Domination and Partnership

Most ancient history books teach us that the first European civilization sprang up in Greece after the so-called Greek Dark Ages. However, as Nicolas Platon, Jacquetta Hawkes, J. V. Luce, and other scholars point out, the Achaean invaders who ruled in Mycenaean times, as well as the Dorian overlords who displaced them, only moved forward after they absorbed much of the material and spiritual culture of the peoples they conquered.[3]

As Luce writes, "Like a fire-ravaged olive tree, Minoan culture went dormant for a time, and then sent up fresh shoots in the shades of the Mycenaean citadels. . . . Minoan princesses, the 'daughters of Atlas,' married into the houses of Mycenaean warlords. Minoan architects designed the mainland palaces, and Minoan painters adorned them with frescoes. Greek first became a written language in the hands of Minoan scribes."[4]

Even after the Dorian devastation, as Luce writes, not everything was lost. Much changed, as powerful earlier goddesses—in such forms as Hera, Athena, and Aphrodite—were now subordinate to Zeus in the official Greek pantheon. Much was forgotten, as even the memory of Minoan civilization began to fade into legend. But there were still elements of Greek civilization that better fit the partnership system: the Athenians' love of art and beauty, their attempts at democracy, and their valuing of philosophical wisdom.

Nonetheless, ancient Athens largely conformed to the configuration of the domination system, with its top-down social and economic structure, a high degree of built-in abuse and violence, the subordination of women and "femininity" to men and "masculinity," and beliefs and stories that idealize domination and violence.[5] ■

ture chamber for the routine torture of slaves in legal proceedings, since a slave's testimony was admissible in court only if given under torture. Slaves worked in their masters' houses and fields, as well as in mines, where conditions were so bad they often died within a year. Slaves manned the oars of the Athenians' famous warships or *triremes*, where they also faced early death should the ship sink in a storm or battle. Household slaves were often put in what Athenians called a "gulp preventer," a wooden device closing the jaws, which was placed on slaves who handled food to keep them from eating it.[6]

As for women, there are some accounts of women who were poets, philosophers, and even political advisers, like Aspasia, the companion of the famous Athenian ruler Pericles during the Greek Golden Age. But these were exceptional cases.

As classicist Eva Keuls notes, women were not even second-class citizens in Athens. "Like a slave," Keuls writes, "a woman had virtually no protection under the law except insofar as she was the property of a man."[7] A woman who was left property by her father had no right to use it. That power was in her guardian's hands. Indeed, "respectable" free women were not free. They were confined to the women's quarters, or *gynaikonitis*.

There was in Athens an official women's police, the *gynaikonomoi*. As Aristotle wrote, it served to restrict the movements of women to "protect their chastity." Girls were often married off when they were mere children, and they had no access to education. Nor were "free" women permitted to freely associate with men, even in their own homes.

Men seem to have relied on "respectable" women largely as managers of their households and breeders of their sons. Men's sexual relations were often with prostitutes or in homosexual liaisons between older men and young boys. Of course, under the dominator double standard for sex, men had complete sexual freedom. And they exercised this freedom in many ways, including the famous Greek *symposia*, which—despite the term's current scholarly usage—were orgies hosted by Athenian men in the *andrones* or men's quarters at the front of the house.

Slave girls were often used by men as prostitutes, and as Keuls writes, "automatically subject to the unfathomable horrors of that institution, which included abuse by their owners, torture, random execution, and sale at any time to the highest bidder."[8] Even those prostitutes who were not slaves were strictly controlled. As Aristotle writes, price control of prostitution was an important Athenian institution. Laws even ensured that "girl flute, harp, and kithara players do not charge more than two drachmas for their services."[9] In other words, the income that women could independently generate through one of the very few—indeed, in some situations only—professions open to them was severely limited.

In sum, only a small minority of the Athenian population enjoyed the benefits of their famous democracy. The majority—male slaves and both slave and "free" women—were basically there for the use of free men.[10]

So while Greek philosophers such as Socrates and Plato sometimes espoused partnership values, this ancient society, from which we inherited many of our values, oriented largely to the domination system. As we saw earlier, this is also true for Judeo-Christian tradition, the other major influence on Western culture. Caring, nonviolence, and empathy are at the core of Judeo-Christian values. But many biblical traditions came out of brutal tribal societies. And we can still see the effect of these dominator Greek and Judeo-Christian traditions in Western economic systems to our day.

ECONOMIC INHUMANITY AND INEFFICIENCY

One of these traditions is top-down economic control. In dominator tribal societies, chiefs owned more wives, cattle, and land than other men. Through raids, and later through wars of conquest, some of these chiefs came to control the bulk of productive resources, including the conquered peoples' labor. Then, as these men passed on their wealth to their sons and they to theirs, the divide between higher and lower classes grew.

In Europe, these higher classes were "noblemen" who traced their lineage to warrior-kings who had amassed enormous landed wealth by the sword. And the laws these elites made to enforce their rule often literally gave them the right to appropriate and exploit the bodies of those they ruled.

In the slave societies of Western antiquity, as in the preabolitionist American South, the bodies of many men and women (as well as little girls and boys) were legally sold and bought, like we today buy groceries, furniture, and clothes. Since they were property, slaves had no choice in what services (including sexual ones) they were forced to render. They had little if any legal protection, and faced terribly painful punishments or starvation if they escaped. As for women who were not slaves, they too were under strict male control, first as daughters and then as wives.[11]

Under medieval feudalism, the bodily labor of both male and female serfs could still lawfully be appropriated by the ruling elites. Serfs lived on the feudal lord's estate, tilled his land, and served him in war. The lord of the manor was sometimes entitled to what historians call *le droit du seigneur* or *ius prima noctis*, the right of the master to first "deflower" or sexually possess a serf's new bride.[12]

Women of the ruling feudal elites were also an underclass, with few economic options or legal rights. Only when men went off to war, as during the Christian Crusades, did women such as Eleanor of Aquitaine and her daughter Marie hold real power, as laws continued to treat married women as their husband's property.

For example, under English common law, which was exported to the American colonies, a woman could not sue or be sued in her own right. When she was negligently injured, her husband could go to court to seek recompense for her lost services to him, but she had no right to compensation for her injuries.[13]

The legal disempowerment of women continued under capitalism well into the nineteenth century even in the West. Women were still deprived of the most basic political, civil, and property rights—from the right to vote and own property to access to higher education and professions such as law and medicine.

> *For much of recorded history, control of productive resources, including people's labor, was in the hands of those on top.*

Under the "robber baron" capitalism of the nineteenth- and early twentieth–centuries, women, men, and children were often forced to work long hours for little pay in unsafe and unsanitary conditions—once again, with little or no legal protection. If they failed to do so, they faced starvation. When they rebelled and tried to organize, they often faced violence.

After the twentieth-century communist revolutions, top-down economic control remained largely in place. In the former Soviet Union, a "dictatorship of the proletariat" sharply circumscribed the life choices of most men and women through force and fear of pain. Their labor—along with the nation's other economic resources—were basically the property of a state in which, once again, a small elite of men ruled from the top. Women's unpaid life-supporting services of caring for children, the sick, and the elderly were still considered men's due. Women had the triple burden of cooking, cleaning, and caring for children in the home, standing for hours in long lines for scarce necessities, and working at outside jobs that generally paid less than those of men.

Today, at least in principle, the ownership of a person's body and the appropriation of a person's services by another are almost universally illegal. Yet despite this, traditions of economic domination remain extremely resistant to change. Slavery, including child slavery, is still openly practiced in some parts of Asia, Africa, and the Middle East. Many indigenous peoples in Latin America are still basically serfs of the landed classes. Inhuman working conditions in fields and factories prevail in many nations. Children, particularly girls, are still denied access to education and expected to work from dawn to dusk.

Even in more "advanced" nations, the work of caring and caregiving is still generally relegated to women for little or no pay, without old age pensions, health care, or other economic safety nets. Hierarchies of domination in businesses and governments are still often justified as not only natural but necessary for economic efficiency. All this is our heritage from times that oriented more closely to the domination system.

Indeed, the modern workplace was built to meet the requirements of a dominator social organization. It was the role of the manager, whether as foreman or top executive, to control those below him. Monopolies or dog-eat-dog competition were the norm, women were relegated to low-pay and low-status jobs, and caring and empathy were seen as having little, if any, relevance.

There were, of course, also bonds based primarily on trust and caring, as without these people could not have functioned. But while the value of these informal relations was often extolled, what counted was one's position in the more formal vertical structures. So while there were industrialists and managers who were noted for their caring and empathy, they were by and large exceptions to the norm.

The industrial workplace was supposed to be governed by stereotypically masculine "hard" qualities, with little attention to caring for workers' safety, health, or other needs. Workers were seen as cogs in the industrial machine. And as is characteristic of hierarchies of domination rather than hierarchies of actualization, accountability and respect flowed only from the bottom up and orders were to be unquestioningly obeyed.[14]

The human costs to both men and women of this imbalanced, fear-based, institutionally insensitive, and all too often abusive and dehumanizing way of running business were enormous. But it was said, and generally believed, to be necessary for economic productivity.

Even now, some people believe that economic efficiency requires a dominator business structure and culture. However, as we saw in chapter 3, these once hallowed beliefs and institutions are not spurs but impediments to productivity and creativity.[15]

Today, many studies demonstrate that the domination system decreases an organization's relational resources—the resources critical for economic success, particularly in the postindustrial economy.[16] Empirical evidence also disproves that "soft" feelings and behaviors are impediments to productivity. On the contrary, as we also saw in chapter 3, studies show that, to again borrow the words of University of Michigan professor Jane Dutton, when people feel cared for they become fully alive—with all this implies for business productivity and economic development.

PERPETUATING HUNGER AND POVERTY

As we have seen, a core aspect of domination systems is the subordination of women and anything stereotypically considered feminine. Over the last decades, the declared goal of international development policy has been ending chronic poverty and hunger. But both government officials and the press continue to ignore a staggering statistic: women represent 70 percent of the 1.3 billion people in our world who live in absolute poverty.[17] Consequently, as Joan Holmes, president of the Hunger Project, points out, any realistic efforts to change patterns of chronic hunger and poverty require changing traditions of discrimination against women.[18]

This is by no means to say that only women suffer in societies that orient to the domination system. Men also suffer, and this is particularly true of the men at the bottom of the dominator pyramid.

◻ *Business Success and Business Ethics*

Another feature of dominator economics is lack of ethics. Like popular sayings such as "all's fair in love and war," the old Latin slogan *caveat emptor* (let the buyer beware) is our heritage from earlier times when the idea that business should be ethical would have been scoffed at.

Today, as Marjorie Kelly, editor of the journal *Business Ethics*, writes, it's clear that lack of ethics lies behind massive business failures such as the Enron, WorldCom, and Refco bankruptcies. She notes that there's growing recognition that unethical business practices not only harm customers, creditors, and employees but also put business value at risk.[19] As David Korten, one of the most vocal voices for ethical economics, writes, there is growing awareness that "a healthy market economy relies on more than profit and market competition; it must operate in the context of both an ethical, life-affirming culture and a sound framework of public policy and regulation."[20]

The bad news, as both Kelly and Korten note, is that irresponsible ways of doing business are still encouraged by many economic indicators and rules. For example, the requirement for quarterly corporate financial reports encourages businesses to focus on the short term rather than the long term, and to pass social and ecological costs on to society. When businesses deplete natural capital by strip-mining, clear-cutting forests, and dumping hazardous wastes, these are simply considered "externalities" in present economic indicators and rules. The same is true when human and social capital is exploited and depleted. As long as economic indicators and rules treat harm to people and nature as externalities, companies can treat workers as expendable commodities and damage the health of whole communities—all in the name of greater profits.

The good news is that the conversation about business is changing. As more people recognize the need for replacing dysfunctional economic rules with rules that encourage and reward caring and ethical business practices, more businesses are making ethical, long-term, life-affirming choices. ■

Growing up in Cuba, where my parents and I fled when we escaped from Vienna in 1939, I know the toll poverty takes from men, women, and children. Since my parents had to leave everything they owned behind, we were plunged from a life of comfort in Vienna to living in rancid-smelling ramshackle hotels and boardinghouses. Even after my parents managed to build a successful business in Havana and our lives changed for the better, I still witnessed the suffering of others around me while Cuban elites, including corrupt officials such as then-President Fulgencio Batista, lived in opulent luxury. I saw families crowded into cockroach-infested one-room hovels, homeless children begging on the streets, men breaking their backs lifting huge loads in the Havana docks. But I also saw that the heaviest burdens were those on women who toiled from dawn to dusk as maids, seamstresses, or beggars, and sometimes became prostitutes in the then-infamous Havana red-light district to feed themselves and their children.

This is still the lot of millions of women in many developing nations. Women continue to work longer hours than men, often doing the hardest work, like carrying huge jugs of water and heavy loads of firewood, as is customary for African women. Yet despite this, in Africa too woman-headed families are the poorest of the poor.

Globally, women earn an average of two-thirds to three-fourths as much as men for the same work in the market economy. And most of the work women do in families—including child care, health and elder care, housekeeping, cooking, collecting firewood, drawing and carrying water, and subsistence farming—is not counted as economically productive, and is therefore not supported by economic policies.

Even in the rich United States, woman-headed families are the lowest tier of the economic hierarchy. One consequence is that one out of every five children lives in poverty—the highest child poverty rate of any industrialized nation.[21] In addition, according to the U.S. Census Bureau, the poverty rate of women over sixty-five is almost twice that of men over sixty-five.[22]

The fact that worldwide poverty and hunger disproportionately affect women and children is neither accidental nor inevitable. It is the direct result of political and economic systems that still have a strong dominator stamp. For example, that even in an affluent nation like the United States older women are so much more likely to live in poverty than older men is largely due to the fact that government and business policies fail to protect elderly women through equal Social Security, pension, and retirement stipends.

If we look at financial resource allocation from a gendered perspective, we see that the poverty of women and children is in key respects the direct result of political and economic priorities. Specifically, it is the result of government, business, and family budgets skewed to privilege men and discriminate against women—budgets that are still considered normal by the vast majority of both women and men.

We see this discriminatory pattern most sharply in poorer nations. For example, education outlays in many African and Asian nations are much greater for males than for females. So also is spending for health care and other public services. In addition, as the economist Moni Mukherjee writes, "A much larger share of the outlay on public order and safety is needed for men than for women because the latter are less prone to criminal activities than men. . . . Outlays for economic services are also skewed, with the lion's share going to men."[23] In other words, spheres occupied primarily by men have funding priority.

The fact that world-wide poverty and hunger dispropor-tionately affect women and children is neither accidental nor inevitable. It is the direct result of political and eco-nomic systems that still have a strong dominator stamp.

The same patterns are found in intra-family allocation of resources. These skewed allocation patterns further perpetu-ate hunger and poverty—and stand in the way of economic and human development.

THE ECONOMICS OF THE HOUSEHOLD

The economics of the household are still generally ignored in conventional analyses. The household is viewed as a unit of either production or consumption, rather than as a microcosm of the larger economic and political system. As a result, most analyses don't take into account intrahousehold resource allocation.

The common assumption is that the male head of household is the prime provider. This assumption, however, ignores the reality documented by scientific studies.

This reality is that, in many of the poorest world regions, women, not men, are the primary providers for the nutrition, health, and other vital aspects of life of their families.[24] In many households women are actually the sole providers. In most African nations, for example, women do the subsistence farming that keeps their families alive. They are either single mothers or their husbands have left for urban areas where they often take another wife.

Over the last decades, there have also been many studies of how economic resources are used in two-parent households. These studies shed further light on how dominator assumptions and policies impede both human and economic development.

As Judith Bruce and Daisy Dwyer write in their book *A Home Divided*, it is quite common that cultural tradition supports the notion that men have a right to personal spending money, which they are perceived to need or deserve, and that women's income is for collective purposes.[25] Consequently, as Cynthia B. Lloyd and Judith Bruce report, "There is considerable empirical evidence across diverse cultures and income groups that women have a higher propensity than men to spend on goods that benefit children and enhance their capacities."[26]

How much higher this propensity can be is shown by Duncan Thomas in his report "Intra-Household Resource Allocation." He found that "in Brazil, $1 in the hands of a Brazilian woman has the same effect on child survival as $18 in the hands of a man."[27] Similarly, Bruce and Lloyd found that in Guatemala "an additional $11.40 per month in a mother's hands would achieve the same weight gain in a young child as an additional $166 if earned by the father."[28]

Of course, there are men who give primary importance to meeting their families' needs even in rigidly male-dominated cultures. Typically, however, men in these societies are socialized to believe it's their prerogative to use their wages for nonfamily purposes, including drinking, smoking, and gambling, and that when women complain, they are nagging and controlling. As Dr. Anugerah Pekerti, chair of World Vision, Indonesia, notes, many fathers seem to have no problem putting their own immediate desires above the survival needs of their children.[29]

Yet traditional economic theories, whether capitalist or socialist, are based on the assumption that the male head of household will expend the resources he controls for the benefit of all family members. This has been the assumption in conventional analyses, which treat the household as a unit, and is one of the assumptions behind the fact that the bulk of aid to people in the developing world has been given to men.

Development aid programs still allocate enormous funds to large-scale projects in which women have little or no say—and from which poor women and children derive few if any benefits. Even the recent microlending or "village loan" programs that largely target women provide only minimal amounts. The bulk of bank loans go to businesses owned by male elites or to male "heads of household."

Much of the humanitarian government aid from developed to developing nations winds up in the hands of elites who deposit it in Swiss banks, build mansions, and otherwise line their pockets with it. Even when funds go directly to the poor, these too often end up in the pockets of men who use them for themselves rather than for their families. The effect of this on the general quality of life is not hard to see.

Again, I want to emphasize that what I'm reporting is not intended to blame men for our world's economic ills. We're dealing with a system in which both women and men are socialized to accept the notion that one half of our species is put on Earth to be served and the other half to serve, and that mothers, but not fathers, must subordinate their needs and desires to those of their families.

This economic double standard flows from the male-superior, female-inferior view of humanity we inherited from more rigidly dominator-oriented cultures. It not only hurts women, but is a template for equating all difference—be it of race, religion, or ethnicity—with superiority and inferiority, with serving and being served, with dominating or being dominated.

In the domination system, there is no partnership alternative. There are only two perceived choices: you dominate or you're dominated. This has clearly had disastrous effects on human relations. It has also led to an inefficient economic system.

CREATING SCARCITY

Probably the most inefficient and destructive aspect of dominator economics and politics is that they artificially produce scarcity. The creation and perpetuation of scarcity is a prerequisite for dominator systems maintenance. It is largely through the production of scarcity that this system, which uses fear of pain as its major motivation for work, maintains itself.

Certainly, environmental or other circumstances can lead to real scarcities. But artificial scarcities are constantly created by dominator politics and economics through overconsumption, wastefulness, exploitation, war or preparation for war, environmental despoliation, and failure to invest in high-quality human capital by not giving value to caring and caregiving.

Overconsumption and wastefulness by those on top is a perennial feature of dominator cultures. Whether it's the opulent Roman feasts or the million-dollar parties of today's super-rich, the grandiose palaces of kings, emperors, and dictators or the extravagant mansions of Enron and WorldCom CEOs, Imelda Marcos's thousands of shoes, or the immense bank accounts of the Sukarno and Suharto families, it comes to the same. Those on top waste resources and those on the bottom scramble for the scraps.

Competition for scraps often takes on racial, religious, and ethnic overtones. Smoldering prejudice is easily fanned into flames of hate and often violence. Jews are accused of evil economic conspiracies, and people of different races or religions are vilified as unfairly taking away resources from those entitled to them.

This scapegoating serves two functions. It divides those on the bottom, pitting them against one another. And it channels frustration and rage away from those whose policies and habits are largely responsible for the scarcity of resources for those below them. All this maintains a system of domination and exploitation in which inadequate wages and lack of a social safety net further lead to the belief that there is not enough to go around.

> *Probably the most inefficient and destructive aspect of dominator economics and politics is that they artificially produce scarcity.*

A mentality of scarcity affects the wealthy as well as the poor. It discourages a more equitable distribution of wealth by those on top, out of fear that they too will find themselves having to do without. A mentality of fear and scarcity also leads to economic rules and policies that permit, even promote, predatory business practices as necessary for survival. This creates more scarcity of resources by eliminating competitors who, along with their employees, lose their livelihoods.

Chronic scarcity of resources that support life is caused by still another prototypical feature of the domination system: funneling resources into weapons and warfare. Today's trillion-dollar-per-year financing of technologies of destruction and domination drains away funds that could be used to care for people's health, education, and welfare. Warfare then compounds the problem, destroying resources as well as people, producing even more scarcity and misery.

According to *World Military & Social Expenditures*, the cost of a U.S. intercontinental ballistic missile would feed 50 million children, build 160,000 schools, or open 340,000 health centers.[30] According to a UNICEF report, the cost of one nuclear submarine would provide low-cost rural water and sanitation facilities for 48 million people, and the cost of eleven radar-evading bombers could provide four years of primary education for 135 million children.[31]

In 2005, the Institute for Policy Studies (IPS) and Foreign Policy in Focus (FPIF) calculated that the cost to taxpayers of U.S. military operations in Iraq came to $5.6 billion per month.[32] But the same Congress that authorized these astronomical military expenditures cut federal investments in health, education, and welfare on the grounds that there wasn't enough money to fund them.

Dominator economic systems also chronically create scarcity through low investment in caring for children's physical, mental, and emotional development. This, coupled with the allocation of enormous sums to armaments—money that could be used to promote more general abundance through investment in a society's human capital—prevents the creation of the "high-quality human capital" we hear so much about. All this retards the economic development that can prevent scarcity, chronic hunger, and poverty.

But it's not only material resources that are wasted in dominator systems; it's also emotional resources. Rigid top-down rankings, whether in the family or state, are artificial barriers to trust, empathy, and caring. Control over possessions as well as over other humans becomes a substitute for meeting basic human needs.

Modern mass marketing has successfully capitalized on these unmet needs by manipulating people's yearning for love, security, and trust. Ads for everything from deodorants to diamonds promise love. Sex with gorgeous women is implied in commercials for soft drinks, hamburgers, and cars. Security, trustworthiness, even emotional involvement, are pledged by insurance and stock brokerage advertising campaigns.

The not-so-subtle message of these kinds of promotions is that if we want to satisfy our yearning for love, fulfillment, security, and joy, what we have to do is to buy and consume. So the poor crowd the aisles of dollar stores, accumulating gadgets and trinkets, while the

---

◻ Real Welfare Reform

Even when policies to care for those in need are introduced, they have often been implemented in uncaring ways because the "women's work" of caring and caregiving is given no real value. The U.S. welfare program is a case in point. When President Franklin D. Roosevelt inaugurated his famous New Deal during the Great Depression, along with Social Security and other social insurance initiatives, there was a modest program called "Aid to Families with Dependent Children," or AFDC. In principle, AFDC was to help single-mother families not covered by social insurance programs. In practice, it turned into a bureaucratic nightmare for recipients, with police-state methods of control.

Social workers were ordered to conduct surprise, late-night visits to welfare recipients' homes without court warrants to search for extra toothbrushes, men's clothing, or gifts that had not been deducted from welfare stipends. These raids were justified on the grounds that if a woman had a relationship with any man, he should support her and her children. So women were not only economically penalized for sexual relations but also denied the most basic rights of privacy and legal process.

In 1970, after much pressure by welfare mothers' organizations, night raids were declared unconstitutional. But welfare stipends were still defined as charity. AFDC continued to be a bureaucratic version of the dominator family, where the male head of household gives the mother a small allowance to buy food, shoes, and clothes for the children, with no value whatsoever accorded to her work of caring and caregiving.

The "idleness" and "fraud" of welfare recipients could therefore easily be used to justify "welfare reform campaigns," starting with President

rich accumulate houses and yachts. And while all this wasteful accumulation clutters up our homes and our planet, those at the very bottom of the dominator hierarchy continue to die of hunger and disease.

This takes us to yet another way that dominator economics lead to artificial scarcities: environmental despoliation. Critics often blame industrialization for our mounting environmental problems. But environmental problems are not unique to industrial economies. Environmental despoliation is characteristic of the domination system. It goes way back, beginning with prehistoric herders who deplet-

---

Richard Nixon's proposed "Family Assistance Plan." By the 1990s, under Democratic President Bill Clinton and a Republican-controlled Congress, the idea that governments have an obligation to help single mothers and children living in poverty was replaced by the idea that poor mothers must get jobs. As economist Randy Albelda writes in her book, *Lost Ground: Welfare Reform, Poverty, and Beyond*, at the same time that middle-class women were urged to get out of the paid workplace and stay home with their children, poor mothers were sent out to work for less than minimum wages.[33]

As a result, many children were left with inadequate care, or no care at all, with increasing numbers of "latchkey" children—and sometimes terrible consequences for other children as well. While his mother was away traveling between two low-paying jobs, an unsupervised six-year-old Michigan boy shot and killed a six-year-old little girl in his class. The media, of course, headlined this case. But they never made the connection between this tragedy and a "welfare reform" that fails to give value and support to the "women's work" of caring and caregiving—a "reform" that continues to calculate welfare stipends as simply allowances for children's necessities, denying that what mothers do is work.

Real welfare reform requires a very different approach: one that empowers mothers and fathers to be both competent parents at home and skilled workers in the market economy. This is the approach of most Western European nations, where public assistance to the needy is considered a social obligation. This approach contrasts sharply with the United States, where welfare programs have been stigmatized as "tax giveaways"—while millions of dollars in government subsidies to corporations and massive tax deductions for the rich are widely approved. ∎

ed soils through overgrazing, creating scarcities that, in turn, fostered relations based on domination.

THE CONQUEST OF NATURE

What is today the Sahara Desert was once a lush green land. Between 40,000 and 23,000 B.C.E., herds of elephants, waterbuck, ostrich, and giraffe roamed North Africa. Soil samples from 12,000 to 4,000 B.C.E. suggest a rainfall of three hundred to four hundred millimeters per year where today there is only ten millimeters. In this wetter climate, as Brian Griffith writes in his history of desertification and cultural change, rivers flowed across North Africa and the landscape of antelope and big cats probably looked much like the national parks of Kenya do today.[34]

Rather than a wasteland of harsh bare rock and dunes of sand, the Sahara was then not only a base for gathering and hunting. With the invention of agriculture, farming became possible. But by 3000 B.C.E., a period of aridity had set in.

Some of the desertification of the region was due to climate changes. Using a large computerized database correlating information on climate change over thousands of years with archaeological data, geographer James DeMeo has mapped these changes in the great desert belt he calls Saharasia (extending roughly from north Africa through the Middle East into central Asia).[35] He found that gradually what was once a garden of plenty became a barren, cruel land.

But climate change was only part of the story. As Griffith writes, when the land grew drier, farming became impossible, and even raising and herding livestock grew more difficult. As the drought advanced and vegetation became even more sparse, human agency itself became a cause of desertification.

Because the herders grazed their goats and sheep in the same areas year-round, grasslands receded further. Trees were felled to open up more grazing land. As trees and plants disappeared, there was even less rain, as happens when forests are decimated to our day. And as herds overgrazed more and more pastures, soils became even more barren.

These cycles of land exploitation led to ever greater scarcity, as nature's life support systems were gradually exhausted. But the cycles of domination and exploitation were not confined to nature. In this ever harsher environment, habits of domination and exploitation became routine.

Some groups began to fight others for access to grassland and water. And as men increasingly relied on brute force for a livelihood, women lost status and power.

As Griffith writes, "The original tamers of sheep and goats were quite possibly women. After hunters had killed a wild mother goat, perhaps they caught the babies and brought them home, and women decided to raise the little orphans. Such keeping of domesticated animals would have been mainly women's work, as it often is today in India or China."[36] But while women undoubtedly continued to tend domestic animals and perform other economically valuable tasks, as pastures grew sparser and farther apart, men took a more active, and very different role. Now it was their role not only to travel farther and farther with the herds, but also to defend the herds from raiders and to engage in raiding themselves. With time, men's economic contributions—and specifically their use of force to make them—began to be seen as primary and women's work became devalued.

Griffith notes how "scarcity promotes coercion as a means of meeting basic needs."[37] And gradually, as the use of coercion became part of the culture, raiding and killing spread from the deserts to the more fertile areas.

This same conclusion was reached by DeMeo in his geographical review of human behavior and social institutions. There was historically, he writes, a correlation between a harsh environment, the rigid social and sexual subordination of women, and the equation of masculinity with toughness and warlikeness.[38] He also presents data indicating that, as the severest environmental changes took place, incursions by nomadic pastoralists into the adjoining areas intensified.

As they traveled further, the nomadic tribes of the wastelands coveted the wealth and security they saw in watered lands.[39] So these nomadic herders and raiders began to encroach on the more fertile areas, first in occasional incursions and later as conquerors who imposed their rule.

When they settled in the Fertile Crescent, the nomadic rulers brought with them their habits of domination. To them, the women of the conquered regions were booty to be appropriated as concubines or slaves, or just raped and killed at will. As the invaders settled in, the situation of "their" women, too, deteriorated further.

Griffith writes: "Back in the desert, these women had often been regarded as a primarily sexual commodity, but at least they had been free to wander and work in the open country. Now they became a jealously guarded sexual commodity to be isolated from their surrounding community."[40] As their warlord husbands secluded them from contact with the conquered people, their restricted status soon became the ideal for the general population.[41] Women were now confined to special quarters and had to be veiled to go out, as also happened later in India after the nomadic Aryan invasions.

The laws and customs of the conquered lands also changed radically, as women became male possessions. "In early Sumer down to 2371 B.C.E.," Griffith notes, "laws concerning marriage and property were quite equal for men and women."[42] But by the time of Babylon (starting circa 1750 B.C.E.) and Assyria (starting circa 1200 B.C.E.), male control over women became draconian. Women who stole from their husbands could be executed. Women who did not wear the required veil would be flogged with staves. Women who sheltered a runaway wife would have their ears cut off. Women who aborted themselves were impaled in stakes to slowly die.

Everything was now geared to conquest and control—of women, "inferior" men, and the land. The subjected people were ruthlessly exploited. Even the irrigation systems needed to feed the population were neglected to fund ever expanding raids, which, as in the old nomadic days, became a major source of wealth.

The Assyrians' brutal conquests built an empire supported by exorbitant annual tributes. The conquered farmers knew they would be slaughtered if they failed to pay. So they grew crops year-round, and exhausted their soil. None of this mattered to the rulers, since, as Griffith writes, the Assyrians seem to have seen their empire as a huge raiding ground. When one region was depleted, they could just expand their conquests, "like nomads chasing ever scarcer pastures."[43]

This conquest mentality—of nature, women, and other men—was also the trademark of the later Persian King Darius. During his reign (circa 500 to 328 B.C.E.), he milked the Middle East for astronomical sums to support his armies and court. Again, he did not care that there were huge environmental costs from pushing the people so hard. Having to pay taxes worth up to half their crops so the king could hire more mercenaries, farmers had little choice. They were forced to till the soil without letup to comply with annual production quotas. Not only that, since expenditures for war were the first priority, water conservation and irrigation systems were often left to fall apart. As Griffith writes, the cycle kept repeating itself: "Desiccation begot warlords, and warlords begot desiccation."

And this cycle is far from over. These habits of domination continue to our day. Only at our level of technological development, they threaten not just one region but our entire ecosystem. Scientists urge us to shift from conquering and exploiting nature to caring for our natural habitat. Report after report warns that our present course is not sustainable.

The 2005 United Nations–sponsored *Millennium Ecosystems Assessment* reports that over the past fifty years human activity has depleted 60 percent of the world's grasslands, forests, farmlands, rivers, and lakes. Compiled by 1,360 scientists from ninety-five countries, this assessment of the damage to our natural habitat also reports that a fifth of the world's coral reefs and a third of its mangrove forests have been destroyed in just a few decades.[44]

Emissions from cars and power plants are responsible for higher temperatures that are melting polar ice so fast that glaciers in Greenland are slipping into the ocean twice as fast as they were just five years ago, polar bears are drowning, and many other species are threatened with extinction. Yet these emissions continue to release more than twenty-five billion metric tons of carbon dioxide into the air each year—leading to scientific warnings that rising seas may engulf coastal cities in just a few decades.

Scientists urge us to shift from conquering and exploiting nature to caring for our natural habitat. Report after report warns that our present course is not sustainable.

Another 2005 report by scientists from the British Royal Society documents that our oceans are turning acidic. This report warns that chemical reactions to industrial emissions that produce carbonic acid are adversely affecting all organisms that have skeletons or shells. They are irrevocably harming marine life on which we and other species depend for food.[45]

Indeed, almost every day another study details the insanity of our present course. But so deeply embedded in our economic models, policies, and practices are the old habits of domination and exploitation that these warnings go largely unheeded.

It's as if nobody cares—at least not those in a position to do something to change this irrational course. Corporate giants and the governments they control continue to destroy the Earth's rain forests, pollute our air and water, and create artificial scarcity by diverting resources into weapons and wars. The plunder of nature, now aided by powerful technologies that cause terrible harm in a matter of years or even months and days, continues unabated.

Yet none of this is inevitable. It can be changed.

CHAPTER 7

The Economics of Partnership

Our ideas and stories are the blueprints for our future. Of course, ideas and stories don't arise in a vacuum. They come out of particular times and places. In the eighteenth century, a powerful idea gained momentum. People began to believe that the human yearning for a better life on Earth can be realized.

For most of recorded history, whether Eastern or Western, the vast majority of people were poor, and as they had been taught to do, accepted poverty as their inevitable lot. None other than Aristotle had declared that everyone is born to his or her station in life: slaves are meant to be slaves and women are meant to be subordinate to men. "From the hour of their birth," he wrote, "some are marked out for subjection, others for rule."[1] Later, the Church taught Christians that suffering is God's punishment for our evil, selfish nature. As for poverty, had not the Gospel of Matthew quoted Jesus as saying, "Ye have the poor always with you."

But as the industrial revolution gained steam in Europe, so did the possibility that the world can change. Indeed, the world was changing rapidly, as new ways of work and life were replacing the old.

By the middle 1700s, the vision of progress through human intervention was applied to economics. If people could improve the means of production, perhaps they could also improve the economic system. With a better understanding of how economic systems function, we could make them work for the greater good of all.

Out of this new probing of economic patterns, two economic theories emerged. The first theory described what we today call *capitalism*. The second theory is what its proponents called *socialism*.

Theories, we are often told, are merely abstractions with no real practical impact. But nothing could be further from the truth. Indeed, hardly anything has affected modern history more profoundly than these two economic theories.

Each of these theories offered a story of how economic systems function, and how they can be improved. And these stories not only transformed economic policies and practices; they transformed the way people thought and lived.[2]

To move forward, we need an understanding of these theories and the times out of which they came. We particularly need to understand the dominator assumptions embedded in them. This understanding is basic if we are to build a new economic theory—one that really works for the greater good of all.

THE CAPITALIST VISION

Adam Smith, the man who wrote the "bible" of capitalist theory, was born in Scotland in 1723. He was brilliant, eccentric, and gregarious. Although he never married, he had a wide circle of friends, colleagues, and admirers, including some of the most prominent figures in British life. His distinguished professional career ranged from teaching at Oxford to traveling through Europe with the scion of an aristocratic family, for which he was handsomely paid. Smith didn't begin his writing career until 1759, when he published a book that's rarely remembered now: *The Theory of Moral Sentiments*. Then, in 1776, the same year the United States was born, he published his famous *Inquiry into the Nature and Cases of the Wealth of Nations*, better known simply as *The Wealth of Nations*.[3]

Smith's was an optimistic vision of the future. He basically accepted the dominator belief that people are inherently selfish. But in his view, this selfishness could work for the common good—if only the market was left to regulate production and commerce without government interference.

This said, Smith by no means believed that selfishness is the only human motivation, although this stance is often attributed to him. He made it clear in *The Theory of Moral Sentiments* that humans can and do act out of "sentiment" for others, and he believed altruism is an important motivation in families, particularly for women.

Smith is also often called antigovernment. But his railings against state economic control take on a very different meaning when viewed in their historical context.

Smith wrote in a time of massive social and economic dislocation. The gentry had appropriated most of the lands that were commons, and hordes of dispossessed farmers reduced to paupers were roaming the countryside. There were also already signs of what was to come with the advent of full-fledged nineteenth-century industrialization. In some places, young children worked in mines twelve hours a day, as did women, including pregnant women, who sometimes gave birth in mine shafts. Conditions in some manufacturing towns weren't much better, with children tending machines around the clock for twelve to fourteen hours at a stretch.[4] Yet the government—which was entirely in the hands of the landed and merchant classes—did nothing to change any of this. Instead, it often exacerbated matters with shortsighted policies designed to further the narrow economic interests of those in power.

Smith did not say that government has no role, nor did he advocate privatization of government services.

When Smith argued against government interference, he was indirectly challenging the economic control of the upper classes. He would have shuddered at the thought that his economic theory was to be used to justify rapacity and greed. In fact, he severely condemned these. He excoriated the rising merchant class for its "mean rapacity," writing that they "neither are, nor ought to be, the rulers of mankind."[5] He also wrote that " no society can surely be flourishing and happy, of which by far the greater part are poor and miserable."[6]

Smith did not say that government has no role, nor did he advocate privatization of government services. He stated that government has the duty of an "exact administration of justice" for all citizens. He also wrote that governments must erect and maintain "those public institutions and those public works which may be in the highest degree advantageous to a great society"—noting that these "are of such a nature that the profit could never repay the expense to any individual or small number of individuals." And he warned that the rising industrialists "generally have an interest to deceive and even to oppress the public."[7]

Nonetheless, at the center of Smith's thinking was the belief that the primary engine for building a better society is the market—that is, the production and exchange of goods for profit through commercial transactions. He believed the forces of the market would counter selfishness through competition. As he put it, the "invisible hand of the market" would ensure that the public isn't cheated and that living standards rise.[8]

This argument, which he expounded in the nine hundred pages of *The Wealth of Nations*, became the underlying rationale for capitalism.

THE SOCIALIST VISION

In important respects, capitalism was a step forward in the move from a dominator to a partnership way of life. It gave impetus to more socially accountable political forms, such as constitutional monarchies and republics, and was a major factor in the creation of a middle class. Certainly capitalism was preferable to the earlier feudal and mercantile economic systems in which nobles and kings owned most economic resources.

However, capitalism emphasized individual acquisitiveness and greed (the profit motive), relied on rankings (the class structure), continued traditions of violence (colonial conquests and wars), and failed to recognize the economic importance of the "women's work" of caring and caregiving. In these and other ways, capitalism retained significant dominator elements.

By the nineteenth century, when it was clear that capitalism was not fulfilling Smith's vision of an economics that works for the common good, Karl Marx and Friedrich Engels proposed a very different theory. Theirs was to be known as *scientific socialism*, and it challenged just about everything Smith had believed, particularly his faith in the forces of the market.

Engels was born in Germany in 1820, but spent much of his life in England managing his father's Manchester textile factory. Unlike many of his class, he freely associated with the poor. He fell in love with a working-class woman, a liaison that lasted until she died, and later lived with her sister, whom he married on her deathbed. Having seen the desperate circumstances of working-class families firsthand, in 1844 he published *The Condition of the Working Class in England*.[9] It was a passionate exposé of a capitalist system that condemned people to work from dawn to dusk and still live in filthy, ratlike dwellings with barely enough to keep body and soul together. Engels had already embraced the egalitarian ideals of communism when he visited Marx in Paris in the summer of 1844. The visit was to be for only a few hours, but it stretched into ten days of intense conversation and collaboration. In the end, Engels became Marx's lifelong friend, working partner, and as time went on, the sole economic support of Marx, his wife Jenny, and their children.

Marx had not always been poor. His poverty was the result of his political convictions, which he expressed first through newspaper articles and eventually through *Das Kapital*, his monumental economic treatise. Karl Marx was born in 1818 in Germany into a prosperous liberal Jewish family, which later converted to Christianity so Marx's father would be less restricted in his law practice. Karl was sent to the universities of Bonn and Berlin to study law. There he came under the influence of the philosopher Georg Wilhelm Friedrich Hegel's theory of dialectical change—how every historic force has its opposite (antithesis) and how their clash eventually produces a synthesis, which in turn contains its own contradictions. This theory profoundly influenced Marx. He decided to become a philosopher himself, and tried to obtain a university position. But he was forced to choose between placating the reactionary Prussian authorities or giving up his hope for an academic career. He chose the latter, and at the age of twenty-three left the university to try his hand at journalism. He edited a liberal newspaper, got himself in trouble for criticizing autocratic rule, and had to leave Germany. This pattern was to repeat itself throughout Marx's life. He and his family had to wander from place to place. They could not have survived without the generosity of Engels, who saw in Marx a genius who would fashion the means for the downtrodden masses to achieve liberty and prosperity.

The scientific socialism of Marx and Engels was an alternative to what they dismissed as the *utopian socialism* of theorists such as Robert Owen and Charles Fourier.[10] Like the work of the British philosopher John Stuart Mill on political economy,[11] Marx and Engels were concerned with the interaction between political processes and economic variables, especially economic policies. But they went beyond Mill's liberal economic analysis to examine economics in terms of the struggle for control of the means of production.

Marx and Engels believed that class conflicts are historically inevitable, and that the victory of the *bourgeoisie* or merchant class over the feudal landed aristocracy would inevitably be followed by the victory of the working class or *proletariat*. But they were not only committed to constructing a new economic theory; they were also committed to seeing it put into action.

As Marx and Engels developed their theory of class warfare, there were in fact workers' uprisings all over Europe. First in France, then in Belgium and Germany, armed revolts sprang up. But all were countered by massive violence, and squashed.

Nonetheless, Marx and Engels believed time was on their side. In their *Communist Manifesto* of 1848, they wrote:

> Modern bourgeois society, with its relations of production, of exchange and of property, a society that has conjured up such gigantic means of production and of exchange, is like the sorcerer who is no longer able to control the powers of the nether world whom he has called up by his spells. . . . The weapons with which the bourgeoisie felled feudalism to the ground are now turned against the bourgeoisie itself. But not only has the bourgeoisie forged the weapons that bring death to itself; it has also called into existence the men who are to wield those weapons—the modern working class— the proletarians. . . . What the bourgeoisie therefore produces, above all, are its own grave-diggers. Its fall and the victory of the proletariat are equally inevitable.[12]

REVOLUTION AND DEVOLUTION

In time, Marx and Engels' dream of a successful communist revolution was realized. But not in an industrialized capitalist nation, as they had predicted. Instead, revolution came in an agricultural, semifeudal society: the Russia of autocratic czars and nobles.

Although socialist policies ended mass hunger and destitution and vastly improved health care and education, traditions of domination in both the family and state did not change. What Marx called the dictatorship of the proletariat turned into just that—another violent and despotic regime.

The central planners created a top-down form of state capitalism where resources were controlled by a small group of men from the top. In Moscow, government *apparatniks* got perks such as seaside villas and sumptuous banquets, while the mass of people lived in overcrowded flats and often lacked staple foods. In the provinces, warlords became communist commissars and continued to terrorize their people.

Part of the problem lay in communist theory itself. Not only did it dictate the abolition of private property and class warfare; it also failed to abandon the dominator tenet that violence is the means to power, as in the well-known adage "The end justifies the means." But an even bigger part of the problem was the rigid dominator nature of the culture that preceded the Soviet Union.

The Russian czars were despotic autocrats in a largely feudal society. Serfs were not freed until the nineteenth century. And then this freedom, like that of freed slaves in the American South, was largely illusory since the power structure did not really change. Moreover, the Soviet Union took over a culture that was rigidly male-dominated. This domination of one half of humanity over the other, buttressed by traditions of wife beating and other forms of violence, provided a basic model for inequality and exploitation.

This connection between gender, politics, and economics is one of the most instructive lessons of modern history. We see it vividly in Stalin's brutally autocratic regime. When Stalin came to power, he repealed Soviet policies enacted under Lenin to shift to more equal relations between women and men. At the same time, the Soviet Union regressed to even more violence and top-down economic control, including the killing of millions of small landowning peasants and the purging of anyone Stalin viewed as a threat to his absolute control.

In this return to a more rigid dominator configuration, the totalitarian Stalinist regime was no different from the totalitarian fascist regime of Hitler in Germany. For Hitler, as for the famous German philosopher Friedrich Nietzsche, equality, democracy, humanitarianism, and women's emancipation were "degenerate" and "effeminate" ideas. For him, as for Stalin, control was an obsession: just as "socially pure" men must rule over the rest of mankind, men must rule over women.[13]

Through economic and military assistance, conquest, and propaganda, the Soviet Union spread socialism worldwide. For a few decades, half the world was socialist, including Eastern Europe, parts of Africa, China and other Asian nations, and even a few countries in the Americas.

What Marx called the dictatorship of the proletariat turned into just that—another violent and despotic regime.

Then, following the fall of the Berlin Wall in 1989, the Soviet Union's communist regime collapsed. Capitalism became the new economic system for Russia and Eastern Europe. China too turned to private enterprise, and was soon (still under communist party control) on its way to becoming a major capitalist power.

Capitalism was declared the winner in the ideological struggle between it and socialism. But while this was hailed as a great boon for economic prosperity, it soon became evident that it was a hollow victory—at least for the vast majority of the world's people. As stock markets rose, corporate profits soared, and CEO salaries reached astronomical sums, report after report showed that conditions were getting worse for a huge part of the population.

In 2005, the United Nations reported that the globalization of an unregulated market system was actually a major factor in the creation of poverty.[14] Infant and maternal deaths were rising in some regions. In the prosperous United States one-fifth of children were living in poverty. Already in 2003, the United Nations Human Development Report found that compared to 1990, fifty-four countries had become poorer, and in twenty-one countries the number of poor people increased rather than decreased.[15] The much-hailed globalization of a free market was producing more poverty rather than less.

FROM CAPITALISM AND SOCIALISM TO PARTNERISM

The theories of both Smith and Marx and Engels made enormous contributions to our understanding of economics. But because they came out of societies that had only moved a few steps toward a partnership system, the scope of what they examined and proposed did not go far enough. Indeed, their analyses perpetuated a much too narrow view of economics.

Smith's picture of how markets function assumed a free market of small entities. He painted an idealized picture of markets as a kind of *deus ex machina* that would ensure fairness and prosperity. And he basically ignored the interaction between social and economic institutions.

Although Marx and Engels recognized the relationship between economic institutions and the larger social system, by and large they saw this as a one-way street in which who controls the means of production is the primary factor. Moreover, Marx's treatises on economics primarily focused on a critique of capitalist markets. And his solution of a socialism controlled from the top by a "dictatorship of the proletariat" never turned into the ideal communist society he envisioned as the ultimate result.

Neither Marx and Engel's nor Smith's economic theories achieved their goal of creating an economy that works for the greater good of all. Nor could this goal have been achieved in the context of societies still largely orienting to the domination system, where social and economic structures as well as cultural values maintain top-down rankings of domination and inhibit caring practices and policies.

The free market envisioned by Smith was never realized. Smith's assumption that competition would counter self-interest did not factor in the emergence of ferocious financiers, men like J. P. Morgan and Cornelius Vanderbilt, who ruthlessly used chicanery, bribery, and force to smash both competitors and union organizers.[16]

The socialism envisioned by Marx and Engels was also never realized. Instead of a just and egalitarian system, what emerged was a system controlled by ruthless men from the top.

As history demonstrates, it's not enough to change who controls the means of production. If control is exercised within the parameters of a domination system, one kind of top-down control will replace another, as happened in the Soviet Union when Bolshevik overlords took control of Russia's assets.[17] Neither is it enough to focus on the mechanics of the market. To move beyond the inhumanities and irrationalities that cause so much suffering and devastation, we have to consider all economic sectors as well as the interaction between economics and the larger social system.

Economic systems both reflect and perpetuate the underlying social structure and values, in a constantly interactive process. If the social structure and values orient to the domination system, so will economics. But at the same time, as Marx and Engels recognized, how economic systems are structured plays a huge role in what kind of social structures and values we have.

This is why we urgently need a new story of what economics is and can be. A key part of this story is a new theory for economics: one that includes the partnership elements of capitalism and socialism, but goes beyond both to ensure that human needs and capacities are nurtured and our natural habitat is conserved.

I call this evolving new economic theory *partnerism*. It is a theory in progress that will require the input and creativity of many of us. Indeed, a fully formed partnerist economic paradigm probably won't emerge until we loosen the grip of dominator traditions further. But we can—and must—shift to new ways of thinking about economics if we are to more effectively addresses our unprecedented global challenges.

Neither capitalist nor socialist theory recognized what is becoming evident as we move into the postindustrial information economy: that a healthy economy and society require an economic system that supports optimal human development.[18] By contrast, partnerism recognizes that the development of high-quality human capital—that is, of human capacities—is (in addition to a healthy ecosystem) the most valuable component of a successful economy. As Amartya Sen notes, the ultimate goal of economic policy should not be the level of monetary income per person, but developing the human capabilities of each person.[19]

This takes us to the next problem with earlier theories. This is that they failed to recognize the importance for human development of what economists call "reproductive labor": giving life and caring for life.

Today, we know from both psychology and neuroscience that the quality of care children receive directly impacts the degree to which adults develop their full capabilities. Neuroscience shows that the development of our brains is profoundly affected by our early experiences. As neuropsychiatrist Bruce Perry writes, "It is during these times in life when social, emotional, cognitive, and physical experiences will shape neural systems in ways that influence functioning for a lifetime."[20] Perry and other scientists have even found that if children are severely abused or neglected, measures of FOC (frontal-occipital circumference, which in young children is a good measure of brain size, and hence potential for mental and emotional development) can be abnormally low.[21]

This scientific knowledge calls for a reconceptualization of economic theory. It shows that we must take into account the importance of caring and caregiving as a requisite for an optimally productive economy.

Once we recognize the importance of caring in economics, we also see that many of our social and environmental problems are the result of economic rules, practices, and policies that promote, and often even require, lack of caring. That most economists don't mention caring is appalling. It is, however, understandable, since the two theories that shaped modern economics came out of times when most people accepted the superiority of men over women, and with this, the devaluation of anything considered "feminine" rather than "masculine"—including caring and caregiving.

While Smith expected women to selflessly care for others, he saw this "women's work" as unproductive and considered women's subordination natural. Despite their ambivalence about what they called the "woman question," Marx and Engels did condemn male dominance. But rather than recognizing the value of women's economic contributions in the home, they too relegated the work of caregiving to "reproduction" rather than "production." And since their focus was on who controls the means of production, this work was not of much significance in their economic analysis.

As for nature, neither Smith nor Marx factored its life-sustaining activities into their theories. For them, nature was there to be exploited by men for food, shelter, and raw materials for manufacturing.

Because they failed to recognize the importance of life-supporting activities—whether in households, the unpaid community economy, or nature—these theories are based on an incomplete model of economics. They take into account only part of the activities required for economic functioning and sustainability.

Not only that, these theories are based on an incomplete model of human needs. They only take into account our need for material survival—perhaps understandably, considering the widespread hunger and poverty in the Europe of their times. They fail to factor in that we humans have basic needs that go beyond material subsistence.

As we see all around us, current economic structures, policies, and practices are not adequately meeting humanity's material needs, much less our needs for personal dignity, meaning, caring connection, and freedom from violence. To develop systems that better meet both these sets of needs, we need an economic theory based on a more complete understanding of evolution and our place in the unfolding drama of life on this Earth.[22] This theory must recognize that in the course of evolution both men and women developed an enormous capacity for caring, creativity, and consciousness—and that rules and practices that encourage rather than inhibit this capacity are foundational to an economic system that works for all. This is a very practical issue if we are to build economic systems that support the expression and development of those capacities that make us fully human: our great capacities for caring, consciousness, and creativity.

Because they failed to recognize the importance of the life-supporting activities of households, the unpaid community economy, and nature, capitalist and socialist theories are based on an incomplete model of economics.

Moreover, we urgently need an economic theory that shows policymakers that they must take into account more than just short-term considerations. Many current economic rules, such as the U.S. Security Exchange Commission's requirement of quarterly corporate reports, pressure businesses to focus only on the short term. Yet it's clear that long-term planning is essential to protect our increasingly fragile ecological systems, that we need to consider the long-term effects of new technological breakthroughs, and that our children and grandchildren will suffer greatly unless we think further ahead. Long-term planning is also essential if societies are to make the necessary investment in the human capital needed for the postindustrial economy. And this investment, in turn, is a key factor in building a more equitable, less violent world for ourselves and generations to come.

In addition, as noted in chapter 1, to properly calibrate the value of an economic activity, we have to take into account its time horizon. This is beginning to be recognized in relation to the enormous costs of running the current criminal justice system compared to the costs of preventing crime by supporting good caring and education. We need economic theories that factor in the long-term consequences of every economic activity, both their actual costs (for example, expenses stemming from crime that are today "externalized" to be borne by society) and the opportunity costs or lost potential (for example, what a person could have contributed to society had there been more caring support at the beginning of his or her life). Economists use equations to determine value, and this time horizon has been a missing factor in their theories and calculations.

A partnerist economic theory recognizes that in the course of evolution both men and women developed an enormous capacity for caring, creativity, and consciousness—and that rules and practices that encourage rather than inhibit this capacity are foundational to an economic system that works for all.

A partnerist economic theory must also take into account what we are today learning about systems self-organization, and how economic rules and structures are in a constantly interactive feedback loop. It must explore what kinds of economic structures are both effective and equitable. It must also explore how the structure of economic institutions is related to the structure of other institutions, such as families and governments. In short, a new economic theory must recognize that without changing the economic and social structures that lie behind uncaring policies, rules, and practices, we cannot expect a system that promotes long-term economic health, environmental sustainability, and equitable relations across the board.

ECONOMICS AND RELATIONSHIPS

This matter of relationships is critical to the development of a new theory and story for economics. Focusing on relationships can help us see what holds us back and what's needed to move forward.

My research uses a method I call the study of *relational dynamics*. By this I mean studying two key dynamics. The first is how various parts of a social system relate to one another in a constantly interactive, self-organizing process. The second is how the people within that system relate to one another and to their natural environment.

As we have seen, both these sets of relations are different depending on the degree to which a culture or subculture orients to either end of the partnership-domination continuum. In the domination system, those on top control those below them—be it in families, politics, or economics. By contrast, the partnership system supports mutually respectful and caring relations.

As long as a culture is primarily based on the domination system, we cannot leave behind inequitable, inefficient, and environmentally destructive economic policies and practices. It's only as we move toward the partnership system that policies and practices can support both our basic survival needs and our needs for community, creativity, meaning, and caring—in other words, the realization of our highest human potentials.

Making this shift requires that economic theories and models pay attention to the dynamics of relations in every sphere of life, not just in economics. Including these larger relational dynamics in economic thinking makes it possible to draw on important new findings from both the natural and social sciences that are ignored in conventional theories.

We can no longer disregard scientific findings that early childhood experiences and relations play a key role in the development of the capacities needed for a healthy economy. Both psychology and new research in neuroscience demonstrate the importance of these relations for the development of the capabilities that make people effective workers, responsible citizens, and fulfilled human beings.

Nor can we ignore the connection between economic prosperity and equity and the status of women. As we saw earlier, we even have statistical studies such as *Women, Men, and the Global Quality of Life* showing that gender equity or inequity play a major role in a nation's quality of life.[23]

These studies empirically verify what some well-known economists already recognized intuitively over a hundred years ago. For instance, Charlotte Perkins Gilman's popular 1898 *Economics and Women* proposed that a more just and productive economic system requires equal opportunities for women. Thorsten Veblen's 1899 best-seller, *The Theory of the Leisure Class*, denounced "the barbarian status of women," and argued that women's activities must be counted in what he called economic provisioning.[24]

But these ideas did not become part of the economic canon transmitted from generation to generation through textbooks and classes. By the second half of the twentieth century, most of what was taught in U.S. economics classes dealt mainly with market production and consumption, and how "rational economic man" made choices governed by selfish self-interest. When the household was mentioned, it was to reiterate another fiction: that, though selfish in the market, man is an altruist when it comes to his family—even though the studies we looked at show that many men don't use their economic resources for their families' welfare.

There were of course twentieth-century theorists with a different view: John Maynard Keynes and John Kenneth Galbraith, for example. While they too focused largely on markets, they emphasized the need for government regulations, were deeply concerned about human welfare, and in Galbraith's case, wrote about how women were what he called "crypto-servants" even in the democratic West.[25] There were even branches of economics known as institutional economics and economic sociology, based on the recognition that "formalist" analyses give a false picture of reality because they don't consider the cultural context of economics.[26]

But the primary, often sole, focus in U.S. economic schools continued to be market-centered. Indeed, economics largely became a discipline of abstract theorems and mathematical equations that often fail to include what really matters in our lives: our relationships with one another and with Mother Earth.[27]

Today a growing number of economic thinkers are taking a broader view of economics. Highly visible figures such as Amartya Sen, Herman Daly, Paul Hawken, David Korten, Paul Krugman, Manfred Max-Neef, Robert Reich, Hernando de Soto, and Joseph Stiglitz recognize that we live in one of the most challenging times in the history of our planet. They argue that the dislocation of rapid technological and economic change, the escalation of violence and terrorism, the widening gap between haves and have-nots, the extermination of entire species, and the massive threats to our natural habitat call for a more environmentally responsible and equitable economic system.

The need for revisioning economics has also been the theme of thinkers whose works have not been as publicized, such as Barbara Brandt, Edgar Cahn, Nancy Folbre, Janet Gornick, Mona Harrington, Heidi Hartmann, Hazel Henderson, Duncan Ironmonger, Julie Nelson, Hilkka Pietila, and Marilyn Waring. These thinkers take economic analyses an important step further by factoring in the economic contributions from the household and nonmonetized community economy.[28]

A common premise of these women and men is that economic theory must go beyond the market—and more specifically, that it must recognize the value of caring and caregiving. As Nelson writes, "Continuing to think about economics as somehow opposed to caring and ethical behavior simply keeps care in a vulnerable, subordinated position."[29]

This is a central theme of Folbre's book *The Invisible Heart*, where she writes that we can't understand or change economics without taking into account the caring activities traditionally performed by women in the home.[30] Pietila writes that "the biggest single contribution to the daily well-being of most families is still the unpaid or nonmarket work."[31] Like Folbre, she also notes that current economic models fail to take into account the life-supporting activities of nature.

A similar argument is made by Henderson, who notes that current economic thinking (and measures) ignore the unpaid contributions of the household and community economy. She writes that the market economy "cannibalizes" these contributions, and that the entire economic edifice rests on them. She trenchantly critiques economic measures for failing to distinguish between what she calls "goods" and "bads"—that is, between activities that benefit or harm humans and nature. Like Brandt, Folbre, Harrington, Hartmann, Nelson, Pietila, Waring, and other feminist economists, she too repeatedly emphasizes the importance of the work of caring and caregiving.

REVISIONING ECONOMICS

These alternative economic analyses provide important insights for constructing a partnerist economic theory. As we saw at the start of this book, they provide building blocks for an economic model that includes all six of the sectors that actually compose economic systems: the household economy, the unpaid community economy, the market economy, the illegal economy, the government economy, and the natural economy. Once we recognize all these economic sectors, we can envision a new theoretical framework for economics.

This theoretical framework will not come together all at once. There will be many subsets of theories.[32] But as the demand for more caring structures and rules grows worldwide, we can begin to revision economics in ways that support positive changes in economic policies and practices.

These changes start with the first economic sector: the household, where the labor force needed for a functioning economy is produced and cared for. We need new economic indicators that factor in the value of the caring activities performed in households. We also need economic inventions that reward this work in ways that put food on the table and pay the rent. There are already a few such inventions,

---

☐ An Economic Invention That Gives Value to Caring and Caregiving in the Community Economy

Time dollars are a community currency invented by attorney, writer, university professor, and social activist Edgar Cahn. Rather than just relying on government-issued money, people can earn time dollars by using their skills and resources to help others (providing child or elder care, transportation, cooking, home improvement, and so on). People can then use their earned time dollars to get help for themselves or their families, or to join a club that gives them discounts on food or health care from local businesses.

Time dollars are also tools for what Cahn calls *co-production*, a method for changing unilateral charity into reciprocity, or as Cahn puts it, turning decency, caring, and altruism into a catalyst for self-validating contributions by help recipients. "Co-production," he writes, "gives real value to caring and caregiving, redefining productive work beyond that which is recognized in the market."[33]

Professor Cahn's use of time dollars as an economic strategy for addressing social problems is being implemented in thirty-six U.S. states as well as in Sweden, Japan, and Canada. For more information on the Time Dollar Institute, headquartered in Washington, D.C., and co-production, see www.timedollar.org. ■

like child-care allowances and paid parental leave, which should be replicated worldwide. But we need many more, if only because they are essential to producing the high-quality human capital we hear so much about today.

In the second economic sector, the unpaid community economy, the caring and caregiving activities of volunteers can also be recognized through economic inventions such as reduced transportation costs and other "perks" for rendering free services. Barter systems such as local currencies, through which people and small businesses exchange goods and services, are another economic invention that can be used to recognize the real value of this essential work. Time dollars, a community currency invented by Edgar Cahn, are a notable example.

The third economic sector, the market economy, also needs economic inventions that give visibility and value to caring and caregiving. Again, there are already a few such inventions. For example, better training and pay for child care, nursing, elder care, and other caring professions has long been proposed as central to the movement for "comparable worth"—that is, comparable pay for professions that require similar levels of skill and training.

Another economic invention that gives visibility and value to caring in the market is the rapidly growing socially responsible investment fund industry, which provides a vehicle for investors to support more caring business practices and policies. It makes it possible to avoid buying stocks of companies that fail to pay attention to the welfare of employees, customers, consumers, the larger community, and the natural environment.[34]

As the demand for more caring structures and rules grows worldwide, we can begin to revision economics in ways that support positive changes in all economic sectors.

In addition, as I will develop more fully at the end of this chapter, we need economic rules and structures that ensure businesses have real incentives to be more caring. Sadly, some corporate executives are aware of the health and environmental damage they cause, and deliberately conceal this knowledge as long as they think they can get away with it.[35] But for the most part, the issue is not one of bad people. It's bad economic rules that come out of, and help maintain, dominator economic structures and relations—rules that can, and must be changed.

This does not mean replacing markets with central planning. Though some central planning is certainly needed, markets have an important function. Indeed, markets play a key role in a healthy economy. But as we have seen, current market valuations are often based on a distorted system of cultural values. And what is often described as just the dynamics of supply and demand actually consists of artificially created demands for unhealthy products.

Moreover, for markets to work effectively and equitably, price systems can no longer externalize the costs of exploiting nature and people. And present economic rules actually encourage businesses to compute profits in ways that harm both people and nature.

This matter of harm leads to the fourth economic sector: the illegal economy that is so harmful to both people and nature. Because globalization has lowered barriers to illegal as well as legal commerce, the illegal economy is today a multi-billion dollar industry. From 1992 to 2002, the global drug trade more than doubled to $900 billion annually. The counterfeit goods trade accounts for another $630 billion per year. The illicit arms trade, which supplies terrorists and guerilla fighters in Africa, Asia, the Middle East, and Latin America, adds another $100 billion.[36] One of fastest-growing and most lucrative illicit trades is trafficking in people. Hundreds of thousands of people, including children, are sold into slavery in the international sex trade and other forms of servitude every year. According to UNICEF, over one hundred thousand girls and women have been trafficked from Albania alone, many of them sold into prostitution by their own families.[37]

None of this could go on were it not for lack of caring. Nor could the illegal economy have grown so big were it not for the fact that government officials at all levels are often complicit in it through bribes, and even through part ownership of criminal syndicates in some places.

This takes us to the fifth economic circle: the government economy. It is the responsibility of governments to enact policies that ensure the safety and well-being of a nation's people. Most industrialized nations except the United States have realized that caring for basic human needs cannot be left to the market. Indeed, it's a mystery why U.S. corporations don't insist on a government health care program, since health care costs make U.S. companies less competitive in the global economy—while at the same time, as we saw in chapter 3, the current U.S. system is actually more costly and less effective than those of other industrialized nations.

As University of Massachusetts economist Randy Albelda notes, workplaces can and should do some things for their employees, but they can't do it all. It is the role of public policies to set the expectations for what corporations should do and then make provisions to complement workplace policies and programs.[38]

Policymakers must also take into account findings that support for caring and caregiving is needed to solve one of the most troublesome problems of working families in the United States today: the stress of lack of family time. As we have seen, this is a major cause not only of absenteeism and low worker productivity but of the fact that workers are less happy than workers in nations where parental leave, high-quality child care, flexible work options, and other family-friendly policies are the norm.[39]

Since the government sector also provides public services directly or by contracting them to private enterprises, it should enforce standards of care for government employees and contractors. And of course, it should make and enforce rules for business honesty and responsibility, and itself live up to these standards.

As it stands now, the U.S. government gives away billions of tax dollars to major political donors. We must end this corruption through real campaign finance reform and other rules that ensure governments promote a nation's well-being rather than enriching political cronies.

This problem of political corruption is a major factor in the failure of economic policies to protect the sixth economic sector: the natural economy. Although it may not always be called corruption, when powerful corporate interests basically buy protection for environmentally destructive policies through campaign contributions, that's what it is.

Yet even now, when it's clear that the natural resource base on which the entire economy rests is becoming overexploited, the solution offered by some economists is even greater commodification of nature. They argue that if water, energy, and even the Earth's atmosphere are made private property, they will be more efficiently managed.

☐ Creating Global Public Goods

Inge Kaul, Isabelle Grunberg, and Marc Stern, as well as a number of well-known economists including Jeffrey Sachs, Amartya Sen, and Joseph Stiglitz, have proposed a new concept that can help promote human security, survival, and development: what they call *global public goods*.

Economists have long used the term public goods to describe goods or services that can be used by anyone, such as parks, education, and police and fire protection. But the concept of global public goods goes much further. It includes peace, equity, financial stability, and environmental sustainability. And it reaches across borders.

The challenge, as economic innovator Hazel Henderson notes, is to organize and create global public goods through a partnership of markets, civil organizations, local authorities, and national governments. She proposes economic inventions to help prevent what economists call negative externalities and instead promote what she calls positive externalities. "A first step," she writes, "is for all nations to establish externality profiles—i.e., the good and bad 'spillovers' they produce beyond their borders. Such national profiles can facilitate realistic bargaining between nations." Another practical suggestion is to create tax profiles of countries. These economic inventions, Henderson argues, are needed to more effectively address problems such as tax havens, capital flight, and money laundering through international mechanisms.

Both Henderson and Kaul recognize that markets can bring great benefits. But they also recognize the need for rules and mechanisms that balance the globalization of markets with the creation and equitable distribution of public goods. As Kaul writes, "Even the wealthiest person cannot do without public goods, including global public goods. Neither can markets. To function efficiently, they need property rights, legal institutions, nomenclature, educated people, peace, and security." Or as Henderson puts it, there are domains that are "global commons"—from our oceans and atmosphere to the Earth's electromagnetic spectrum and cyberspace. How these resources are used and allocated must be regulated through international treaties in which governments, businesses, local communities, and grassroots groups all have a say.[40] ■

This argument ignores the reality we see all around us, of companies that often operate with the most cynical disregard of the harm they do to our natural life-support systems. As Inge Kaul, director of U.N. Development Studies, points out, what we need are international rules that make it possible to collectively manage our natural resources in more sustainable, equitable ways.[41] These resources are what she and other economic thinkers call "global public goods." And protecting these global public goods requires economic indicators, rules, and practices that recognize that we must accord real value to caring—including caring for Mother Earth.

Indeed, just about everything we just looked at comes down to one thing: creating rules, policies, and structures that encourage and support caring for ourselves, others, and nature.

THE STRUCTURE OF ECONOMIC INSTITUTIONS

I want to end this chapter by more fully addressing the critical matter of economic structures, because without attention to this issue we can't move to a caring economics.

As I noted earlier, unlike houses, machines, and other material structures, businesses, governments, and families are living structures. These structures aren't held together by mortar or screws and bolts. They're held together by habits of thinking and acting and by the stories and rules that mold these habits.

Shifting to an economic system that better meets human needs entails changes in material structures—for example, building factories and offices with green spaces and on-site child care facilities. But even more important are the changes in our living structures: in the patterns of interactions that form families, businesses, governments, and other social institutions.

These patterns are largely determined by the laws, rules, and beliefs that govern their construction. And these laws, rules, and beliefs are very different depending on the degree to which a society orients to the partnership or domination end of the partnership-domination continuum.

As we have seen, the structures we inherited from times that oriented more rigidly to the domination system were designed to concentrate and maintain control in the hands of those on top. This is still the case for many of today's economic structures, including that most central of today's economic entities: the limited liability corporation.

The corporation as we today know it is a descendant of entities chartered under the British Crown, such as the British East India Company and the Hudson Bay Company, which were designed as instruments for the domination and exploitation of British colonies. As economist David Korten writes, they were formed "to exploit colonial territories by extracting their labor and resources and monopolizing their markets."[42]

This dominator heritage still informs present corporate design and practice. While shareholders have replaced kings, the modern corporation is basically a money-making machine, with little regard for anything else, including people and nature. And while the rules for the creation and operation of corporations are made by government charters, these charters still basically define business corporations solely as instruments for making short-term monetary profits for shareholders and accumulating financial assets.

These financial assets are now increasingly concentrated in the megacorporations that have become today's global fiefdoms. Indeed, these megacorporations control more assets than many nations. For example, fifty-one of the world's one hundred largest economies are today corporations rather than nations.[43]

In short, today's megacorporations have become instruments for the domination system by further consolidating the concentration of economic power. They control markets, making the idea of a free market a fiction. Their powerful advertising strategies shape consumer purchasing patterns to enrich their coffers. Through both legal and illegal support for politicians, they control many government policies, obtain massive tax-funded subsidies, and successfully oppose environmental and labor regulations. Moreover, they not only exercise their enormous economic and political power individually; they do so jointly.

These corporate giants exercise their power through a number of international institutions such as the World Trade Organization and International Monetary Fund that lay down the rules for international trade. So ironically, while so-called neoliberal economists adamantly oppose socialist central planning, we today have central planning by corporate interests on an unprecedented global scale.[44]

All this has been thoroughly documented by David Korten, Thom Hartmann, Paul Hawken, and many others, who propose that the laws and charters governing corporations must be changed.[45] Since corporations are fictional creatures created by government permission, changes to make them more accountable, limit their monopolistic powers, and ensure that their activities do not deplete human and natural capital in the name of wealth creation are possible—and urgently needed. For example, charters could require that corporate boards include employee and community representatives as a means of ensuring greater accountability. Antimonopoly laws already on the books can, and must, also be enforced and strengthened if we are to have the free market Smith envisioned.

In addition, we need changes in the rules for another important economic structure: the stock exchanges that serve corporations by facilitating sales and purchases of their shares. Today, many of these transactions are simply speculation, gambles that, as Korten, Jeff Gates, and others note, don't create any real value.[46] Or as Hazel Henderson succinctly puts it, what we now have is a "global casino" where players bet that a stock's price will rise or fall.

All this must, and can be, changed through more sensible laws, rules, and regulations. Stiff national and international taxes on very short-term stock transactions can be used to discourage the rampant financial speculation that doesn't contribute any valuable goods or services. National and international agencies can also institute rules that no longer allow corporations to "externalize"—that is, pass on to society—the human and ecological costs of practices that harm people and nature.

Because the enormous concentration of wealth and economic power in corporations has led to so many abuses, some economists have even proposed that the large publicly traded corporation should be abolished, arguing that its very structure encourages activities that cause social and environmental harm.[47] Some economists have also proposed that we must stop globalization and return to small, localized economic units if we want a more equitable and sustainable economic system. They argue that, in this way, local communities will have more of a voice in economic decisions. They also argue that people running local enterprises are less likely to do severe harm to their communities and environments since they have to live in them.[48]

Certainly, as Korten writes, large corporations have proven ideal vehicles for the concentration of ownership and power in fewer and fewer hands. The rules for globalization imposed by these corporations have also increasingly put corporations beyond the reach of democratic accountability—indeed, even beyond the reach of national governments. In Korten's words, "Today's borderless global economy pits every person, community, and firm in a relentless race to the bottom, as private economic power extends out and governments compete to attract jobs and investment by offering the biggest subsidies and the lowest regulatory standards."[49] Moreover, the very depersonalization of large institutions, with their business or government bureaucracies, also often leads to insensitive practices and policies.

However, historically many smaller structures have had the same problems. Small businesses are hardly immune to price gouging and other dishonest practices, and small mills and factories continue to exploit their workers and pollute the environment. Indeed, some of the most brutal exploitation in today's global economy is that of workers toiling for small local entities. Some of these local enterprises even use slaves, including child slaves: for example, carpet shops where Indian and Pakistani children lose their eyesight from long hours of stitching; Thai, Indian, and Burmese houses of prostitution in which ten- and eleven-year-old girls are brutalized and enslaved; and Middle Eastern camel racing rings, in which child jockeys—little boys bought by merchants and sold as jockeys—are treated more brutally even than the camels.[50] Moreover, the working conditions of many small subcontractors to global corporations are also abysmal—and it is local companies that run these enterprises.[51]

Of course, such inhuman practices are not new. As we saw in chapter 6, they are rooted in long-standing traditions of exploitation and dehumanization inherent in the economics of domination, whether on a small or large scale.

I should add that, following the lead of Rousseau's idealization of the "noble savage," tribal societies are still often idealized. But again, the reality is much more complex. Some tribal societies such as the Teduray mentioned in chapter 5 are more peaceful and equitable. But there are also inequitable and violent tribal societies. For instance, the Masai of precolonial Africa were the scourge of their neighbors, whom they periodically raided, killed, raped, and plundered. Moreover, Masai women were ritually humiliated, sexually mutilated, and economically exploited in the most brutal ways.[52]

All this points to the fact that a shift to a more equitable and sustainable economic system cannot be accomplished merely by reducing size or localizing business operations. While smaller, localized units facilitate more human contacts, a caring economics requires more fundamental changes. It requires that we accelerate the shift to a system that across the board—be it in large or small organizations—supports partnership rather than dominator relationships.

So we again return to some of the central themes of this book. We come back to the need for a shift from domination to partnership in all institutions. We also come back to the need for a shift in cultural values so that the life-supporting work of caregiving, along with "feminine" qualities such as sensitivity and caring, are no longer systematically devalued as they must be to maintain rigid rankings of domination.

An economic system that no longer depletes both human and natural capital requires structural changes in economic institutions and cultural changes in the values that inform these institutions. Above all, it requires a new way of thinking about economics that takes into account matters not addressed in earlier theories.

Constructing an economic system that really works for the greater good of all will take time and require the efforts of many people. But it is essential. Indeed, as we will see in the next chapter, shifting to a caring economics is ever more urgent as we move further into the postindustrial era.

CHAPTER 8

Technology, Work, and the Postindustrial Era

When Czech playwright Karel Capek coined the word *robot* in 1920, devices that act, work, and think like humans were fantasies. Now robotics and other forms of automation are realities. Robots are routinely used in manufacturing in the United States, Japan, and other industrialized nations. Automated devices process millions of Internet sales, handle banking and other business transactions, answer customer phone calls, sort and evaluate military intelligence, monitor stock deals, and perform thousands of other functions that until recently were done exclusively by people.

Humanoid robots like *Star Wars'* lovable R2D2 and 3CPO were also not long ago science fiction creatures. Now they too are becoming realities. In the United States, a Carnegie-Mellon University team developed a mobile robotic companion for the home that uses natural language voice commands and provides information from the Internet, like weather and television schedules.[1] Even robot dogs are on the way. Cynthia Breazeal at the MIT media lab is putting together a computerized dog that reads pedometers and bathroom scales to gather information about weight, activity, and eating habits. The robot dog will help people lose weight by monitoring their daily food intake and exercise levels and warning them not to eat forbidden foods.[2]

Of course, today a future where robots replace humans exists only in *I, Robot* and other science fiction films. But some "smart" robots are already on the market. In September 2005, a three-foot-tall "housesitter" robot that can recognize ten thousand words and ten different faces went on sale from Mitsubishi Heavy Industries. Smart robots will soon be big business. The Japan Robot Association expects the Japanese market for next-generation robots to reach $14 billion by 2010 and more than $37 billion by 2025.[3]

The technological revolution in robotics is only a small part of what scientists call the *new technological convergence*. There's biotechnology, which opens the door to changing the genetic makeup of living organisms. There's nanotechnology, which puts the rearrangement of atoms and molecules in both living and inanimate matter into human hands. There's artificial intelligence, which can do complex human thinking, only thousands of times faster. Still other once undreamed of technological breakthroughs are down the road.

Some scientists and businesspeople see these postindustrial technologies as magic wands. They paint a glowing picture of how technological breakthroughs will create a wondrous new world. Others paint a very different picture. They see huge dangers from these unprecedented powers. Changing cells and atoms, they argue, should be left to nature and God. Some even fear that using these technologies will bring the end of humanity as we know it.

But once a technological genie is out of the bottle, it can't be stuffed back in. History shows that when new technologies are developed, they're used. The solution isn't putting our heads in the sand and pretending new technologies will go away. The solution is ensuring that, rather than being used to destroy and dominate, new technologies are used to help us create a more humane and prosperous world.

This does not mean that technological breakthroughs will in themselves solve our global problems. But how governments, businesses, and all of us direct their use will profoundly affect our social and economic future.

TECHNOLOGY AND THE FUTURE OF WORK

Robotics and other forms of automation have already changed our economic landscape in unprecedented ways. In the United States alone, 50 percent of blue-collar jobs were eliminated between 1969 and 1999 due to robotics and information technology.[4] And this wave of job losses, in which over ten million jobs involving physical labor and repetitive activities were replaced by automation, is just part of the story. Millions of white-collar jobs, such as those of telephone operators and receptionists, were also phased out by automation. In addition, many other well-paying jobs have disappeared.

The loss of manufacturing and white-collar jobs, and increasingly also programming and other high-technology jobs, is in part due to their outsourcing to nations with lower labor costs. But as automation becomes cheaper and more prevalent, many of these jobs, too, will be largely taken over by automation.

A 2005 report by the research firm Strategy Analytics predicts that many first-level jobs in service industries related to customer service, help desk, and directory assistance will soon be lost to intelligent systems.[5] Harvey Cohen, the author of the study, also warns that mid- and high-level jobs are threatened because of the expansion of automated intelligent systems capable of decision-making, advisory, and analytical functions. While these systems are not likely to replace humans altogether, he writes, they will markedly reduce the number of people needed to support business and government activities.[6]

The consequences, not only of unemployment and underemployment but of a less financially secure consumer base, are already being felt in the United States. There is a polarization of jobs, with well-paying jobs largely requiring advanced degrees or high-technology skills on the one hand and large numbers of people relegated to low-wage jobs that are often part-time and without benefits on the other.

As we move further into the postindustrial economy, predictions are that the U.S. industrial job base will shrink as radically as the agricultural job base shrank earlier, from employing a majority of workers to less than 5 percent. But unlike industrialization, automation does not offer large numbers of replacement jobs, especially in the nonprofessional occupations that until now provided mass employment.

The question is what to do with the "surplus" populations that technological advances such as automation, robotics, and artificial intelligence systems leave in their wake. Foreseeing this problem, and the mass suffering it will bring, the liberal economist Robert Theobald proposed a guaranteed annual income to help those in need.[7] For similar reasons, and to prevent extensive violence and the collapse of social and economic infrastructures, the conservative economist Milton Friedman proposed a negative income tax. This too would give people with no or low earnings a government stipend.[8]

These measures, however, are not appropriate responses to projections that much of what has been considered productive work will gradually be phased out by new technologies in agriculture, manufacturing, and the knowledge economy. These measures just entail doling out money, and contribute nothing to either economic or personal development.

Neither a guaranteed annual income nor a negative income tax encourages productivity and creativity. Neither gives recipients the opportunity to do meaningful work, thus robbing people of the feeling that they are doing something of importance.

Nor does a guaranteed annual income or a negative income tax reward positive behaviors and discourage harmful ones. Neither addresses uncaring economic policies and business practices. Neither takes into account the damage to our health and our natural habitat of such policies and practices, as well as the loss of human potential they entail. In short, these measures do not address the power imbalances that lie behind chronic economic inequity and inefficiency.

There is a more appropriate response to the challenges of the postindustrial world: *If we move to a caring economics, the shift to automated postindustrial technologies need not be bad news.*[9] On the contrary, these technologies open the door for redefining what is productive work in ways that utilize our unique human capacities— ways appropriate for a more humane and prosperous world.

The move into the postindustrial age calls for economic policies that support and reward activities that machines and high-technology devices, no matter how sophisticated, cannot perform: being creative, flexible, and caring. It calls for investment in education for caring and in adequate rewards for this essential work.

Instead of a guaranteed annual income or negative income tax, Congress and state governors—prodded by businesses, unions, and activists—must quickly launch programs that invest in developing the high-quality human capital that *can* meet the challenges we face. This means changing the rules of the game so that the essential work of caring for ourselves, our children, and our growing elderly population has high value, with funds allocated for training and support.

Under these new rules, expenditures supporting parental leave, child care, education, and health care will no longer be expensed every year, adding to government deficits, as is now the case. These expenditures will be recognized as essential investments in a nation's most important asset: its future human capital. They will be amortized over the span of a generation, as is done for investments in the other infrastructures that make it possible for organizations to function effectively.

When government stipends are given, they should be to reward the work of caring and caregiving, be it for humans or for nature's life-support systems, in the household and community economy. They should also fund training for the kind of high-quality caring that both psychology and neuroscience show is foundational to optimal human development.

Automated postindustrial technologies open the door for redefining what is productive work in ways that utilize our unique human capacities—ways appropriate for a more humane and prosperous world.

This approach will help ensure that we have the flexible, innovative, and caring people needed for the postindustrial workforce. Indeed, projections are that the fastest-growing U.S. job market will be in the service sector, where caring is supremely important.

Giving high value to caring for people and nature will also help ensure that our natural resources are not polluted and depleted, and that there is less violence and oppression worldwide. It will lead to more caring families and more fulfilled, evolved human beings.

When demanded by the world's people and implemented globally, policies that promote caring will lead to generally more caring and effective business and government practices and policies worldwide. And because people will learn to really value caring, this approach will lead to a more responsible and caring ethos for science, and hence also for the development of technology.

USES AND ABUSES OF TECHNOLOGY

The destructive effects of modern technologies are all around us— from the devastation of high-tech wars to industrial pollution and global warming. Small wonder that some people blame technology for our ills. But the problem isn't technology.

There's nothing predetermined about how a particular technological breakthrough is used. The same technological advance can lead to very different applications, depending on whether social structures and beliefs promote relations of domination and exploitation or relations of mutual benefit and caring.

There was no intrinsic reason why manufacturing plants had to be designed as assembly lines where humans became cogs in the industrial machine. These dehumanizing arrangements were not dictated by the invention of machines, but by an ethos of domination and the social and economic system this ethos supports.

Factories could have used the industrial democracy methods that were later developed in more partnership-oriented Nordic nations like Norway and Sweden. Plants could have been organized in hierarchies of actualization rather than domination. They could have used production methods where people work in teams, workers use their creativity, and managers facilitate rather than control and coerce.

Neither was there anything inherent in industrial technology to make sweatshops, mines, and other business enterprises practically enslave men, women, and children in dangerous workplaces. On the contrary, these technologies could have been used to free humans from backbreaking and dehumanizing work.

Nor was there anything in industrial technologies that demanded their use for ever more efficient environmental despoliation. This too was the result of a dominator ethos in which nature's life-giving and supporting capacities—like woman's life-giving and supporting capacities—are viewed as man's natural due—to use, or abuse, as he sees fit.

The basic question is whether technology is guided by an ethos of domination or partnership. And every day this question becomes more urgent, as scientists make once unimaginable breakthroughs in new fields such as biotechnology and nanotechnology.

Biotechnology can bring enormous benefits. Findings from the human genome project and stem cell research could lead to better health and longer life spans. They could bring cures for diseases that are now incurable, such as Parkinson's, Alzheimer's, AIDS, and cancer. Genetic surgery at the embryonic or fetal stage could prevent abnormalities that cause terrible suffering. Genetically engineered crops are even said to be the answer to world hunger, particularly for the developing world.

But at the same time, these new technological applications raise serious issues. For example, there's concern about health risks posed by genetically modified food. Some scientists fear that genetically modified crops carrying antibiotic genes may generate antibiotic resistance in livestock or humans. There's the environmental risk of transgenes escaping from cultivated crops into wild relatives, or contaminating organic or just regular varieties on nearby farms—as is already happening. Then there's the problem of giant companies such as Monsanto suing farmers for seed patent infringement, as happened recently when their genetically engineered seed blew onto a Canadian farmer's land, who in turn sued Monsanto for contaminating his soil.[10] Even beyond this, there's concern that genetically engineered crops may give rise to unanticipated interactions within the genome, with unknown effects.[11]

Genetic breakthroughs used for military purposes pose a more immediate danger. Biological weapons were already used in Iraq by Saddam Hussein against Kurds, and the Center for Nonproliferation Studies reports that a dozen nations, including Algeria, Canada, China, France, Germany, Iran, and the United States have developed or are developing chemical and biological weapons using substances ranging from anthrax and botulinum toxin to smallpox and typhus.[12] Further, looming on the horizon is the specter of biological terrorism, of chemical and biological weapons used against "enemy" civilians in attacks by individuals as agents of governments or on their own.

There's also the specter of genetic engineering as an instrument of thought and behavior control. Biological substances could be used by the military to control troops and civilians, or by authoritarian and would-be authoritarian regimes to control their own people.

In addition, as Jeremy Rifkin points out in *The Biotech Century*, in a time when racial cleansing and other genocidal policies are a tragic reality, biotechnology also lends itself to eugenics programs designed to eliminate "undesirable" populations. He points out that this was foreshadowed by Nazi eugenics programs that resulted in the murder of six million Jews plus several million other "undesirables" such as Poles and Gypsies, as well as the gassing of Germans with disabilities. And sadly, as the virulent resurgence of white supremacist and neo-Nazi groups shows, the "superman" vision of Nietzsche and Hitler is not necessarily a thing of the past.[13]

As Rifkin also writes, unless there is real forethought in the much touted use of genetic engineering to selectively eliminate "faulty" genes, the result could be a dangerous narrowing of the human gene pool. Mutations have played a major role in the evolution of life, and in the long run this could affect nothing less than human evolution.

The same techno-logical advance can lead to very differ-ent applications, depending on whether social structures and beliefs promote relations of domina-tion and exploita-tion or relations of mutual benefit and caring.

The recent coupling by Italian scientists of brain cells with silicon circuits raises equally hairy (and frightening) issues. Touted as a way to one day enable the creation of sophisticated neural prostheses to treat neurological disorders or develop organic computers that crunch numbers using living neurons, this breakthrough is also a first step toward another possible evolutionary nightmare: a new species that combines human and electronic traits.[14]

Difficult issues also arise in regard to nanotechnology, which combines incredibly tiny components into new atomic and molecular structures. A nanometer is one-billionth of a meter. Working with components this small once seemed inconceivable. But today scientists are doing just that in experiments designed to revolutionize everything from manufacturing to medicine.

It's believed nanotechnology will radically change medicine through biomedical devices inserted into the body for diagnostic and drug delivery uses. There are today, for example, no diagnostic methods that spot cancer in its earliest stages. Nor is there any way of telling what kind of cancer is growing in early stages. Nanofluidic transistors promise diagnosis at a stage when there are only two or three cancer cells—dramatically improving chances of stopping the growth of the disease.[15]

Predictions are that nanotechnology will also radically change the way almost everything is designed and made—from vaccines to computers to automobile tires to objects not yet imagined. So-called nanotubes, tiny but superstrong molecules that self-assemble spontaneously out of carbon and other atoms, could completely alter manufacturing as we have known it.[16] Researchers at the University of California at Berkeley have already created nanotransistors to electrically control molecules, a breakthrough that could lead to labs-on-a-chip for computerized control of chemical and biological processing.[17]

These kinds of discoveries could free humans from rote work. Along with automation, they could usher in a time when humans are free to develop and use those abilities that make us unique. Nanotechnology could even change economic valuations that depend on scarcity.

For example, experiments indicate we may be able to rearrange the atoms of coal to produce diamonds. If we rearrange atoms to produce diamonds from coal, diamonds will no longer be scarce; in fact, they will be a glut on the market. This opens the door to a new conversation about what is truly valuable—like the life-sustaining activities of households, communities, and nature.

But despite predictions of dazzling breakthroughs in medicine, supercomputing, and energy, nanotechnology also poses terrifying risks. Nobody is quite sure how products so small that they are invisible to the human eye would behave, particularly when the nanoworld's basic design elements—atoms and small molecules—are governed by the little understood laws of quantum mechanics rather than the more familiar Newtonian physics of large objects.

One concern is that without much more rigorous testing, nanotechnologists could release Frankenstein-like monsters. Dr. Mark Weisner, a Rice University professor, warns that nanotubes, because of their needlelike shape, could become the next asbestos. Other scientists worry whether the characteristics that make carbon nanotubes and similar nanoscale particles attractive candidates for carrying drugs into the brain could also allow such particles to transport toxins. Still others worry about the lack of research into how nanoparticles absorbed by bacteria might enter the food chain.[18]

The ultimate nightmare is what some scientists call the Gray Goo catastrophe. That scenario is that self-replicating microscopic robots the size of bacteria fill the world and wipe out humanity.[19]

FROM DETACHMENT TO CARING

How scientific breakthroughs are applied largely depends on the ethos guiding science. Today, the governing scientific ethos is still one of "detached objectivity." On the face of it, detached objectivity may sound good, as it connotes lack of bias. But in truth, every one of us, including scientists, has internalized many biases that maintain domination systems. So being "values-neutral," as many scientists proclaim they must be, simply reinforces and maintains prevailing assumptions and beliefs. Moreover, if we look more closely, what passes for detachment is often a suppression of "soft" qualities such as empathy and caring disguised by the argument that it's not appropriate to inject "subjectivity" into "objective" science.

This view of science is our heritage from more rigid dominator times. As the historian of science David Noble shows in his book *A World Without Women: The Christian Clerical Culture of Western Science*, modern science came out of a Christian clerical (often monastic) culture that was grounded in a worldview of contempt for women and anything soft or stereotypically feminine. So deep-seated was this denigration of women and the "feminine" that the clergy not only excluded women; monks even avoided any contact with the women who came to do their cleaning.[20]

Although modern science broke with religious dogma, it continued the earlier clerical culture's denigration of women and anything connected with them. One result, as Noble documents, was a science characterized by the suppression of empathy and caring. Another result was a science characterized by lack of holism or relational thinking.

In recent years, the entry of women into science has begun to change the exclusion from scientific methodology of empathy and other traits stereotypically considered feminine. For example, Barbara McClintock's work in plant genetics, for which she won a Nobel prize in 1983, used the approach described by Evelyn Fox Keller as "feeling for the organism." Another example of a more empathic and holistic scientific approach is the work of animal ethnologists such as Jane Goodall, Dian Fossey, and Cynthia Moss. These women revolutionized their fields by combining an empathic approach with painstaking observation. As a result, a growing number of scientists of both genders are shifting toward a blend of intuitive/empathic and objective methods.[21]

Many scientists are also rejecting the notion that science must be values-neutral. More and more scientists are expressing concern about the development of ever more powerful technologies with little attention to long-range effects on us and our planet.

The theme of a 2000 article by Sun Microsystems' chief scientist Bill Joy was the danger from new technologies gone amok. And because Joy has been so visible as a pioneer in information technology, his article "Why the Future Doesn't Need Us," received international attention.[22]

Joy noted that twentieth-century nuclear, biological, and chemical (NBC) technologies require access to vast amounts of raw (often rare) materials, technical information, and large-scale industries. By contrast, the twenty-first-century technologies of genetic manipulation, nanotechnology, and robotics (GNR) require neither large facilities nor rare raw materials. Not only that, some of these new technologies can replicate—that is, build new versions of themselves. Nuclear bombs did not sprout more bombs and toxic spills did not grow more spills. If the new self-replicating GNR technologies are released into the world, they could be nearly impossible to recall or control. Therefore, Joy warned of what he called "knowledge-enabled mass destruction (KMD)." Unless we stop the helter-skelter development and use of GNR technologies, he wrote, we could be the last generation of humans.

This scenario may be overly catastrophic. But Joy is clearly right that we urgently need standards guided by an ethos of caring and responsibility for the development of biotechnology, nanotechnology, robotics, and other powerful new technologies.

This does not mean we should stop research. On the contrary, we must continue to make substantial investments in both pure and applied research. Scientific research is not only economically profitable but also of great human benefit. It has led to wonderful technological applications—from computer chips and lasers to the Internet and heart transplant surgery. But we need regulations that ensure adequate risk assessment before technological applications are commercially exploited.

Yet responsible risk assessment is actually discouraged, rather than encouraged, by current economic models and rules of the game. If economic productivity is only measured by short-term sales and profits in the market, policies will follow suit. They will continue to ignore "externalities" such as health and environmental risks and their social and economic costs.

Indeed, even though their long-term effects are far from known, commercial applications of nanotechnology are already part of our day-to-day lives. Nanoscale particles are already embedded in consumer products like sunscreens, stain-resistant khakis, and wound dressings. Other applications using the much-touted nanotubes are on the design tables, without any real testing of their long-term effects.

❏ When Unhealthy Market Rules Get in the Way of Healthy Technologies

The notion that all that matters is short-term financial profit not only gets in the way of responsible assessments of the effects of new products, as when Merck had to pull the painkiller Vioxx off the market because of fatal side effects. Economic rules that put profits above all else can also prevent products that really heal from becoming available to sick people.

For example, it's been known for centuries that birch bark has healing powers. American Indians still hold birch in almost sacred status for its practical, medicinal, and spiritual properties. Ancient Russians knew that wounds healed faster when birch bark was applied. And birch bark is cheap and widely available. But according to Robert Carlson, University of Minnesota-Duluth chemistry professor and a pioneer researcher on birch applications, even though he and other scientists demonstrated that birch extract can heal herpes, "because it wasn't synthetic, pharmaceutical companies balked." Carlson summed up what happened as follows: "While you can patent processes, you can't patent nature. So possibly the best medicine for herpes remains unavailable a decade after it was discovered."[23]

The problem here is not one of patent laws, which are actually being altered under pressure from biochemical companies to even permit patenting genes. The problem is that the pharmaceutical giants that manufacture synthetic compounds have generally opposed low-cost medicines such as herbs and other traditional remedies—a pattern that will only change when corporate charters require attention to the long-term interests of all stakeholders, not just a company's short-term profits. ∎

Many of us are concerned about this situation. But while there is much talk, there has been very little change in the scientific and technological rules of the game.

A NEW PERSPECTIVE ON TECHNOLOGY

Ensuring the postmodern technological convergence is used for positive ends requires attention to the cultural values and social institutions that shape our ideas about what kinds of technologies we should, or should not, develop and market. We can start by broadening our definition of technology to include all the tools we humans use to achieve our goals.

Technologies are not just what the technology historian Lewis Mumford called *technics*: material artifacts such as hammers, vacuum cleaners, and computers. Building on the ideas of the legendary futurist Buckminster Fuller, I propose a broader definition of technology that includes not only technics but our uniquely human tools for creating new realities: our hands and our brains.

The artifacts and processes our brains imagine are human creations. It is our brains that are, and were from the beginning, our primary tools for achieving human-defined goals. The ideas our brains generate, not the technics themselves, determine the ends for which technologies are used.

By focusing on ends, we can distinguish between positive and negative uses of the same technological base. Instead of seeing technology as one big category into which we toss everything from can openers to hydrogen bombs, we can divide technologies into three basic types.

The first are *technologies of life support*. These technologies are designed to maintain the life and health of our bodies and our environment. They include farming, weaving, construction, and other ways of meeting basic survival needs. In addition, they include a vast array of technologies of communication and transportation, from our language and our legs to jet airplanes, radios, telephones, and emails.

Technologies of life support also include methods that facilitate healthy childbirth and enable parents to space out the birth of their children so they can adequately provide for them. They include technologies to prevent and heal disease and technologies that prevent the depletion and pollution of our natural environment.

The second type are technologies designed to help realize our highest potentials: our capacities for consciousness, reasoning, empathy, creativity, and love. I call these *technologies of actualization*. These technologies help us meet our deep human yearnings for caring connections, meaning, justice, and freedom.

Technologies of actualization also include both material and nonmaterial processes. Ancient examples of technologies of actualization are music, the arts, meditation, and other techniques for spiritual growth. Many technologies of actualization are relational technologies, such as better methods of child care and education. They are also social technologies, such as public education, representative democratic politics, equitable economics, and other human inventions.

The third type are what I call *technologies of destruction*. These technologies are very different from the first two. Their aim is destruction rather than creation. They include all the technics of terror, beginning with the sharp blade of the ancient warrior and culminating with today's weapons for nuclear warfare and bacteriological terrorism.

Of course, technologies of life support and actualization are not necessarily used for the common good. Guided by an ethos of domination, these technologies will be used in ways that primarily benefit those on top, with only "trickle-down" benefits for the rest of the population. Or they will be used in ways that dehumanize us. And this is so even for technological breakthroughs that in a partnership-oriented system could free humanity from mind-numbing drudgery.

But the greatest danger for our future lies in the fact that in cultures orienting primarily to the domination system there's no way to prevent the use of technological breakthroughs for destruction. History shows that in such cultures technologies of destruction have always been a top priority.

Today, the destructive power of nuclear and biological technologies is as great as that once attributed only to an all-powerful, angry Father God: the power to destroy all life. And research in biotechnology, nanotechnology, and robotics is pushing military technology into as yet unheard-of realms.

A Pentagon agency recently tested unmanned logistics vehicles that can reason about their immediate environment, distinguish sky

◻ *Technology and Our Lives*

Today's electronic technologies—from television, computers, and videos to faxes, email, and cell phones—offer us amazing new ways of learning, creating, and communicating. We can watch events as they happen in the farthest corner of the world, communicate instantly across vast distances, and use our computers to write and edit whole books—even to publish them ourselves.

But these technological marvels are also implicated in a panoply of new problems. We've seen an epidemic of childhood obesity and crime, as children sit long hours watching TV programs (including cartoons where there are on average twenty-five violent acts per hour),[24] or playing brutally violent video games. Psychologists have even identified a new addiction: children's obsession with video gaming, surfing the Internet, or visiting chatrooms, which is interfering with their homework and lives.

Of course, many adults are also electronically addicted. And that's not all. Advanced electronic technologies—from the Internet, cell phones, and fax machines to voicemail, email, and BlackBerries—are taking up more and more of our time. As TV and Internet news bombard us with sound bytes, we're also in such information overload that it's hard for us to understand what is really happening in the world. And instead of shortening the workday in the United States, the speed of communication made possible by new electronic technologies has largely been used to push people to work harder and longer.[25]

That this is not inevitable is shown by Western European nations where employees are working fewer hours than they were before. We too can shorten the workday in the United States so both women and men can spend more time with their families and friends—a step that won't cut into productivity, as people are more effective when they're less tired and stressed. Nor is the social isolation, alienation, and mind-numbing brought by electronic technologies inevitable. Technologies can be designed to take human needs into account. We can move to an economic system that uses advanced technologies in ways that take the rhythms of our bodies into account rather than pushing us into an ever more frantic pace—just as we can design and use technologies in ways that take the rhythms of nature into account. ∎

from ground, road, and trees, and make lightning-quick decisions. And that's just the beginning.

In 2004, an official of the U.S. Joint Forces Research Center told the *New York Times* that the robotization of the military is not a question of if, but rather a question of when. There's no question that advanced computerized machines that can decide whether to kill will be developed, he said. "The lawyers tell me there are no prohibitions against robots making life-or-death decisions."[26]

Using robots to make life-or-death decisions may sound like madness. But in the dominator mind it makes great sense. Humans sometimes hesitate to maim and kill. Robots will have no such qualms. So unless the postmodern technological convergence is used for positive ends, this is still another way the scenario envisioned in Joy's "Why the Future Does Not Need Us" might come to pass.

FROM TECHNOLOGICAL FANTASIES TO GLOBAL REALITIES

Every parent—and every policymaker in government and industry—should be concerned about whether the development and use of new technologies is guided by an ethos of caring and responsibility. Yet business and government reports on new technologies rarely touch on this vital issue.

Most business reports focus entirely on the profits from new technologies to the United States and other technologically advanced nations. For instance, a 2002 Economic Research Institute report forecast that the wiring of intelligent networks into homes, cars, and offices will soon become a $350 billion industry. It predicted that the new industry of genetically modified species or organisms (GMOs) will soon reach $140 billion, and the automation of agriculture will be a $160 billion industry in a few years. Optical computers operated by light wave (lasers/fiber-optics) rather than electricity will soon be a $120 billion business, and smart robots able to handle tasks everywhere, from the home to the factory, will shortly become a $90 billion industry.[27]

U.S. government reports also enthuse about how new technologies will bring enormous benefits. The CIA's National Intelligence Council's *Global Trends 2015* report rhapsodizes about the economic impact of a host of new products that are smart, multifunctional, and environmentally compatible, predicting they will greatly benefit manufacturing, logistics, and personal lifestyles.[28] A U.S. government report sponsored by the National Science Foundation and the Commerce Department asserts that these technologies will usher in "a golden age that would be an epochal point in human history," predicting that nanotechnology, biotechnology, and artificial intelligence will alter human evolution within twenty years.[29]

Occasionally, these reports contain short asides acknowledging that new technological breakthroughs raise moral, legal, environmental, and social issues. But they rarely mention the risks of barreling ahead with their commercial or military applications. Nor do their rosy projections of a technological utopia make any mention of what's actually happening to the vast majority of people in our world as we move into the postindustrial age.

In nation after nation, conditions for a majority of people have actually worsened in the last decade, as the gap between those on top and bottom grows. A U.N. report released on August 25, 2005 reported that in sub-Saharan Africa alone, the number of poor people increased by almost ninety million in little more than a decade (from 1990 to 2001). In Latin America, unemployment rose from nearly 7 percent in 1995 to 9 percent in 2002.

Despite claims that the globalization of capitalism is raising living standards for all, this 158-page U.N. report, *The World Social Situation: The Inequality Predicament*, noted that greater economic globalization has gone along with greater inequality both between and within countries. Even comparatively wealthy nations like the United States, Canada, and Britain have failed to escape this trend. And although China and India have seen considerable economic growth, inequality continues in these two largest Asian nations, or, as in China, is getting worse.[30]

One of the most pervasive forms of inequality, *The World Social Situation* report found, continues to be gender discrimination. While greater entry of women into the labor force has given many women more economic independence, women worldwide still earn substantially less than men. And particularly in the developing world, women are often confined to the unregulated or informal market economy, where, as human rights activist Lin Chew writes, working conditions are "aptly described by the three Ds: dirty, dangerous, and demeaning."[31]

About 60 percent of the world's workers in the informal market sector are women—a huge proportion given the fact that women have a lower level of labor force participation than men. And while more women and girls are being educated, formal employment figures for women have stagnated or even decreased in some parts of the world, with millions of women trying to support themselves and their children barely eking out a living—and all too often unable to do so.

According to the UNICEF report *The State of the World's Children 2005: Childhood Under Threat*, more than half the world's children are

☐ *Globalization, Domination, and Partnership*

Sometimes globalization is blamed for our world's ills. Actually, the globalization picture is more complex.

Certainly, as David Korten and other critics of globalization point out, trade agreements that require open borders and unregulated markets have often encouraged lower wages, exploitive working conditions, and the rapacious exploitation of nature. As Korten and others also point out, local communities can be more economically secure when most of their basic needs for goods, services, and employment are met locally. In contrast to absentee-owner corporations, local businesses may also be more likely to manage local resources more responsibly, since they depend on them for their own well-being and have to live with any environmental and health damage their activities cause.

But localization of economics is no cure-all. Local cultural traditions, as well as social and economic structures, can be extremely inequitable.

As Augusto Lopez-Claros, chief economist and director of the Global Competitiveness Network, points out about the failures of globalization, "Many of the problems laid at its door are more properly the result of unwise social policies, or the imposition of cultural habits and traditions which have nothing to do with the phenomenon of globalization itself." Lopez-Claros gives as an example that "how money from cash crops is spent by the men who earn it has far more to do with deeply entrenched social problems, such as alcoholism or sexism, than with globalization." He also notes that, in regions where there is still extreme male dominance, globalization is helping women gain access to employment, and

suffering extreme deprivation because of poverty, war, and HIV/AIDS. This deprivation is causing permanent damage to children and blocking progress toward human rights and economic development.[32] According to a World Health Organization report released in 2005, rather than living longer, 35 percent of African children now face a greater risk of dying than they did ten years ago.

These statistics are shorthand for horrible suffering. They don't show us the faces of the millions of children dying for lack of food. They don't show us the pain of the orphans who end up on the street,

---

therefore access to the possibility of escaping violent or abusive situations. So once again, we see that economic practices and policies cannot be changed by focusing on economics alone. The shift to a more equitable and sustainable economic system requires attention to the larger culture.

Whether the globalization of markets has positive or negative effects largely depends on the rules and policies that govern it. It depends on whether or not there are safeguards for workers and consumers, protection of natural resources, and other caring national and international policies. For global trade to really raise living standards for all, as its proponents claim it will, requires changes in economic structures and rules. It requires international rules that prevent megacorporations from dominating not only economics but politics. It requires regulations that demand social and ecological responsibility and attention to long-term rather than just short-term corporate goals.

To again borrow the words of Lopez-Claros, "The economics of globalization must go hand in hand with social policy intervention which preserves and enhances the positive effects of globalization." And ultimately, whether it's locally or internationally, whether economics works only for a few or for the greater good of all, depends on whether the underlying social structures and cultural values orient to the domination or partnership system.

What it comes down to is this. Trade globalization is a fact of economic life in the postindustrial age. The issue is whether it is governed by an ethos of domination or of partnership.[33]

of the men and women who toil from dawn to dusk, of the women who die in childbirth for lack of medical care.

As the authors of *The World Social Situation* write, to focus exclusively on economic growth and income generation as a development strategy is both inhuman and ineffective. They point out that this approach is not only leading to the accumulation of wealth by a few and deepening the poverty of many but also to social instability, "for which every one will have to pay the price."[34]

Clearly, if the majority of the world's people continue to live in poverty, the projections of advanced technologies taking us to "a golden age" are absurd. To move to a better era for humanity, we have to deal with the realities of people's lives.

We have to deal with the fact that every minute a child dies of preventable causes and that every year hundreds of thousands of women die from pregnancy-related complications, often due to illegal abortions sought by those desperate not to bear another child. We have to deal with the exponential growth of population at a time when postindustrial technologies are already replacing people with intelligent machines and the production of many basic goods and services will no longer require a large human workforce.

We have to deal with the fact that, largely due to exponential human population growth, over one-third of all nonhuman species are now at risk of extinction. According to scientists, in addition to species already lost, about 24 percent (1,130) of mammals and 12 percent (1,183) of bird species are threatened.[35]

We have to deal with the concern of a growing number of scientists that human activities are destroying our natural life-support systems. According to *The UN Millennium Ecosystem Assessment*, over the past fifty years, as the world population doubled, we have lost more than half of the Earth's grasslands, forests, farmlands, rivers, and lakes. The consensus of the scientists from ninety-five countries who compiled this assessment was that, unless there are major changes in policies and institutions, as population soars from the current 6.5 billion to the projected 9.1 billion in the next fifty years, increased demands for food, clean water, and fuel will have disastrous results. Among their projections are the emergence of new diseases, deteriorating water quality, "dead zones" along the coasts, the collapse of fisheries, and large shifts in regional climates.[36] And we are already beginning to see some of these problems.

Population growth and economic disparities are also fueling global terrorism and warfare. Of course, this violence is not only a matter of have-nots struggling for control of economic resources, as is often asserted. It goes much deeper, to traditions of using violence to control others, beginning in dominator families. For example, most of the 9/11 terrorists came from wealthy Saudi families where women and children are under strict, often brutal, control. But rising populations, a large percentage of young people in poor nations, and wide economic discrepancies within and between nations are important factors in fueling international violence.

New technologies are not going to solve these problems. Certainly new technologies can help people survive and have better lives. But this means focusing economic investments not just on technologies that yield short-term corporate profits but on those that yield long-term social and environmental profits. It means heavy investment in family-planning technologies to help stabilize population growth, and greater use of technologies of communication to change norms that define women as male-controlled technologies of reproduction. It means massively funding decentralized energy sources such as low-cost solar cells, and investing in solar ovens for developing nations to prevent denuding land of trees and save lives lost from the fumes and flames of wood and coal stoves. It means standards for science and technology that channel the postmodern technological convergence into technologies of life support and actualization rather than destruction.

However, even if nanotechnology, biotechnology, and robotics are used as technologies of life support and actualization, that won't suffice to meet the challenges we face. There are no quick fixes, much less quick fixes through breakthroughs in material technologies. We have to focus not just on material technologies but on social technologies.

The most critical issue for our future is not technological. It is how fast we can come out of denial about what's actually happening in our world and what we must do to shift to a way of living and making a living that promotes caring for humans and our natural environment. As we'll see in the next two chapters, we can make this shift, but only when we change deeply entrenched beliefs about who we humans are and can be.

CHAPTER 9

Who We are and Where We Are

Ryan Hreljac was six years old when his first-grade teacher in North Grenville, Canada, told his class that children in Africa were getting sick and dying because they had no clean water. Ryan decided to start raising money to help. He did extra household chores to earn his first $70, and then enlisted others to raise the $2,000 needed so that in 1999 a water well could be drilled near the Angolo School in Northern Uganda. Since then, with the support of nonprofit organizations such as WaterCan and Free the Children, the Ryan's Well Foundation has raised over $1 million to help build 196 wells in ten countries serving over 350,000 people.[1]

When Clara Hale died in 1992 at the age of eighty-seven, she had taken care of over eight hundred children: children with AIDS, children of drug-addicted mothers, children no one wanted. At first, she cared for abandoned children in her little Harlem apartment, where within six months she had twenty-two babies, all with HIV. As time went on, with the support of local officials, she was able to acquire a brownstone. There, she and her staff continued to put into action her credo that all children need and deserve love.[2]

These are just two examples of people who reached out to help total strangers. There are thousands of them, all over the world. Sometimes they even risk their lives to save those of people they've never met. They jump into dangerous waters trying to rescue someone who's drowning, or run into a burning building to save someone trapped inside. Some even risk the lives of their entire family to help strangers, like the people who hid Jews from the Nazis during World War II—knowing that if discovered, not only they but their whole family would be summarily shot.

These unselfish acts of kindness counter the conventional belief that a more caring world goes against our inherently selfish, evil nature. Yet this belief is deeply entrenched in popular stories about human nature: from the religious myth about a fatally flawed humanity guilty of "original sin" to sociobiological theories that human evolution was driven by "selfish genes" that program us to only help others when it directly or indirectly benefits us.[3]

Of course, in today's interconnected world where events in a remote corner of the planet can affect us all for good or ill, it can be argued that helping people in faraway places does benefit us. So caring and empathic actions even toward strangers could still be chalked up to self-interest, which is obviously an important human motivation.

But there's much more to human behaviors and human nature than pure selfishness. We're certainly capable of insensitivity, cruelty, greed, and violence. But we're also capable of sensitivity, caring, generosity, and empathy.

Our capacity for caring is just as wired into us by evolution as our capacity for cruelty—perhaps even more so. Caring is required for the perpetuation of our species. Some caring for offspring was already a requisite for the survival of other mammals. But because human infants are totally dependent on care for a very long time, caring became even more indispensable when our species emerged on the evolutionary scene.

By the grace of evolution, we humans are equipped with a neurochemistry that gives us pleasure when we care for others. We've all experienced this pleasure. We feel good when we care for a child, a lover, a friend, even a pet. We feel good when we're helpful, even to strangers.

The human impulse to care for and help others is already present in babies. This was recently demonstrated by Felix Warneken, a scientist at the Max Planck Institute for Evolutionary Anthropology. Warneken designed an experiment where eighteen-month-old babies watched him "struggling" with ordinary tasks such as hanging towels with clothespins or stacking books. Over and over, as he "accidentally" dropped a clothespin or knocked over books, each of the twenty-four toddlers in the experiment offered him help within seconds. But they only did this if Warneken appeared to need help. When he threw a pin on the floor or deliberately knocked over a book, the babies did not respond. On the other hand, if it looked like he needed help, the babies quickly toddled over, grabbed the object, and eagerly handed it back to him.[4]

To test the babies' motivations, Warneken made a point of not thanking them. What he found confirmed that their motives were empathy and altruism, rather than an expectation of praise or other reward. The babies were simply responding to a stranger's need by coming forward to help.

So a case can be made that we humans are strongly programmed by our biology to act in helpful, caring ways. Why then, we may ask, is there so much lack of helpfulness and caring in our world? To answer that question, we move from biology to culture.

ECONOMIC LESSONS FROM NEUROSCIENCE

Over the last decades, scientists have made great strides in understanding how our brains interact with our environments. The old nature-versus-nurture argument is slowly giving way to the understanding that the two act in tandem.

Scientists have shown that brain development occurs largely after birth, and that our early experiences play a major role in the direction of this development. The neural architecture of the brain is shaped by the interaction of our genes with our early environment—particularly with our human environment and the kind of care we receive.

This does not mean that our behaviors are determined by our early experiences. While early experiences are critical, the brain continues to change in our adult years through the interaction of our genes, our environment, and our choices.

The choices we make play a large part in how we behave. Of course, our choices are affected by both our life experiences and our genes. But we humans are uniquely equipped to make conscious decisions.

We have been equipped by evolution with frontal lobes that enable us to transcend unconscious impulses and make deliberate choices. And these choices, in turn, affect our life experiences and our cultural environments.

Indeed, the choices we make have been shown by scientific studies to affect what happens in our brains. In 2002, neuroscientists at Emory University used a new technique called functional magnetic resonance imaging (fMRI) to look at what happens in people's brains when they choose to act purely out of greed or for mutual benefit.[5] To their surprise, the researchers found that the most powerful reactions of the brain were *not* associated with winning or losing in a game for monetary gain. What really made the brain light up was when the players chose mutualism over "me-ism." And what lit up was the brain circuitry associated with pleasurable sensations.[6]

As Dr. Gregory S. Berns, one of the experimenters, told the *New York Times*, the brightest signals arose in cooperative alliances. And these signals came up in the areas of the brain known to respond to desserts, pictures of attractive faces, money, cocaine, and any number of licit or illicit delights.[7] In other words, they came up in the brain's pleasure centers.

The longer the players engaged in a mutually beneficial strategy, the more strongly the blood flowed to the brain's pathways of pleasure. However, if they played against a computer rather than a person, they were less likely to cooperate. And while the incentive for joining the study was monetary gain, in the game itself the pleasure of mutualism often overrode a monetary motivation.[8]

> *By the grace of evolution, we humans are equipped with a neurochemistry that gives us pleasure when we care for others—be it for a child, a lover, a friend, or even a pet.*

That the thought of a human bond rather than the thought of monetary gain produced the greatest pleasure would indicate that we're wired by evolution for reciprocity and mutual caring as an effective survival strategy. It would also indicate that if, like the players in this experiment, we have clear options, we are inclined to choose reciprocity and mutual caring over greed and pure selfishness, because this choice gives us more pleasure.

We usually think of choice as an individual matter. Ultimately this is true. But the choices we make are limited by the options we have or think we have.

In the Emory experiment, the players' options were dictated by the researchers. But in real life, our options are largely shaped by the kind of culture we live in. If our culture orients heavily to the domination system, people's actual and/or perceived options will be limited, and choices will often be made with little or no caring for those lower in the pecking order.

For example, a poor family in India may choose to sell their eleven-year-old daughter into the sexual slave trade, even knowing this will condemn her to a life of degradation, violence, and eventual HIV infection. They may think they have no alternative, that this is the only way for them to get some badly needed money, avoid the expense of a dowry for her, and get funds to send their son to school. To them, this choice seems a reasonable option, simply an extension of the "child bride" custom traditional in parts of Southeast Asia.[9] Even the little girl will probably choose to assent, because she too has learned to devalue herself in this culture where girl children are considered less valuable than boys, and in any case, she has nowhere to run away to, since such sales are condoned in her village.

We may ask, how could parents be so cruel to their own child? Certainly cultural factors are a major factor. But again, findings from neuroscience provide some more basic answers. They show that severe or chronic stress inhibits our capacity for empathy, as well as our capacity for perceiving options and making reasoned, conscious choices.

As neuroscientist Debra Niehoff has documented, the neurochemistry of stress makes it harder to be conscious of others, or even fully conscious of oneself, since a great deal of energy goes into ways of escaping from pain or at least becoming less aware of it. "Empathy," she writes, "takes a back seat to relief from the numbing discomfort of a stress-deadened nervous system."[10] And of course, empathy is a major component of caring. Stress also inhibits our capacity for perceiving alternatives. As stress expert Bruce McEwen puts it, "People say 'stress makes you stupid.' But what it really does is limit your options."[11]

Of course, there are always stresses in life. Sometimes stress can be a challenge to explore new opportunities and develop new skills. But when stress is extreme or chronic, as it is for many people in domination systems, its effects are quite different.

One of the side effects of chronic stress is to make us less conscious of what is happening to us and around us. To again quote Niehoff: "As stress wears away at the nervous system, risk assessment grows less and less accurate. Minor insults are seen as major threats. Benign details take on a new emotional urgency. . . . Surrounded on all sides by real and imagined threats, the individual resorts to the time-honored survival strategies: fight, flight, or freeze."[12]

So stress gets in the way of our capacity to make good choices, and even to perceive our full options for choices. At the same time, stress hinders the expression of our natural capacity for empathy and caring.

This stress-related suppression of empathy and caring helps explain how the Indian family could be so cruel. With their emotional and cognitive capacities numbed by the stress of grueling poverty and all the other stresses built into relations of rigid top-down rankings, they could justify doing this terrible thing to their own child. And since their culture considers girls less valuable than boys, they could even rationalize it on the grounds that it was necessary to give their son an education.

The Indian family's cruelty is an extreme case. But generation after generation, many parents have treated their children in cruel and abusive ways because in dominator cultures child care is associated with unquestioning obedience and severe punishments—in short, with coercion and pain. This kind of child rearing requires suppression of consciousness. So we find parents professing love for their children at the same time that they mistreat them.

We could dismiss these protestations of love as hypocrisy. But most parents do love their children. What makes it possible for parents to treat children in unempathic ways is a stress-induced mechanism for domination systems maintenance: denial. In denying their own cruelty, parents in domination systems often repeat the denial of the cruelty they themselves suffered as children in dominator families.

Denial is the suppression of authentic human perceptions and experiences into the unconscious. In rigid dominator families, children often learn to deny that there's anything wrong with abuse and violence against those who "deserve it," as they're often told about themselves. Out of fear of more pain, they learn not to express anger or frustration at adults who cause them pain. Since they can't express these negative feelings directly, they often deflect them toward people they're taught to perceive as inferior, immoral, or less powerful.[13]

Fortunately, this doesn't happen to everyone who grows up in a dominator family. Some people grow up to reject this kind of child rearing, and even to work against insensitivity, cruelty, and injustice in other spheres of life. It also doesn't mean that people can't change. They can and do.

But to change, people have to become conscious that there are alternatives. And to learn about alternatives to dominator beliefs, institutions, and behaviors, people must be exposed to the possibility of partnership-oriented ones.

ECONOMICS, POLITICS, AND STRESS

Many cultural stories worldwide present the domination system as the only human alternative. Fairy tales romanticize the rule of kings and queens over "common people." Classics such as Homer's *Iliad* and Shakespeare's kings trilogy romanticize "heroic violence." Many religious stories present men's control, even ownership, of women as normal and moral.

These stories came out of times that oriented much more closely to a "pure" domination system. Along with newer stories that perpetuate these limited beliefs about human nature, they play a major role in how we view our world and how we live in it.[14] But precisely because stories are so important in shaping values, new narratives can help change unhealthy values.

Of particular importance are new stories about human nature. We need new narratives that give us a more complete and accurate picture of who we are and who we can be—stories that show that our enormous capacities for consciousness, creativity, and caring are integral to human evolution, that these capacities are what make us distinctively human.[15]

Of course, changing stories is not sufficient. Cultural stories and social structures go hand in hand. We must also work to replace dominator structures with partnership structures in all institutions, both in the public sphere of politics and economics and the private sphere of family and other intimate relations.

As we've seen, dominator structures artificially produce stress, and the production of stress is a means of imposing and maintaining relations of domination and submission. As we've also seen, severe or chronic stress, particularly in people's early years, plays havoc with our innate capacities for consciousness and caring.

Children raised in family environments where rankings of domination are painfully enforced frequently take the view that these kinds of relations are inevitable into other relations. They often take this view into their peer groups, sometimes acting it out by bullying other children. And if other elements in their culture—from toys and games to education, religion, and the mass media—also portray this way of structuring relations as normal, moral, and even fun, these patterns become part of a child's cognitive and emotional map for all relations.[16]

Add to this that children in dominator families are taught a male-superior/female-inferior view of our species, and the belief that hierarchies of domination are normal is further reinforced. In such families, children observe that difference is equated with superiority or inferiority, with dominating or being dominated, with being served or serving. Unless they are exposed to another alternative, they are often prone to accept economic and social inequality as "just the way things are."

As psychologist Else Frenkel-Brunswick showed in studies of what she called the authoritarian personality, in families that rely heavily on fear and punishment, and where "relationships are based on roles clearly defined in terms of dominance and submission . . . certain aspects of experience have to be kept out of awareness." In these chronically stressful families, the suppression of awareness serves "to reduce conflict and anxiety and to maintain stereotyped patterns."[17]

Frenkel-Brunswick, whose research was part of an effort to understand what happened in Nazi Germany, also found that children in dominator families tend to overemphasize hostility and danger, because this conforms to their own daily experiences. This leads to an adversarial view of the world in which perceptual rigidity and blindness to what is actually happening often results in maladaptive personal and political behaviors.

These dynamics help explain the policies of leaders trapped in dominator mindsets and emotional habits. Leaders brought up in dominator families, where the strong are always right and the weak are always wrong, often replicate these conditions unless they're exposed to more equitable alternatives. And since in these families the "women's work" of caregiving is considered less valuable than activities assigned to men, they also learn to devalue caring and caregiving.

Family relations based on domination and submission also often teach important lessons about violence. When children experience violence, or observe violence against their mothers, they learn it's acceptable to use force to impose one's will on others. This attitude is then often transferred to other relations, including international ones. People with this attitude tend to believe that national security must rely on violence, and to not support polices to change social and economic conditions that foster violence.

In short, when people grow up in situations where partnership relations are not modeled, they often believe that the only alternative is to dominate or be dominated. They also often believe that human nature is uncaring and violent, and that anything associated with women and the "feminine"—such as caring and caregiving—is inferior to anything stereotypically associated with men and the "masculine."

These are the kinds of dynamics that lie behind political and economic decisions that ignore, and even aggravate, global problems such as chronic hunger and poverty, overpopulation, and environmental devastation. They lie behind policies that evidence lack of empathy for those they harm, and in our interconnected world, ultimately harm us all.

Dominator structures artificially produce stress, and severe or chronic stress, particularly in people's early years, plays havoc with our innate capacities for consciousness and caring.

I again want to emphasize that not everyone exposed to the stress of dominator families accepts and perpetuates relations of domination and submission. People sometimes reject these dominator traditions, and may even work to change them.

I also want to again emphasize that stressful childhood experiences in dominator families are not the only reason why many people accept unjust relations. It's much more complex: dominator families, education, the media, religion, and other institutions interact with dominator child rearing and other early experiences to reinforce each other. And dominator economic policies and practices play a key role in this vicious cycle.

As we saw in chapter 6, anthropological and archeological data indicate that rigid dominator cultures originated in inhospitable environments—deserts, steppes, drought-blighted areas—where resources were scarce.[18] But as we also saw, even in hospitable environments such as fertile valleys or coastal areas, dominator economic systems maintain themselves by creating chronic scarcities, and with this, chronic stress.

Domination systems create artificial scarcities by misdistributing resources to those on top. They destroy material and human resources through environmental exploitation, chronic wars, and other forms of institutionalized violence. Dominator policies also

⊡ Policy Implications of Neuroscience

The choices we make affect our brain neurochemistry all through life. We are learning that meditation, changes in diet, and exercise affect brain neurochemistry. Changes in the kinds of relationships we experience can make a huge difference. And so can changes in beliefs and social structures. All these affect our brain neurochemistry, and thus how we think, feel, and act.

Even radical changes in consciousness and behavior can occur in adults. However, early experiences play a key role in shaping our neural and biochemical development. As Dr. Bruce Perry and other neuroscientists point out, childhood experiences provide the organizing framework for our brains—and for many of our traits and behaviors.[19]

The studies of Perry and other neuroscientists show that abused or neglected children are more inclined to withdraw into depression than children who have experienced supportive, respectful environments. They're more inclined to have a high tolerance for abusive relationships. They're also more likely to become abusers themselves. These patterns are most extreme in severely abused or neglected children. But all of us are affected by our early experiences.

This evidence from neuroscience calls for policies that support good care for children. If enough people and organizations demand this, governments will support education for caregiving in schools and communities, fund universal health care and quality child care, and develop economic inventions that reward good caregiving.

Consider the enormous community expense of *not* investing in good child care—from crime, mental illness, drug abuse, and lost human potential to the economic consequences of lower-quality human capital. Community investment in caregiving will pay for itself in less than a generation—and make a huge profit in the bargain. ▪

create scarcity through their low social investment in caring for children's physical, mental, and emotional development. This limits the availability of high-quality human capital, retarding the economic development that can help prevent scarcity. And particularly these days, when weapons systems carry huge price tags, dominator economics create artificial scarcities by expending enormous sums on armaments, money that could be used to promote more general abundance through the funding of basic education, health care, and other investments in a society's human capital.

The stress of scarcity often produces emotional (and thus neurochemical) reactions similar to those produced by dominator child rearing. It also often produces feelings of dependency on, and fear of, those who control economic resources. Like children who are dependent on abusive parents, people on the lower rungs of the dominator economic pyramid often tend to identify with those in control. They suppress consciousness of the real situation, and even idealize those who exploit and oppress them. So we often find poor people venting their frustration and pain against minorities or those designated as enemies by political and religious leaders.

However, the negative effects of stress on those on the bottom of dominator hierarchies are not only a matter of poverty. This was dramatically demonstrated by the Whitehall Studies, so-named for the street where much of the British civil service is housed. These studies, conducted by the British physician Sir Michael Marmot and his colleagues during the 1970s, showed that those on the lower rungs of the civil service hierarchy suffered disproportionately from stress-related health problems.[20] These people were *not* poor. The stress that made them more susceptible to heart attacks, diabetes, depression, alcoholism, respiratory illness, and cancer came from the dominator hierarchy itself.

Like many other bureaucracies, whether governmental or corporate, the structure of the British civil service was one of top-down commands. There was little if any discretion for those on the lower rungs, as expressed by the bureaucratic refrain, "I wish I could help, but these are the rules." In such situations, violating rules is grounds for dismissal. So the further down people are in these hierarchies, the fewer options they have, and the more they must suppress initiative, creativity, and caring as well as consciousness—otherwise, it would be too painful to enforce rules that are often uncaring. This suppression is stressful and so is the fear that maintains hierarchies of domination. And all this stress has adverse health consequences.

Studies also show that it's not the richest nations that are home to the healthiest populations, but the nations where there is more equality. British medical epidemiologist Richard Wilkinson and other researchers have found that less income inequality predicts better health for *both* the poor and the wealthy.[21] One of the reasons is that the more unequal income is in a community, the greater the psychosocial stress will be. Of course, the poor are generally more stressed than the well-off. But even the relatively well-off are stressed in cultures where there is a large concentration of wealth at the top. This stress, Wilkinson found, comes from competitively comparing their situation with those who have even more material goods. And as Stanford neurobiologist Robert Sapolsky noted in his analysis of the stress of inequality, "In our global village, we are constantly made aware of the moguls and celebrities whose resources dwarf ours."[22]

So the large social inequalities built into domination systems are stressful not only for those on the bottom economic rungs but even for those on higher ones. Once a certain level of material affluence is reached, more material goods don't seem to make people happier and are no substitute for the real satisfaction of close family and other bonds.[23]

Many other aspects of domination systems cause stress and health problems. The uncaring use of industrial technologies causes environmentally linked diseases and deaths. And although these effects are often most severe for those in the bottom socioeconomic tiers (toxic waste dumps, for example, are typically located in poor neighborhoods), industrial technologies that pollute our air and food adversely affect us all. Violence, be it in families or in the family of nations, is of course also stressful. Fear is stressful. Yet both fear and violence are built into domination systems, for rigid top-down rankings are ultimately maintained by fear and force.

In sum, starting in early childhood through family relations based on domination and submission, stress serves to constrict both people's actual life options and their consciousness of alternatives. When children are taught the "normality" of domination and submission—and society doesn't offer alternatives—they often learn to go into denial and inhibit their capacity for empathy and consciousness. They then tend to build family, educational, religious, economic, and political institutions based on these principles when they grow up. And so the cycle repeats itself generation after generation.

Under these circumstances, the wonder is not that there's so much insensitivity and irrationality in our world, but that there's so much sensitivity and good sense. Yet the story that human nature is purely selfish, or as some sociobiologists claim, that we're unconsciously run by "ruthlessly selfish genes," persists. And this, despite all the evidence that humans are capable of a much larger range of motivations and that integral to our genetic equipment is a deep yearning for justice, mutuality, and caring.

CURRENTS AND CROSSCURRENTS TO OUR FUTURE

The human yearning for justice, mutuality, and caring lies behind massive advances in Western culture from the Middle Ages to our time. Countering the story that, because it was more religious, the medieval age was a better and more caring time, history shows that with its Inquisition, Crusades, and witch-burnings, it was actually an incredibly brutal time.[24] Indeed, in critical respects it was not very different from what we see today in despotic fundamentalist Muslim theocracies, where publicly chopping off people's hands, stoning women to death, "holy wars," and terrorist attacks on helpless civilians are still considered moral.

This so-called European Age of Faith was a time of chronic wars and the most horrible public tortures, which not only terrorized people into conforming but also served to desensitize them to cruelty and suffering, including their own. Although parents undoubtedly had loving feelings for their children, severe child abuse and neglect was common. Women in most families worked from dawn to dusk on house and farm chores, with little time left for child care. As continued to be common practice later, children were often apprenticed out at an early age, and child labor in the most appalling conditions was the norm.[25] In well-to-do families, babies were regularly farmed out to wet nurses. Many women abandoned babies on roads, hoping strangers would pick them up, or put them in orphanages, even though the death rate in these institutions was astronomical.[26] It was also a time²of rigid male dominance. If a woman killed her husband, she was subject to the same horrible execution by torture as someone who killed the king.²⁷ And just as men had the legal power to beat their wives and children, despotic rulers had almost absolute powers over their subjects.

But as the gradual shift from agrarian to industrial technologies increasingly destabilized existing patterns of work and life, one social movement after another challenged entrenched traditions of domination. The "rights of man" movement of the seventeenth and eighteenth centuries challenged the "divinely ordained" rule of kings. The eighteenth- and nineteenth-century feminist or "rights of women" movement challenged another tradition of domination: "divinely ordained" control by men over women and children in the "castles" of their homes. The nineteenth-century abolitionist and economic justice movements challenged still other traditions of domination: the enslavement of "inferior" races by "superior" ones and the economic exploitation of "working men." The movement to humanize the treatment of the mentally ill challenged the practice of beating and chaining them to tame their "antisocial instincts." Educational reform movements challenged corporal punishment to control children in schools. The twentieth-century civil rights, anticolonialism, women's liberation, indigenous peoples' rights, peace, and gay rights movements took the challenge to traditions of domination even further. The international peace movement challenged the use of force by one nation to control another. And the environmental movement challenged the once-hallowed conquest of nature.

These organized challenges to traditions of domination brought enormous gains. Without the eighteenth-century challenge to the "divine right" of kings to rule, we would still be living under despotic monarchs. Had it not been for the abolitionist movement, slavery would still be legal. Without the nineteenth- and twentieth-century feminist movements, women would still be under absolute male control, legally deprived of the right to manage their own property, gain custody of their children, be admitted to universities, go into business on their own, or vote. Had it not been for the challenges of organized labor, unsafe and unsanitary workplaces, twelve-hour workdays, child labor, and other features of early robber-baron capitalism would still be legal. Without the civil rights movement, we would still have segregated water fountains, buses, restaurants, hotels, and hospitals. And were it not for a new movement challenging domination and violence in intimate relations, crimes such as rape, wife beating, and child abuse would still not be prosecuted.

However, every one of these movements was met by fierce resistance. And this resistance has intermittently led to regressions in which gains already made were lost.

If we look at the last three hundred years from the perspective of the underlying tension between the partnership and domination systems, a new story of modern history comes to the fore. We see that underneath what may seem like random and unconnected events there is a pattern: the thrust toward partnership countered by the push back to domination.

Hitler's Germany, Stalin's Soviet Union, Khomeini's Iran, and the Taliban of Afghanistan are dramatic examples of regressions in modern times to a "pure" domination system. And even in the United States, there have been intermittent regressions to a more rigid domination system.

The latest such regression began in the 1970s, and we are still in it as I write this book. In our "cradle of democracy," politicians talk of American ideals such as democracy, equality, and freedom. But their rhetoric is often a smoke screen for pushing back partnership gains.

Many politicians today talk about the need for a free market, free enterprise, and freedom from environmental regulations. But what they really mean by freedom when they take regulatory power away from federal agencies set up to protect us and our environment, is freedom for those in economic control from any governmental curtailment of their power.[28] They see nothing wrong with strict government control over those they want to keep "in their place." Despite all their talk about freedom from government interference,

As the gradual shift from agrarian to industrial technologies destabilized patterns of work and life, one social movement after another challenged entrenched traditions of domination. However, every one of these movements was met by fierce resistance and periodic regressions.

they're all for government interference when it comes to denying women reproductive choice or quashing street protests against powerful economic interests.

Along the same lines, politicians who promote "supply-side" trickle-down economic policies often talk about democracy and equality.[29] But in reality these policies have led to more economic inequality, and as political economist Jeff Gates points out, pose a threat to any real democracy.[30]

U.S. government figures show that over the last decades the earnings of the American middle and lower classes have stagnated or declined when inflation is taken into account. At the same time, upper-class incomes have risen sharply. According to the Internal Revenue Service, in 1979 the richest 1 percent's share of reported income was 9.6 percent, but by 2003 it had risen to 17.5 percent. Yet during the same period, the bottom 40 percent's share fell from 11.3 percent to 8.8 percent.[31]

Between 1965 and 2004, salaries of CEOs in the United States jumped to unheard-of levels. Their pay in salary, bonus, and other compensation such as exercised stock options and vested stock grants averaged $10.2 million in 2004. That same year, full-time worker pay averaged just $32,594. That's 11 percent less than 1973's average worker pay of $36,629 (adjusting for inflation).[32]

This widening of the economic gap between those on top and those on bottom both in the United States and other nations is not an isolated phenomenon. It is part of a larger regression toward more rigid top-down rankings in all spheres of life.

One of the most dangerous aspects of this regression is the worldwide rise of so-called religious fundamentalism. Actually, this movement should be called *dominator fundamentalism*, because its aim is to reinstate the fundamentals of the domination system: rigid top-down control in both the family and the state, rigid male dominance, violence as a means of control, and beliefs that all this is not only normal but moral.

The leaders of the Christian Right in the United States have focused on two goals: theocratic rule in the state and patriarchal rule in the family. Beginning in the 1970s, when they mobilized to defeat the Equal Rights Amendment (which would simply have prohibited gender-based government discrimination), they have invoked Christianity to advance policies that are often the polar opposite of the teachings of Jesus. Whereas Jesus taught caring, compassion, empathy, and nonviolence—the fundamentals of partnership—most leaders of the Christian Right preach the fundamentals of the domination model.

They preach fear, as in "You've got to put the fear of God into people"; guilt, as in "You're a sinner"; hate, as in their promotion of "holy wars"; and prejudice, as in their vilification of people of different races, religions, or sexual orientations. Above all, the aim of funda-

---

Moving Beyond Myths of the "Good Old Days"

We hear a great deal about the good old days, when families were "intact" and people were more caring. But the assumption that care was so good in the past flies in the face of history. Not only neglect but abuse and violence against children were common in earlier times. Even as late as the eighteenth and nineteenth centuries, autobiographical accounts tell of severe bodily violence as routine in homes and schools (with several reports of brothers and sisters killed by violence at the hands of teachers or parents).[33]

Of course, there were always people who cared. But the fact that most women in the agrarian economy had to work from dawn to dusk meant they had little time to spend caring for their children. They were also handicapped by lack of knowledge about hygiene and diet, and by traditions of highly punitive, force-based child rearing.

Today's huge market for books and magazines on good parenting shows that more and more people recognize the need for knowledge of stages of child development and how best to care for children. It is true that women in the United States spend less time at home because they are no longer barred from education and entry into the professional world and because two incomes have become more necessary even for middle-class families. But the solution is not to return to a time when women were what economist John Kenneth Galbraith aptly called crypto-servants: essentially, unpaid household help.

The solution is to give real value to the work of caring and caregiving in homes, schools, and society at large—whether it's done by women or men. ■

mentalist leaders, whether in the United States, Iran, India, or Pakistan, is to push us back to families where the authority of the father is absolute.[34]

In the Muslim world, the repressive legal code known as *Sharia*, which brutally enforces strict male control over women, is being reinstituted. Hindu fundamentalists defend traditions of male dominance, child marriage, and even the old practice of *sati*, or widow burning. In the United States, the Promise Keepers and similar groups have been urging men to reassert control over women and telling women God orders them to submit.[35]

Fundamentalists also preach that children must be taught absolute obedience, on pain of severe punishment. U.S. fundamentalists promote methods they call raising children "God's way," advising parents to harshly punish children.[36] And unfortunately, because these methods are familiar, and hence feel natural to many people who carry the pain, frustration, and anger of their own dominator child rearing, these books and programs have a wide following, perpetuating family traditions of domination that in turn support rankings of domination across the board.

THE ECONOMICS AND POLITICS OF DENIAL

The fundamentalist family values agenda isn't just influencing families; it's profoundly influencing politics and economics. Studies show that men from authoritarian, abusive families tend to vote for "strongman" leaders. They also tend to support punitive rather than caring social and economic policies.[37] So a U.S. survey showing that, since the rise of fundamentalism, a substantially higher percentage of respondents believe that "the father of the family is master of the house" doesn't just reflect a shift to an authoritarian family ideal. It reveals some of the psychosocial dynamics that lie behind the election of U.S. politicians who rely on force in foreign relations, suppress domestic dissent, and promote policies that economically privilege those on top at the expense of those on the bottom.[38]

These unconscious psychosocial dynamics also help explain why the rank and file of the Christian Right have supported politicians whose policies benefit the super-rich and megacorporations. This support may seem strange, since most of the Christian Right's rank and file are lower middle class or poor. But it makes sense if we consider that many of them come from authoritarian, punitive families, where they learned to identify with those in control and to deny that "superiors" can do wrong.[39]

I again want to emphasize that not everyone from a family based on domination and submission is trapped by unconscious psychological dynamics that lead them to vote against their own economic self-interest. But many people are if they don't gain access to more egalitarian relationship models.

As we have seen, in a top-down, authoritarian family that relies on fear and force, children often learn to be in denial about their parents' behavior since they depend on them for survival: for food, shelter, and protection from strangers.[40] This makes it easy to later be in denial about "strong" leaders who abuse power, and to identify with them, particularly in times of actual or perceived external danger.

People's willingness to close their eyes to skyrocketing CEO salaries (while these same CEOs "downsize" companies by eliminating thousands of jobs) and to tax cuts that mainly benefit the very rich (while social programs are slashed) is to a large extent due to habits of denial that many people carry from their childhoods. Similarly, people's willingness to countenance the erosion of democratic safeguards, such as freedom from secret government surveillance, and their support for the preemptive Iraq War, even though it was justified by false information, are also largely due to early habits of obedience to authority figures coupled with denial that "strong" leaders can be wrong.

Of course, there are other factors. There's the reconcentration of U.S. media control, so that by 2000 only six companies controlled most of America's mass media.[41] There's the constant media message that what's good for the rich and powerful is good for the masses. There are all the media stories telling us that for the United States to be competitive in the global economy, workers' wages and benefits must be cut. There are all the political spins playing on people's fear of losing their jobs and benefits, including health care, as is happening to many U.S. workers.

On top of the fears engendered by economic insecurity, there's also the fear of rising fundamentalist terrorism. This fear is unfortunately based on reality, as 9/11 tragically showed. But the authentic threat of terrorism has also been exploited to justify greater top-down control.

The social instability stemming from the rapid shift into the postindustrial era is another cause of fear, particularly for people with the psychological rigidity characteristic of the dominator personality. Add to this the consumption frenzy stoked by marketing moguls and the quickening speed of life through electronic technologies such as the Internet, cell phones, iPods, fax machines, email, and voicemail, and it's not surprising that many people have little time or energy to reflect on their lives and our world, much less to do things that bring about positive change.

Yet despite all this, the movement toward partnership is alive and well. Even in this period of fear, fanaticism, corruption, alienation, and confusion, the values we treasure—equality, fairness, justice, dignity, and ultimately kindness and caring—continue to inspire millions of people to work for a better world.

THE GLOBAL MOVEMENT TO PARTNERSHIP

Kindness and caring are integral to our humanity. In *The Theory of Moral Sentiments*, Adam Smith recognized this positive side of human nature. While he did not focus on this in *The Wealth of Nations*, behind his advocacy of a free market was the assumption that self-interest will be tempered by consideration for others.[42]

These two sets of motivations are not contradictory. Enlightened self-interest includes concern for others. Today, the growing awareness of this connection lies behind the efforts of millions of people to change customs, institutions, and practices in a partnership direction.

On the one side is the pull of the old domination system to reassert its hold through the psychosocial dynamics we've been examining. For some people, the destabilization of old institutions through our rapid move into the postindustrial era is a terrible threat. They cling to the old and familiar, and frantically try to push us back to what they see as the safety of authoritarian, punitive, male-dominated families. They yearn for a reconsolidation of top-down control in all institutions—from family, religion, and education to politics and economics.

On the other side is the push to free us from these kinds of institutions. For the people on this side, rapid technological and social change, and the destabilization it brings, are an opportunity to move forward.

Hundreds of thousands of nongovernmental organizations are working to change patterns of poverty and economic injustice, preserve our environment, change unhealthy lifestyles, promote nonviolent conflict resolution, and protect the human rights of children, women, and men. Although they focus on many different issues, all these organizations have a common goal: shifting to a more caring economic and social system.

Organizations like Amnesty International, Human Rights Watch, and a myriad of smaller groups campaign against torture of political prisoners, genital mutilation of girls, and the sale of children into the multi-billion dollar global sex industry. Friends of the Earth, Scientists for Social Responsibility, the Earth Island Institute, the Sierra Club, and hundreds of other organizations work for policies that protect our natural life-support systems, prevent toxins and pollutants from contaminating our environment and harming our health, and curtail carbon dioxide emissions that contribute to global warming. Other organizations promote organic farming, organic food, and what is now called holistic, alternative, or integrated health care, encouraging healthy, less stressful, and more caring lifestyles.[43]

Co-op America's Fair Trade Alliance helps build U.S. markets for imports from companies that treat employees well rather than those whose workers toil in sweatshops, plantations, or other places of exploitation. Its Corporate Responsibility program helps communities pressure Wal-Mart and other companies to change uncaring employment practices. Its Green Pages list environmentally and socially responsible companies in the United States.

The Hunger Project, the Global Fund for Women, the Women's Environment & Development Organization, the International Museum of Women, the Older Women's League, and thousands of smaller grassroots organizations, from Women Living Under Muslim Laws to the Tostan project in Senegal and the Teen Talking Circles in Seattle, are dedicated to raising the status of women. Planned Parenthood International, Population Action International, the Population Institute, and other organizations promote family planning and reproductive health services for women worldwide.

Of particular importance are organizations working for the rights of children, such as the international Centers for Compassion for Children and the U.S.–based Children's Defense Fund. Women's studies, African-American studies, peace studies, and men's studies programs are other important new developments. So are thousands of international, national, and local conferences where people on every continent share ideas for economic and social transformation.

Also unprecedented are the scores of books countering the old story that humanity is inevitably trapped in relations of domination and submission, violence, and male dominance.[44] These alternative narratives about our past, present, and possible future are helping many people move forward, with books challenging dominator gender stereotypes opening new life options not only for women but also for men.

Men's groups such as the Canadian Center for Violence Intervention (CIRV), the Swedish Manscentrum, and the U.S. Mentors in Violence Prevention (MVP) program, which works with U.S. Marines and college athletes, are dedicated to ending traditions of male violence against women. Groups such as Dads and Daughters are helping men become more caring and involved fathers.

Progressive schools and other organizations that promote education for children's emotional as well as physical and mental development and model caring behaviors are also important in the movement toward a more equitable and caring society. So also are groups such as the Center for Media and Democracy, Fairness, and Accuracy in Reporting (FAIR), and Media Watch, which provide analyses of the mainstream media as well as alternative sources for news and political and economic perspectives.

There are a myriad of networks for progressive action: organizations working for racial equality, indigenous rights, religious tolerance, peace, and economic justice. There are also progressive spiritual networks, such as those of Quakers, Unitarians, and the *Tikkun* Community's Network of Spiritual Progressives, whose "Spiritual Covenant with America" offers an alternative to the old dominator "morality."[45]

Organizations such as Ashoka and Avina fund social entrepreneurs, women and men who use their initiative, leadership, and organizational skills to promote equity, peace, sustainability, and economic development. Socially responsible investing—that is, investing only in companies screened for sound environmental and social policies and practices—is another new phenomenon, with the Calvert, Domini, and Pax funds doing as well, and often better, than conventional funds. There are also microlending programs such as the Self-

Employed Women's Association (SEWA) founded by Ela Baatt in India and the Namaste Direct program in Latin America, which pro-

□ Social Entrepreneurs

Social entrepreneuring is a new profession dedicated to building a more caring and sustainable future. It is a core element of the nonprofit organizational sector, or civil society, that has grown exponentially in the last decades.

Hafsat Abiola, daughter of the first democratically elected president of Nigeria, is one of these social entrepreneurs. After both her parents were killed by the Nigerian military, Abiola found herself alone in the United States, where she worked to help return political democracy to her homeland. She later returned to Nigeria and founded KIND, an organization that prepares young women to become leaders and fight against gender discrimination.

In Bangladesh, another social entrepreneur, Shamsul Momenn Palash, mobilizes environmental activists at universities. Palash's passion for the environment goes back to his childhood, when the Sitalakha River, where he used to swim, was polluted by a fertilizer factory. He now trains students to work for environmental sustainability.

In the United States, Ocean Robbins co-founded YES!, Youth for Environmental Sanity, when he was sixteen. Robbins has been an activist since age seven, when he organized a peace rally in his elementary school. YES! holds camps for young activists and leaders from all over the globe, inspiring them to build a better world.

In Rio de Janeiro, another social entrepreneur, Thais Corral, founded CEMINA (an acronym for the Portuguese words for Communication, Education, Information on Gender), which provides communities Internet facilities where local women broadcast and produce programs that go to over four hundred radio stations. Corral calls these women cyberelas, that is, cyber-Cinderellas. Corral also runs a number of other organizations and travels all over the world to work for peace, sustainability, and economic and social justice.

There are today thousands of such social entrepreneurs: women and men, sometimes even boys and girls, with innovative ideas for solving social problems and the dedication to put these ideas into action. ■

vide small loans for women entrepreneurs, making it possible for them to better care for their families. These are highly successful ventures, with a repayment rate that averages close to 100 percent.

Organizations such as Businesses for Social Responsibility, the World Business Academy, and the Social Venture Network have proposed new charters for corporations, social responsibility assessment measures, and other means for moving toward the triple bottom line of business, social, and environmental profits. Conferences and seminars on spirituality in the workplace focus on imbuing work with more meaning and supporting more caring ways of doing business.

Largely as a result of these kinds of efforts, a growing number of corporations are now considering the social and environmental concerns of their employees, shareholders, and the communities in which they operate. Businesses are beginning to recognize that organizational cultures where caring is valued and rewarded lead to greater competence, effective communication, and successful collaboration. Parental leave for both mothers and fathers and flexible work options are becoming more prevalent.

More and more people are changing their purchasing habits. They favor companies that pay workers a living wage and don't use child labor.[46] They look for environmentally safe products, such as cosmetics from the Body Shop stores, which employ indigenous peoples and sell natural products that have not been cruelly tested on animals.

Also largely as a result of grassroots pressure, the governments of most industrialized countries provide universal health care as an investment in their human capital. Many nations, for example, Sweden, Norway, Finland, France, Germany, New Zealand, and Canada, also provide paid parental leave and subsidize child care.

Thanks to government incentives, many European nations are way ahead of the United States in shifting from coal and oil to renewable resources that don't emit carbon dioxide and other "greenhouse" gases. Germany gets over 5 percent of its energy from renewable non-polluting sources such as biomass, wind, and solar panels. Spain produces 10 percent of its electricity from wind power and aims to triple this by 2010. In Sweden, renewable energy in the form of hydropower and biofuels accounts for about 20 percent of energy supply, almost as large a percentage as oil.[47]

European Union countries require manufacturers to recycle and dispose of product packaging, which has led to more environmentally friendly packaging, including the elimination of styrofoam inserts and plastic wraps for many products. The European Union also requires that genetically engineered products not be sold until tested for long-range effects.

Nordic schools have courses on caring gender relations and parenting. In U.S. schools, antibullying and nonviolent conflict resolution programs are beginning to spread. Modeling environmental responsibility, a growing number of school districts are replacing diesel-burning school buses with vehicles that use natural gas, or better still, electricity.

Politicians of all stripes are at least beginning to talk about a more caring world. Some are putting their rhetoric into practice through more just and caring policies. A plethora of United Nations Conventions and Resolutions supporting human rights and just economic development have also been influenced by global changes in consciousness. UNESCO sponsors the distribution of solar ovens and training for their use in refugee camps. The United Nations Population Fund (UNFPA), the United Nations Children's Fund (UNICEF), and the United Nations Development Fund for Women (UNIFEM) are dedicated to protecting the human rights of women and children. Other important international initiatives include the United Nations Millennium Development Goals, the Global Marshall Plan, and the Earth Charter, now ratified by hundreds of municipalities, companies, and NGOs in over one hundred countries.

These and thousands of other initiatives, organizations, and programs, are making a huge difference in the world, challenging traditions of domination and developing partnership alternatives. Indeed, never before has there been such a strong movement toward partnership. Nonetheless, we haven't yet been able to free our world from the fetters of domination. We will look at what we can do to help change this in the next chapter.

CHAPTER 10

The Caring Revolution

As Gandhi said, we shouldn't mistake what is habitual for what is normal. We were not born with unhealthy habits. We had to learn them. We can unlearn them, and help others do the same.

Many of our economic habits were shaped by a warped story of human nature and an economic double standard that gives little or no value to the essential work of caring and caregiving. The measures of productivity we habitually use include market activities that harm our health and natural environment while assigning no value to the life-supporting activities of households and nature. The money that central banks create and circulate bears little relation to any tangible assets.[1] Quarterly corporate reports fail to factor in the health and environmental damage a company's products or activities cause. Government policies, too, are often based on fantasies rather than realities, as dramatically shown by the George W. Bush administration's denial of the urgent need to take action against global warming.

We have a choice. We can keep complaining about greed, fraud, and cutthroat business practices. We can put up with the daily stress of unsuccessfully juggling jobs and family. We can tell ourselves there's nothing we can do about policies that damage our natural environment, create huge gaps between haves and have-nots, and lead to untold suffering. Or we can join together to help construct a saner, sounder, more caring economics and culture.

FROM AWARENESS TO ACTION

As we become aware of better possibilities, we can change how we think, feel, and act. But that's just the beginning. When a sufficient number of us change our beliefs and actions, our culture changes. As we build more partnership-oriented families, workplaces, and communities, we change the rules for our day-to-day relations. These new rules, in turn, support more partnership-oriented relations across the board. We then also begin to change the rules for the wider web of economic and political relations around us. And all this supports further changes in how we think, feel, and act, and in the structures and beliefs around us.

I can attest to this process based on my own experience. Like many people, I used to think there wasn't anything I could do to make ours a better world. I didn't even think there was much I could do to change things that made me unhappy in my day-to-day life. But I found out that I was wrong on both counts.

Once I freed myself from the dominator trance, from the stories I had been taught is the natural order and my natural place in it as a woman, my consciousness, my energy, and my life took off in directions I never thought possible. From feeling helpless and overwhelmed, I moved into an action mode—including social and political action.

Animated by my new consciousness of how the gender double standard had constricted my life and that of those like me, I joined with others to work for change. I worked to end the then-customary segregation of want ads into Help Wanted Male and Help Wanted Female, with all the good jobs under Help Wanted Male and all the dead-end ones under Help Wanted Female. I founded the Los Angeles Women's Legal Program, the first U.S. program on women and the law, offering lectures on the discrimination against women that was then legal, as well as providing free legal services to poor women. I used my legal training to write a Friend of the Court brief to the United States Supreme Court, making the then-radical argument that women should be considered persons under the Equal Protection Clause of the Fourteenth Amendment to the Constitution, and that laws discriminating on the basis of sex should be struck down.

These efforts, coupled with those of other women and men who envisioned a better society, succeeded. Want ads were desegregated. Legal aid programs for poor people were instituted. The courts struck down one discriminatory law after another.

However, I gradually began to understand that while changing laws is essential to advance civil rights, women's rights, economic justice, and environmental protection, it is not enough. As gains we had already made were lost or co-opted, I saw that we must go deeper: to fundamental cultural and structural change.

The question I had to ask at that point was: Change from what to what? I saw that categories such as capitalism versus socialism, religious versus secular, Right versus Left, and industrial versus pre- or postindustrial were not adequate to answer this question. These conventional categories fragment our consciousness because they don't take into account the social importance of the primary human relations, even though this is where people first learn either to respect human rights or to accept human rights violations as normal.

When I included the construction of relations between women and men and parents and children in my cross-cultural and historical analysis, the configurations of the partnership system and the domination system began to emerge. I saw that these two configurations affect our habits of thinking, feeling, and acting. I saw that they affect families, religions, economics, and politics. I saw how they affect the stories we live and die by. I even saw that they affect nothing less than the development of our brains.[2]

I also saw that high technology guided by an ethos of domination and conquest threatens our lives and the lives of our children. I began to look for interventions that can most effectively change our potentially lethal course. And I saw that one of the most critical interventions is a fundamental economic restructuring.

THE URGENT NEED FOR ECONOMIC RESTRUCTURING

I am certainly not alone in seeing that a fundamental economic restructuring is urgently needed. As Earth Policy Institute founder Lester Brown points out, the present economic course is unsustainable. Brown documents that forests are shrinking, deserts are expanding, water tables are falling, soils are eroding, fisheries are collapsing, and arctic ice is melting. Consumption of basic commodities such as food and water is rising exponentially, with China already consuming more than the United States in grain, meat, and steel.[3] Present energy use patterns are also unsustainable. If its economic growth continues

at the present rate of 8 percent, Chinese oil consumption alone is projected to reach ninety-nine billion barrels per day in 2031—twenty
million barrels per day more than the entire world currently produces. Indian economic growth of 7 percent, and a population projected to surpass China's by 2030, will make similar unsustainable
demands.[4]

Brown warns that to prevent economic and ecological collapse we
must restructure the global economy, implement a comprehensive
poverty eradication strategy, and restore damaged ecological systems.
He urges us to change consumption patterns, switch to wind, solar,
and other alternative energy technologies, and slow down global population growth.[5] "Plan A, business as usual, is no longer a viable
option," he writes. "We need to turn quickly to Plan B before the
geopolitics of oil, grain, and raw material scarcity lead to economic
instability, political conflict, and disruption of the social order on
which economic progress depends."[6]

Of course, Brown is right about all this. But much of what he
describes are symptoms of deeper problems that stem from dominator economic policies and cultural norms. Economic restructuring
must go beyond changing patterns of resource consumption, introducing new technologies, and slowing down population growth.
Even if these essential changes are effectively implemented—which is
doubtful under present norms and rules—new crises will inevitably
erupt.

We need more fundamental changes. Economic systems are
human creations. Every economic institution and program, from
banks and corporations to unemployment insurance and Social Security, is a human invention. The economic rules we take for granted are
human inventions. We must decide which economic rules we want to
keep and which we want to leave behind, and invent new economic
rules that meet our authentic human needs. If we join together to
demand these new rules, we can each play a part in moving toward a
more caring economics and a more caring world.

We urgently need changes in the economic rules guiding the market. As it stands, consumers and taxpayers often end up paying the
costs of uncaring business practices. There's little incentive for companies to be more responsible. Tax credits for companies that are
environmentally and socially responsible can make a big difference.

Levying high taxes on practices that harm our environment and our health can also provide important incentives for change, and at the same time provide funding for more caring government policies.

Another way to raise funds for caring policies and at the same time restructure the market economy is to tax stock market speculation. Taxing very short-term stock transactions will discourage speculation and provide revenue for health care, child care, education, and other programs that promote well-being worldwide.

We also need economic policies that encourage local production of food and other essentials. Control over basic resources such as water should not be outsourced to absentee-owner corporations, as happened in Bolivia when Bechtel took over a local water supply and raised prices to outrageous levels.[7]

But while economic policies should support small, local enterprises, small is not necessarily beautiful. Small enterprises too have often been inequitable and exploitive.

We need universal standards that protect workers, consumers, and nature in local, national, and international enterprises—be they large or small. And the globalization of commerce can be an opportunity to establish these universal standards.

With technologies of transportation that span the globe in hours and communications that span it in seconds, globalization of trade is inevitable. But uncaring economic rules, policies, and practices are *not* inevitable. As the following table shows, we can—and must—restructure economic systems in ways that are equitable and sustainable.

We must build economic structures, rules, policies, and practices that support caring for ourselves, others, and nature in the full spectrum of economic sectors, from the household economy to the natural economy. At the same time, we must accelerate the shift to partnership cultures and structures worldwide so that caring is given higher value.

It stands to reason that if we want more caring social and economic policies we can't continue to devalue caring and caregiving. If we want a clean and healthy environment, we have to take better care of it. If we want more humane and productive workplaces, if we want our children to get the care and education that equips them to live good lives, if we want safer streets and more loving homes, if we want

RESTRUCTURING ECONOMIC SYSTEMS

Unsustainable Economic Systems	**Sustainable Economic Systems**
Ignore contributions of the life-sustaining activities of households, communities, and nature.	*Recognize* contributions of the life-sustaining activities of households, communities, and nature.
Driven by dominator beliefs and institutions that *devalue* caring and caregiving.	Driven by partnership beliefs and institutions that *value* caring and caregiving.
Rules, policies, and practices *inhibit* human development, creativity, equitable relations, mutual responsibility, and concern for nature and future generations.	Rules, policies, and practices *support* human development, creativity, equitable relations, mutual responsibility, and concern for nature and future generations.
Technological applications are driven by an ethos of *control and domination.*	Technological applications are driven by an ethos of *caring and partnership.*
Measurements of economic productivity *include* activities that harm people and nature, and *fail to include* essential non-market life-supporting activities.	Measurements of economic productivity *exclude* activities that harm people and nature, and *include* essential non-market life-supporting activities.
Economic structures are designed to support *concentration of assets and power at the top,* with little accountability to those on bottom.	Economic structures are *participatory and equitable,* designed to support mutual accountability and benefit.
Human needs and capacities are often *exploited,* and nature is *depleted* and polluted.	Human needs and capacities are *nurtured,* and our natural habitat is *conserved.*
Investment in developing the high-quality human capital needed for the postindustrial age is *inadequate.*	Investment in developing the high-quality human capital needed for the postindustrial age is *a top priority.*
Is not sustainable at our level of technology in an inextricably interconnected world.	*Can help us meet the social, economic, and ecological challenges we face.*

to live in a more peaceful world, then we have to do a better job of supporting and rewarding caring and caregiving in all areas of life.

WHAT GOVERNMENT AND BUSINESS LEADERS CAN DO

Under present economic rules, people are supposed to serve the needs of the market as workers and consumers. This is backward. Economic rules should ensure that the market serves our needs as human beings living on an increasingly threatened planet.

To achieve this, government and business leaders must change economic rules so they support both structural changes and changes in values. Structures play a major role in shaping behavior. Just as we can't sit in a corner in a round room, we can't expect relationships based on mutual accountability, benefit, and respect to flourish, or even exist, in hierarchies of domination. We need policies that promote a shift to hierarchies of actualization in all structures, from families and schools to businesses and governments. At the same time, since values and structures reinforce each other, we need policies that promote caring as a core cultural value.

An essential step for changing the economic rules of the game is launching more accurate economic measures. Government and business leaders must see to it that economic indicators include the essential work of caring and caregiving performed in the household and the unpaid community economy.

These measures must also factor in the costs of environmentally and socially destructive products and activities. Without these changes, the public won't understand that we all pay the costs of uncaring policies and practices, and policymakers will continue to get a distorted picture of what are, and are not, economically productive activities.

Fortunately, there is growing consciousness of the need for changes in national and international accounting methods. As we have seen, new measures such as the United Nations Human Development Reports and the Redefining Progress and Calvert-Henderson Quality of Life Indicators have begun to emerge. There are also initiatives to change World Bank and International Monetary Fund statistics to add nations' public investments in education and health care to asset accounts and amortize them over twenty years—the time it takes to raise a child to become a healthy, well-educated, productive adult.[8] But we must work to speed up this process. And we must make sure that when changes are made particular attention is given to including the unpaid work still primarily performed by women in the household economy.

As discussed in chapter 4, a number of nations have already quantified the value of this unpaid caring work, and found that it is extremely high. Nongovernmental groups are also beginning to focus on the economic value of caring work in households. For example, the U.S. company Salary.com estimated that a fair wage for a typical stay-at-home parent would be $134,471 a year.[9]

This information must be integrated into the economic indicators that policymakers use to guide decisions. Economist Duncan Ironmonger's proposal that government leaders replace GDP and GNP with gross economic product (GEP) can be a starting point. This new economic indicator would consist of two equally weighted indices: the gross market product (GMP) Index, which measures the value added to the economy from the market, and the gross household product (GHP) index, which measures the value added to the economy from unpaid household work. The sum of the two, the GEP, can then guide both national and international economic policies in a sound direction.[10]

But new economic measurements are only one of the foundations for a caring economic system. Government and business leaders must also change economic policies and practices so they encourage and support caring and caregiving.

As we have seen, behind the devaluation of the essential human work of caring and caregiving lies the economic double standard that ranks men and the stereotypically masculine over women and what is perceived as feminine. This gender system of valuations has directly affected economic priorities so that less money goes into supporting activities that make for a high quality of life for everyone, including caring for children's material and emotional needs.

Many governments allocate enormous resources to manufacturing weapons and fighting wars. At the same time, government leaders often claim there isn't enough money to fund health care, child care, and other caring activities. We must counter these false claims by showing that these policies are not a question of money but of values.

It is estimated that the true cost of the Iraq War may reach $2 trillion: enough to fund schools worldwide that teach caring and mutually respectful relations rather than hatred and violence, and at the same time end hunger and provide universal health care.[11]

We must see to it that policymakers make a massive investment in high-quality child care. We can easily counter the argument that we can't afford this with data showing that investing in children is extraordinarily cost-effective. As the Canadian study we looked at in chapter 3 shows, the return on investment in universal, high-quality child care and early education is a whopping 200 percent—not to speak of the enormous human benefits. As I also mentioned, the costs of parenting education, paid parental leave, and publicly subsidized high-quality child care should be amortized like other investments in infrastructure such as machines and buildings, rather than viewed as merely expenses.

We must show policymakers and the public the enormous benefits of investing in human development, and the enormous costs of failing to do so, particularly as we move into the postindustrial economy. More capable, skilled, and caring workers increase economic productivity, and their tax contributions in turn make more funding available for government and business policies that support caring and caregiving, from Social Security for the elderly to good care for children. We must build a political movement to pressure policymakers to make these changes—or change the policymakers.

Policymakers need a new perspective on what makes sense for economic policy. For example, today governments fund training for soldiers to learn how to kill and pensions (an economic invention that recognizes and rewards socially valued work) to reward them. But we don't have government funding for education to prepare both women and men to effectively care for children, or pensions for those who do this work. Governments must change this, if only to change the shameful fact that older women, even in an affluent nation like the United States, make up one of the poorest segments of society.

Again, there will undoubtedly be objections. Some may argue that we can't measure the effectiveness of training for good child care. But we can remind them that the effectiveness of combat training is not a condition for paying soldiers and awarding them pensions. As for those who argue that we don't know what makes for good child care, we can point to the huge body of scientific data on what kind of child care fosters, or inhibits, healthy human development, data showing that "traditional" methods such as using physical violence are not only ineffective but often stunt human capabilities.[12]

The real issue here is how power is defined and used: whether it's as power to dominate and disempower or to nurture and empower. Our policymakers have been in the habit of giving less value to the caring and caregiving stereotypically associated with women than to the conquest and domination stereotypically associated with "real men." Now is the time to build on the growing frustration with the economic and ecological disasters this irrational system of values is causing, and change the rules and social structures that support it.

WHAT SOCIAL ACTIVISTS CAN DO

As we have seen, many of our values and structures were shaped by traditions of domination. During the shift from the agrarian to the industrial age, many of these traditions were challenged. However, the social movements that over the last several hundred years challenged these traditions focused primarily on the top of the domination pyramid: relations in the so-called public sphere of politics and economics from which women and children were barred. As a result, the foundations on which this pyramid rests, and continually rebuilds itself, were not sufficiently modified.

The destabilization of our move into the postindustrial era is an opportunity to continue the shift from domination to partnership. It opens the door to a second stage in the challenge to traditions of domination, one that encompasses *both* the public and private spheres.

Shifting from domination to partnership as the main cultural model does not mean that we will have a pure partnership society. It's not realistic to expect an ideal society. But to reverse the current regression to the domination system and prevent further such steps backward, we have to build the foundations on which a more democratic, peaceful, economically equitable, and environmentally sustainable world can rest. This requires a powerful national and international movement to change the foundational relations that have been ignored in mainstream economic theory: the primary human relations between women and men and between parents and children. It requires that the thousands of organizations worldwide today working for economic and social justice promote an integrated agenda that no longer splits off the rights of the majority—women and children—from the purview of human rights.

One reason policies raising the status of women are needed is, of course, that women make up half the population. But there is much more. As we saw earlier, in societies where women have higher status and make up almost half the government, such as the Nordic nations, more fiscal priority is given to caring policies such as universal health care, high-quality child care, parenting education, and generous paid parental leave. Greater status and power for women and policies that promote a higher quality of life for all go hand in hand.

The 1995 Center for Partnership Studies' statistical study based on data from eighty-nine nations, which we looked at earlier, shows just that. When the status and power of women is greater, so also is a nation's general quality of life; when they are lower, so is the quality of life for all.[13]

These findings, as we also saw in chapter 4, are corroborated by the 2000 World Values Survey. Based on data from sixty-five societies representing 80 percent of the world's population, this survey also shows a powerful correlation between support for equality between men and women and a more democratic, equitable, and prosperous society.[14] Another important finding from this survey is that greater acceptance of gender equity goes along with a shift away from traditional authoritarian styles of child rearing, and that these changes in attitudes toward women and children are in turn linked with greater trust, less reliance on outside authority, a greater sense of well-being, and other aspects of "self-expression" values.

The 2000 World Values Survey corroborates the conclusion that dominator-oriented societies keep us arrested at lower levels of motivation and development. It also confirms the conclusion that partnership-oriented societies are more successful in meeting human needs. It further corroborates the conclusion that gender equity is central to economic development. As Inglehart and his colleagues write, "The most important social change of the past few decades has been the revolution in gender roles that has transformed the lives of a majority of the population throughout advanced industrial society."[15]

Studies such as these illustrate the need for a gender-specific approach to economic analysis if policymakers are to have the data they need to make informed choices. This approach has profound implications for policies to end chronic poverty and hunger in the developing world. As Ann Crittenden writes, researchers in Africa, Latin America, the Caribbean, Asia, and the Indian subcontinent have all found that when mothers are educated and have some control over the family income, children are healthier and get more schooling.[16]

The time is now for women and men who care about the future of the planet to mount a global movement to change laws and customs that in large regions (for example, much of Africa, Southern Asia, and the Middle East) deprive women of health care, education, and the right to own property.[17] We must work to make the public and government officials aware of the studies we looked at in chapter 6 on intrahousehold economic relations, which show that men in many world regions allocate less of their earnings than women do to caring for children's needs.[18]

The key to this movement is for women to play an equal role in the formulation of government and business policies around the world. As illustrated by the Nordic world, as women rise in status through entry into more positions of social governance, stereotypically feminine qualities such as caring and nonviolence attain more social priority—as men no longer fear that embracing these is an "unmanly" loss of status. We cannot really talk of representative democracy as long as women still hold only a small minority of political positions.[19] Neither can we halt population growth unless women have reproductive freedom, education, and equal rights. And we cannot expect to eradicate poverty unless we take into account the fact that the mass of the world's poor and hungry are women and children.

I again want to emphasize that none of this is a matter of blaming men. Both women and men have been taught to accept and enforce traditions of domination. And stereotypically feminine traits, such as caring and nonviolence, can be found in both women and men, as can traits stereotypically considered masculine, such as venturesomeness and assertiveness.

But to move to a more equitable and effective economic system, social activists worldwide must work to ensure that the treatment of women and children conforms to universal standards of human rights. As the famous children's troubadour Raffi writes, we must create a child honoring society that respects its most vulnerable members.[20] This means that rules and practices that violate the human rights of children and women can no longer be justified on traditional or moral grounds. Multiculturalism, tolerance, and cultural sensitivity must not be used to justify abuse, violence, and injustice in family and other intimate relations, as they still often are today.[21]

In short, respect for women's rights and children's rights is a prerequisite for a more equitable, sustainable, and prosperous future. It is not sufficient to build this better future. But without it, we don't have a foundation on which this future can rest.

□ Population Growth, the Status of Women, and Caring Policies

Raising the status of women is foundational to stemming population growth. If a woman in a rigidly male-dominated culture has no sons, she has to keep breeding until she does. Hence, many women are afraid to stop having children, despite the devastation to their health of constant pregnancies—sometimes six or seven before they are in their mid-twenties.

Countries that are moving toward equality for women have lower birth-rates.[22] We even see the same inside countries where the national birth-rate is high. For example, birthrates are lower in the Indian province of Kerala where women's status is higher than in other parts of the country.

Some people believe that caring policies such as parenting education, parental leave, and child care will add to the population explosion at a time when a large workforce is no longer needed. In reality, such national policies have not led to high birthrates. On the contrary, studies show that parenting classes coupled with sex education *reduce* teenage pregnancies. What actually lies behind the high birthrates of many of the poorest, most overpopulated world regions is lack of knowledge about family planning, lack of access to contraceptives, and the subordination of women. ∎

THE DYNAMICS OF TRANSFORMATION

Imagine a world where economic systems are what they should and can be: means to meet human needs and aspirations. Lauralee Alben, a pioneer in the field of interactive design, points out that the first principle of design is a vision of desired outcomes. When you design the intentions and relationships you desire, she writes, profound changes are possible.[23]

These changes begin with what Alben calls ripple effects. Once initiated, these ripples extend outward, forming currents. When these currents come together, they become massive waves. And when the momentum of these waves builds up, the result is a sea change in the entire system.

A caring revolution is a sea change. It is the cumulative effect of all the ripples flowing from giving visibility and value to the most important human work: the work of caring and caregiving.

When the economic importance of caring and caregiving in the household is made visible, workplace rules such as flextime, job sharing, and other partnership economic inventions gain currency. Men do more of this work as its value is more generally recognized, and women and men participate more equally in the formal labor force and have the same opportunities and responsibilities at home. Schools offer education for good parenting and teach skills for caring personal relations. Governments help fund universal health care and high-quality child care, as well as parental leave for both fathers and mothers so they can take better care of themselves and their families. People are happier at home and in workplaces. All this promotes better care for children, and helps produce the high-quality human capital needed for a healthy, equitable economy.

As the general quality of human capital rises, more capable, skilled, and caring workers contribute to a more productive economy. This more productive economy in turn makes more funding available for government and business policies that support caring and caregiving. And this in turn enhances the quality of life for all.

Care for the elderly is facilitated by adequate monetary pensions as well as business and government policies that give adequate support to their caregivers. Women who have spent years caring for children no longer face an old age of poverty.

In the unpaid community economy, volunteers receive reduced transportation costs and other rewards for rendering free services.

Barter systems such as community currencies give more value to caring work in the exchange of services. As caring is seen to be more valuable, human relations improve across the board. Rather than being disparaged as "do-gooders" or "bleeding hearts," people who work for social and economic equity are rewarded and honored.

The market economy gradually changes. Businesses reward caring behaviors. They recognize that employees who feel cared for are more productive and that customers who feel cared for are more loyal. The rules of the market prevent monopolies, require companies to "internalize" rather than pass on costs of uncaring practices to society, and generally encourage companies to become more caring of all stakeholders: employees, shareholders, families, communities, and the planet.

Government policies also change as support for caring is recognized as a sound and essential investment. Problems that seemed intractable begin to wane. Poverty and hunger are more effectively addressed as support for caring and caregiving increases. Pensions and other rewards for caring and caregiving are created. The status of women rises, and with this, there is a generally higher quality of life.

These ripples of change affect every economic sector. As greater value is placed on caring, the illegal economy begins to shrink. As our material, emotional, and spiritual needs are increasingly met, the market for drugs, illegal arms, sex slavery and prostitution, and other economic activities now in the hands of crime syndicates is reduced. This too brings huge economic and social benefits.

With the savings in criminal justice courts and prisons comes more fiscal fluidity. Other social costs deriving from uncaring policies and practices, all the way from high school dropout rates and job absenteeism to terrorism and warfare, also decrease.

Along with the higher value given to the life-sustaining activities of the household comes a higher valuing of the life-sustaining activities of nature. There is greater respect for other life forms that share our planet with us, and the destruction of species after species ceases. As maintaining a clean home environment is no longer disparaged as "just women's work," not polluting and cluttering up our natural environment becomes routine. Caring for Mother Earth isn't viewed as a financial liability but recognized as essential for economic health and long-term sustainability.

As family, educational, business, and government structures shift from hierarchies of domination to hierarchies of actualization, democracy moves from rhetoric to reality. Trust, dignity, and creativity flourish. New technologies replace those that pollute and degrade our life-support systems. Exponential population growth is halted as women gain reproductive freedom, education, and equal rights. Gaps between haves and have-nots shrink. There's no longer an underclass that can barely meet its survival needs, or elites who amass enormous wealth as substitutes for meeting their yearning for caring connection, fairness, and meaning. Rather than investing resources in technologies that take life, societies invest primarily in technologies that support and enhance life.

Ripple by ripple, a caring economics that meets basic human needs and promotes optimal human development emerges. Individuals and families take more responsibility for one another and our natural environment. Economic policies are coordinated with social policies to support healthy, equitable relations across the board.

Morality becomes a vehicle for caring and love rather than a tool for coercion and domination. Spirituality is no longer an escape from the suffering inherent in a dominator world but an active engagement in creating a better life right here on Earth. Love becomes a commitment to create a world where the wonder and beauty latent in every child can be realized.

Making these changes won't be easy, and it won't be quick. But every one of us can set in motion the ripples that will cumulate in the caring revolution that will transform our lives and our world.

WHAT EACH OF US CAN DO

Obviously we must enlist people in positions of power to support the caring revolution. We can, and must, change the political landscape by electing leaders that back caring values. We can do this by voting for such leaders, donating to them, and campaigning for their election. We can also run for office ourselves on a caring economic platform.

In addition, we must inform national and international leaders of the benefits of caring policies. We must demand more caring values from those who are already in office, and see that a caring economic platform is backed by our political party.

But we can't wait for our national and international leaders to act. Every one of us can be a leader by using our imagination and initiative to change consciousness, practices, and policies. Indeed, it is only through the growing global demand for human rights, economic equity, and environmental sustainability that the caring revolution will succeed.

We can start with something simple: changing the conversation about economics. All the modern partnership movements have shifted normative ideals by changing the terms of the social conversation. Just as words like *freedom* and *democracy* helped introduce new political models, we can all help introduce new economic models by changing the economic discourse.

A first step in expanding the conversation about economics is simply to include the word *caring*. This may seem like a small thing. But it's an important step toward a new economics that gives visibility and value to what really makes us happy and healthy, and in the bargain leads to economic prosperity and ecological sustainability.[24]

Every one of us can talk about caring in our day-to-day conversations, at home, at work, at parties, at meetings, in schools and universities, and in public spaces. If we go to PTA meetings and other places where parents congregate, we can talk about how policies that support parenting are not only good for families but for the economy. We can engage our friends and colleagues in discussion groups to talk about what a caring economics means for our economy, our natural environment, and our lives. We can write letters to the editor about caring economics. We can put blogs about it on the Internet. We can make presentations about caring economics at meetings and conferences.

We can't wait for our national and international leaders to act. Every one of us can be a leader by using our imagination and initiative to change consciousness, practices, and policies.

Business and economic schools are key sites for changing the conversation about what economics is and can be.[25] This is why I have been working to build an Alliance for a Caring Economy through the Center for Partnership Studies to hold symposia, conferences, and leadership training programs for creating and implementing new caring economic inventions.[26]

As we change the conversation about economics, we can draw on the materials in chapter 3 showing that companies implementing caring policies are highly successful. We can present business managers some of the statistics we looked at. Those of us who are managers can

---

▢ Resources for Promoting Family-Friendly Political and Economic Policies

Here are examples of organizations working for family policies and practices needed for a healthy, equitable, productive society:

- The National Partnership for Women and the Family has for over thirty-five years introduced and obtained passage of family-friendly legislation, ranging from laws that require large companies to provide some family and medical leave to laws prohibiting pregnancy discrimination. See www.nationalpartnership.org/.

- For a Work & Family Bill of Rights that includes rights to quality, affordable child and elder care; annual paid family leave for full- and part-time employees; adequate health insurance for all; and a minimum wage, see www.takecarenet.org/WorkFamilyBOR.aspx.

- The MOTHERS Economic Empowerment Agenda includes the refundable Caregiver Tax Credit proposed by Theresa Funiciello (www.caregiver-credit.org/) for anyone caring for a family dependent; a Social Security Credit for mothers and other unpaid family caregivers; inclusion in GNP of unpaid labor in the home; and living wages and improved professional training for paid caregivers and early childhood teachers. See www.mothersoughttohaveequalrights.org/cando/meea.html.

- Mom's Rising has created the Motherhood Manifesto, which proposes similar measures, as well as TV ratings and afterschool programs. See www.momsrising.org/.

- The Institute for Women's Policy Research has conducted studies on the benefits of family-friendly policies with a particular focus on women and social justice. See www.iwpr.org/index.cfm.

- The Center for Partnership Studies' Caring Family Policy Agenda includes many of the preceding proposals. See www.partnershipway.org. This agenda consists of policies to implement the following:

offer incentives for practices that care for people and nature. We can go further, and propose that standards for caring policies and behaviors be included in corporate charters. We can propose that conformity to these standards be required for membership in chambers of commerce and other business associations.

A *Bill of Rights for children* that includes the right to loving care, shelter, nutrition, education, health care, freedom from violence, and a clean environment

Caring family values based on partnership, mutual respect, nonviolence, and a high valuing of caring and caregiving

Family-friendly governments and workplaces needed for healthy, prosperous families and a healthy, prosperous, postindustrial economy

- The Spiritual Alliance to Stop Intimate Violence (SAIV) is dedicated to stopping the use of force in family and other intimate relations. See www.saiv.net.

- Raffi, the internationally known troubadour and founder of Child Honoring, has proposed the Child Honoring Covenant and Principles. See www.raffinews.com/node/17.

Books and articles on these issues include:

- Raffi Cavoukian and Sharna Olfman (eds.), *Child Honouring* (New York: Praeger, 2006).

- Joan Blades and Kristin Rowe-Finkbeiner, *The Motherhood Manifesto* (New York: Nation Books, 2006).

- Ann Crittenden, *The Price of Motherhood* (New York: Metropolitan Books, 2001).

- Riane Eisler, *The Power of Partnership: Seven Relationships That Will Change Your Life* (Novato, Calif.: New World Library, 2002), particularly the Partnership Political Agenda.

- Riane Eisler, "Spare the Rod," *YES: A Magazine of Positive Futures*, Winter 2005, pp. 30–32.

- Riane Eisler and Frances Kissling, *The American Family* (2005; www. partnershipway.org). ■

We can show how current economic measures distort reality, and point to alternatives that accurately reflect the benefits of caring policies and practices and the costs of uncaring ones. We can talk to people concerned about job outsourcing to low-wage nations and the takeover of human work by automation, and show why these trends are further reasons to move to a caring economics.

We can buy from companies that have caring personnel, consumer, and environmental policies, and vote for political candidates who sponsor bills to support these. If we're in government, we can introduce caring economic policies ourselves. Those of us who live in the United States can point to what other nations are doing, and how investments in health care, child care, paid parental leave, and other caring economic inventions produce higher-quality human capital and a less stressful, more pleasurable life. We can show that government programs that invest in people are not "giveaways" but foundations for a safer, saner, more prosperous and just world for us all. We can support initiatives such as the Center for Partnership Studies' Caring Family Policy Agenda and the Work and Take Care Net's Family Bill of Rights.

We can talk to our friends and colleagues about how mass marketing teaches us to confuse amassing possessions with real satisfaction and pleasure, and point to how this problem is inherent in dominator economics. We can show how resource misdistribution, failure to invest in human capital, and other dominator economic practices not only lead to economic scarcity but to emotional and spiritual scarcity as well.

We can remind ourselves and others that because people first learn what is normal or abnormal early in life, equitable and democratic relations have to be fostered in families.[27] We can support organizations that work for women's rights and children's rights. We can work to end traditions of abuse and violence against women and children, and enlist others to join us. We can, and must, do this not only for the sake of the millions whose lives are blighted by this violence, but for the sake of us all, because violence in the family trains children to use violence to impose their will in all relations.[28]

We also can, and must, teach caring skills to both girls and boys, not only in homes but in schools.[29] In our time, when the constant assaults of television, movies, pop music, and video games teach that uncaring, cruel, and violent behaviors are exciting and fun, we must teach children to value caring. It's also important that we model caring—for example, as volunteers in our communities.

Equally important, since so much of what has become our defining culture portrays injustice and violence as simply human nature, we must see to it that children, and adults, get a more complete and accurate story of human nature and human possibilities. The reason is simple: unless people think something is possible, they won't even try to create it.

ECONOMICS AND HUMAN EVOLUTION

The most important human creations are our cultures. The cultures we create largely determine whether we kill one another and destroy nature's life-support systems, or live in a humane and sustainable world. And economic systems are a key element of all cultures.

I have in this book argued that we need a caring economics more congruent with the direction in evolution toward greater consciousness, creativity, and caring. I realize that speaking of direction in evolution is today a kind of scientific heresy. At best, it's acceptable to say there is evolutionary movement toward greater complexity and variability. But as Darwin himself noted, the movement in evolution goes beyond greater complexity and variability to the emergence of needs, capacities, motivations, and possibilities of a different order than those present in earlier life forms.[30]

Education for Caring

Valuing or not valuing caring is a basic lesson learned early in life. As I propose in *Tomorrow's Children: A Blueprint for Partnership Education in the 21st Century*, teaching caring for life—for self, others, and our Mother Earth—should be part of the curriculum, from preschool to graduate school. Teaching caring skills is particularly urgent to counter the staggering brutality today dispensed through television news and "entertainment," including video games sold to children that simulate mayhem, rape, and murder.[31] ∎

This does not mean that our species, as one of the latest to emerge, is the apex of evolution, and thus entitled to lord it over other life forms. Nor does it mean there is a divine plan or intelligent design. We don't have any way of knowing what ultimately lies behind evolution, and this is so whether we think evolution is directionless or not. But it does mean that as life evolved on our Earth, it developed an ever greater capacity for consciousness, creativity, planning, and choice. And while these capacities are not unique to us, they are most highly developed in our species.

Whether these human capacities are expressed, however, largely depends on the kinds of social and economic systems we create. This makes us, quite literally, cocreators of our evolution.

We certainly can't determine everything about our future. But we *can* join together to create the social and economic conditions that nurture, drive, and promote the expression of our positive rather than negative genetic capacities. Indeed, having unprecedented biological capacities means that it's our evolutionary responsibility to use these gifts in positive rather than negative ways.

All life forms—from the smallest to the largest, from amoeba and plankton to elephants and whales—have to some extent altered our planet. Some have done so by simply appearing on the evolutionary scene. Others have built new structures: birds make nests and beavers construct dams. But no species has come close to what we humans have done.

We have used our imagination and our capacity for turning visions into realities to create a whole new human-made world. Some of what we created is extraordinary: buildings as tall as mountains, airplanes that fly higher than birds, and technologies that reveal subatomic structures, explore outer space, and probe the mysteries of the brain. Some of it is exquisite: beautiful music, poetry, and art. But some of it is horrendous: gas chambers, torture chambers, nuclear bombs, and invisible biological weapons for instant mass annihilation.

We stand at an evolutionary crossroads in our human adventure on this Earth. We can continue with "business as usual"—even though both science and our native intelligence tell us that the mix of high technology and an ethos of domination and conquest may take us to an evolutionary end. Or we can use the great gifts we were given by evolution to create a new economic story and reality—a caring economics that supports both human survival and human development and actualization.

It is in our power to imagine the world we want for ourselves and our children. For most of us, this is a world where our basic needs for food, shelter, and safety, as well as our yearning for nurturing and love, for justice and peace, and for a sense that what we do has meaning and helps others as well as ourselves, are fulfilled. Above all, it is a world where our children survive and thrive.

We stand at an evolutionary cross-roads in our human adventure on this Earth.

It is up to us to help create the conditions that support this vision. We have been endowed by nature with an amazing brain, an enormous capacity for love, a remarkable creativity, and a unique ability to learn, change, grow, and plan ahead. If we act now, we can use these capacities to co-create the economic and social systems that support the great gifts we were granted by evolution.

Notes

Introduction: Reasons to Care

1. For example, I was a co-founder of the General Evolution Research Group (GERG), a multinational group of scholars from disciplines ranging from astronomy, chemistry, and physics to biology, history, and sociology who are interested in the development and application of an updated view of evolution to our global problems. For a history of GERG, see David Loye (ed.), *The Great Adventure: Toward a Fully Human Theory of Evolution* (Albany, N.Y.: State University of New York Press, 2004), appendix C.

2. See, for example, Riane Eisler, "Technology, Gender, and History: Toward a Nonlinear Model of Social Evolution," in Ervin Laszlo, Ignazio Masulli, Robert Artigiani, and Vilmos Csanyi (eds.), *The Evolution of Cognitive Maps: New Paradigms for the Twenty-First Century* (Langhorne, Penn.: Gordon and Breach Science Publishers, 1993); Riane Eisler, "Cultural Transformation Theory: A New Paradigm for History," in Johan Galtung and Sohail Inayatullah (eds.), *Macrohistory and Macrohistorians* (Westport, Conn.: Praeger, 1997); Riane Eisler and Daniel S. Levine, "Nature, Nurture, and Caring: We Are Not Prisoners of Our Genes," *Brain and Mind*, Apr. 2002, 3(1), 9–52.

3. See, for example, Riane Eisler, *The Chalice and The Blade: Our History, Our Future* (San Francisco: Harper & Row, 1987). In this and other earlier books, I wrote interchangeably of the partnership and dominator *models* and the partnership and domination *systems*. In this book I use the term systems rather than models because model has a specific technical meaning in economic parlance and system is less academic and more appropriate for the general reader.

4. As I will discuss later and others have also pointed out, Smith actually wanted an economics that works for the greater good of all, in line with his earlier book, *Theory of Moral Sentiments*. See, for example, Alberto Martinelli and Neil J. Smelser (eds.), *Economy and Society* (Newbury Park, Calif.: Sage, 1990); Kenneth Lux, *Adam Smith's Mistake: How a Moral Philosopher Invented Economics and Ended Morality* (Boston: Shambhala, 1990).

Chapter 1: We Need a New Economics

1. Estimates are that unemployment in Saudi Arabia has been growing steadily since 1999, with unofficial estimates of 35 percent. High rates of youth unemployment are blamed for a large increase in crime rates, despite Sharia laws with draconian punishments, such as chopping off hands for theft. See, for example, "Downward Spiral of Unemployment and Juvenile Delinquency," *Asia News*, Apr. 17, 2004. See www.asianews.it/view.php?l=en&art=637.

2. According to the Population Reference Bureau, a think tank based in Washington, D.C., the Middle East region's population growth rate has become the highest in the world. See Hassan Fattah, "The Middle East Baby Boom," *American Demographics*, Sept. 1, 2002.

3. Some scholars argue that there is nothing about sex for "martyrs" in paradise written in the Koran, that the passages simply refer to every male believer getting seventy-two wives. But according to the Middle East Media Research Institute (MEMRI), an independent nonprofit organization that translates and analyzes the media of the Middle East, the popular belief—as well as the propaganda by those who recruit terrorists, the media, and many clerics—is that martyrs do receive virgins in paradise. An article published by MEMRI reported that the Palestinian terrorist organization Hamas educates the children in its schools, beginning in kindergarten, to believe that a suicide bomber is given virgins in paradise. See www.memri.org.

4. See, for example, Joseph Stiglitz, *Globalization and Its Discontents* (New York: Norton, 2003).

5. See Nancy Folbre, *The Invisible Heart: Economics and Family Values* (New York: New Press, 2001).

6. For critiques of the focus of mainstream neoclassical economics on markets, see Karl Polanyi, *The Great Transformation* (Boston: Beacon Press, 1941); Paul Elkins (ed.), *The Living Economy* (New York: Routledge & Kegan Paul, 1986); and Martinelli and Smelser, *Economy and Society*. Many socialist theorists have also critiqued classical and neoclassical capitalist economic theory, and so have feminist theorists. See, for example, Marianne Ferber and Julie Nelson (eds.), *Beyond Economic Man* (Chicago: University of Chicago Press, 1993).

7. *Caring* has many definitions, ranging from a feeling or emotion to an activity or series of actions. It is used here in all these senses. In this broad definition, I draw from the work of feminist philosophers such as Carol Gilligan and Nel Noddings, who have written extensively on the subject of an ethic of care. See Carol Gilligan, *In a Different Voice: Psychological Theory and Women's Development* (Cambridge: Harvard University Press, 1982) and Nel Noddings, *Caring, a Feminine Approach to Ethics & Moral Education* (Berkeley: University of California Press, 1984). In *Starting at Home: Caring and Social Policy* (Berkeley: University of California Press, 2002), Noddings argues that caring should be a foundation for ethical decision making because care is basic in human life and all people want to be cared for. She challenges the moral theory of the famous philosopher Immanuel Kant, who held that it is only through reason that we can control our natural selfish impulses. Noddings asserts that real morality is based on our inherent need for giving and receiving care and on our capacities for empathy (or as she puts it, sympathy). One of my aims is to show how and why economic rules and policies have blocked the expression of this basic human need and what is required to move to an economic system that has as its aim promoting both human survival and the development of human capabilities, including our human capabilities for caring, meaning, and self-actualization. See, also, Amartya Sen, *Development as Freedom* (Oxford: Oxford University Press, 1999);

Mona Harrington, *Care and Equality: Inventing a New Family Politics* (New York: Knopf, 1999); Martha Nussbaum, *Sex and Justice* (New York: Oxford University Press, 2000); Riane Eisler, *The Power of Partnership: Seven Relationships That Will Change Your Life* (Novato, Calif.: New World Library, 2002). For other writings on an ethic of care, see Rosemarie Tong, *Feminist Thought: A Comprehensive Introduction* (Boulder, Colo.: Westview Press, 1989); Alison M. Jaggar (ed.), *Living with Contradictions: Controversies in Feminist Social Ethics* (Boulder: Westview Press, 1994); and Virginia Held (ed.), *Justice and Care: Essential Readings in Feminist Ethics* (Boulder, Colo.: Westview Press, 1995).

8. I use the term economic rules to describe governmental and business rules governing economic structures and policies, including their legal framework, not in the sense used by some economists to denote dynamics that are presumably inherent in market operations.

9. For Aristotle, there were two parts of the economy. The first, *oikonomike* (running a household), is natural and good, whereas the second, *chrematistike* (the market) can be unnatural when it is an end in itself, directed toward the accumulation of money for its own sake. So for Aristotle, wealth can be true and natural (that is, useful) or spurious and banal (for example, capital accumulation as a means of coercion), where "money is the starting point and the goal." See Aristotle, *Nicomachean Ethics* (350 B.C.E.), translated by W. D. Ross, especially Books IV and VIII. See http://classics.mit.edu/Aristotle/nicomachaen.html.

10. Others, including Hazel Henderson, Thais Corral, Edgar Cahn, Elisabet Sahtouris, and I, were equally adamant that this work must be considered in economic measures and models.

11. In later chapters, particularly chapter 4, we will look at various approaches to quantifying the work of caring and caregiving. As economist Nancy Folbre points out, this is not a simple issue. However, the fact that a growing number of scholars, as well as national and international officials, are examining this issue is an important signpost to a more caring economy.

12. Marilyn Waring, *If Women Counted: A New Feminist Economics* (San Francisco: Harper & Row, 1988).

13. Barbara Brandt, *Whole Life Economics: Revaluing Daily Life* (Philadelphia: New Society Publishers, 1995); Ann Crittenden, *The Price of Motherhood: Why the Most Important Job in the World Is Still the Least Valued* (New York: Metropolitan Books, 2001); Ferber and Nelson, *Beyond Economic Man*; Folbre, *The Invisible Heart*; Janet C. Gornick and Marcia K. Meyers, *Families That Work: Policies for Reconciling Parenthood and Employment* (New York: Russell Sage Foundation Publications, 2003); Heidi Hartmann, "Thirty Years from Today: Visions of Economic Justice," *Dollars & Sense*, Nov. 1, 2004; Hazel Henderson, *Beyond Globalization: Shaping a Sustainable Global Economy* (Bloomfield, Conn.: Kumarian Press, 1999); Julie A. Nelson, *Economics for Humans* (Chicago: University of Chicago Press, 2006); Hilkka Pietila, "Nordic Welfare Society—A Strategy to Eradicate Poverty and Build Up Equality: Finland as a Case Study," *Journal Cooperation South*, 2001, 2, 79–96; Genevieve Vaughan, *For-Giving: A Feminist Criticism of Exchange* (Austin, Tex.: Plain View Press, 1997).

14. See, for example, Devaki Jain and Nirmala Banerjee (eds.), *The Tyranny of the Household: Women in Poverty, Investigative Essays on Women's Work* (New Delhi: Shakti Books, 1985); Edgar Cahn, *No More Throwaway People: The Co-Production Imperative* (Washington, D.C.: Essential Books, 2004); Herman E. Daly and John B. Cobb, *For the Common Good: Redirecting the Economy Toward Community, the Environment, and a Sustainable Future*, 2nd ed. (Boston: Beacon Press, 1994); David C. Korten, *The Great Turning: From Empire to Earth Community* (San Francisco: Berrett-Koehler, 2006); Paul Krugman, *The Great Unraveling: Losing Our Way in the New Century* (New York: Norton, 2004); Amartya Sen, *Development as Freedom* (Oxford: Oxford University Press, 1999). Others who are contributing to new approaches to economics include Shirley Burggraf, *The Feminine Economy and the Economic Man: Reviving the Role of Family in the Post-Industrial Age* (New York: Perseus Books, 1999); Mona Harrington, *Care and Equality: Inventing a New Family Politics* (New York: Knopf, 1999); Paul Hawken, Amory Lovins, L. Hunter Lovins, *Natural Capitalism: Creating the Next Industrial Revolution* (Boston: Back Bay Books, 2000); Jody Heymann, *Forgotten Families: Ending the Growing Crisis Confronting Children and Working Parents in the Global Economy* (New York: Oxford University Press, 2006); Prue Hyman, *Women and Economics: A New Zealand Feminist Perspective* (Wellington, New Zealand: Bridget Williams Books, 1996); Joan C. Williams, *Unbending Gender: Why Family and Work Conflict and What to Do About It* (New York: Oxford University Press, 2000); Jeffrey Sachs, *The End of Poverty: Economic Possibilities for Our Time* (New York: Penguin, 2006).

15. GDP is the value of all economic production inside a nation's borders; GNP is the value of economic production undertaken by a nation's residents, regardless of where they are working. Profits from a Honda factory based in South Carolina, for example, contribute to the U.S. GDP (production inside U.S. borders) but also contribute to Japan's GNP (production with assets owned by Japanese residents). A major difference between GNP and GDP is that GNP includes only production that generates income for a nation's residents, whereas GDP includes all production that generates income, whether for a nation's residents or foreign investors.

16. *The Occupational Handbook* (Washington, D.C.: U.S. Department of Labor, Bureau of Labor Statistics, Aug. 2006) reports that in May 2004 median hourly earnings of wage and salary child care workers were $8.06. The middle 50 percent earned between $6.75 and $10.01. The lowest 10 percent earned less than $5.90, and the highest 10 percent earned more than $12.34. See www.bls.gov/oco/ocos170.htm#earnings.

17. Cahn, *No More Throwaway People*.

18. For details on the benefits-cost analysis of the Abecedarian Early Childhood Intervention project done by the National Institute for Early Education Research (NIEER), see http://nieer.org/docs/?DocID=57. The researchers found substantial benefits not only to the children and their families but also to school districts, which can expect to save more than $11,000 per child because participants are less likely to require special or remedial education.

19. See Ontario Ministry of Health and Long-Term Care, www.health.gov.on.ca/english/public/pub/ministry_reports/healthy_babies_report/hbabies_report.html.

20. World Economic Forum, *Global Competitiveness Report, 2006–2007*. See www.weforum.org/en/initiatives/gcp/Global%20Competitiveness%20Report/index.htm.

21. See Mom Salary Wizard, http://swz.salary.com/momsalarywizard/htmls/mswl_momcenter.html. Other estimates have been lower. As noted in chapter 4, there is also some movement toward incorporating information about the monetary value of household work into measures of national productivity, but only as satellite accounts to GDP and GNP.

22. Daniela Estrada, "The Challenge of Paying for Unremunerated Work," *Other News: Information That Markets Eliminate*, June 7, 2006. See http://other-news.info/index.php?p=1510.

23. Jeffrey Kluger, "The Tipping Point," *Time*, Apr. 3, 2006. The phrase tipping point gained currency through Malcolm Gladwell's *The Tipping Point: How Little Things Can Make a Big Difference* (Boston: Back Bay Books, 2002).

Chapter 2: Economics Through a Wider Lens

1. Again, for brevity I use the term economics in its popular sense as a shorthand for economic systems and not just to describe the discipline that studies these systems.

2. Eisler, *The Chalice and The Blade*.

3. Riane Eisler, *Sacred Pleasure: Sex, Myth, and The Politics of the Body* (San Francisco: HarperCollins, 1995); Eisler, *The Power of Partnership*. In *Tomorrow's Children*, I also applied my research to education. (Riane Eisler, *Tomorrow's Children: A Blueprint for Partnership Education in the 21st Century* (Boulder, Colo.: Westview Press, 2000).)

4. Robert Ornstein, *The Psychology of Consciousness* (New York: Viking, 1972). Or as the American psychologist William James pointed out in his *Principles of Psychology*, "It is hard to focus our attention on the nameless" (Mineola, N.Y.: Dover Publications, 1955 [originally published 1890]), chapter 7.

5. For example, nations such as Norway, Sweden, Finland, Iceland, and Denmark consistently rate high in the United Nations annual Human Development Reports, which include such basic measures as life spans, infant mortality rates, literacy rates, environmental protection, and other measures of the general quality of life.

6. I want to clarify that I use the term communism to refer to a Soviet-style regime in which "the dictatorship of the proletariat" was supposed to pave the way for the better future that nineteenth-century philosophers called communism. I do not use the term, as is sometimes done in popular parlance, as a synonym for socialism. Nor do I use *communist* as a synonym for communist parties in the former U.S.S.R. and the present People's Republic of China. I also want to clarify that nations that have embraced some socialist principles, such as most Western European nations, can be marked by democracy and civic freedom. In these nations, the state has a certain role as supplier and regulator, whereas "pure" capitalism would rely only on regulations through markets.

7. Barbaric practices, such as public drawing and quartering, disemboweling, and other horrible tortures were commonplace even in "civilized" places such as Great Britain as late as the Elizabethan Age. And publicly burning women accused of witchcraft continued in both Europe and some American colonies well into the eighteenth century.

8. See, for example, Louisa Lim, "China Warns of Water Pollution," *BBC News Beijing*, Mar. 23, 2005. http://news.bbc.co.uk/2/hi/asia-pacific/4374383.stm.

9. See, for example, *Report on the World Social Situation: The Inequality Predicament* (New York: United Nations and Division for Social Policy and Development, U.N. Department of Economic and Social Affairs, 2005). This report, which is prepared on a biennial basis, has served as a background document for policy analysis of socioeconomic matters at the intergovernmental level. For details, see www.un.org/esa/desa/.

10. This definition of economics is still found in encyclopedias as well as the websites of many universities and other institutions. A definition proposed by Adam Smith is "the science relating to the laws of production, distribution, and exchange." Among more recent definitions is "the branch of social science that deals with the production and distribution and consumption of goods and services and their management."

11. See, for example, David Morris, *Measuring the Condition of the World's Poor* (New York: Pergamon Press, 1979).

12. *Human Development Report 1995*. United Nations Development Programme (New York: Oxford University Press, 1995).

13. For a discussion of some of these attempts, see Hazel Henderson, "Changing Paradigms and Indicators: Implementing Equitable, Sustainable and Participatory Development," in Jo Marie Griesgraber and Bernhard G. Gunter (eds.), *The World Bank: Lending on a Global Scale: Rethinking Bretton Woods, Vol. 2* (London: Pluto Press, 1996).

14. "Teure Haushaltproduktion" ["Expensive Household Production"], *Neue Zürcher Zeitung*, Nov. 11, 2004.

15. See, for example, John Roach, "Greenland Glaciers Losing Ice Much Faster, Study Says," *National Geographic News*, February 16, 2006, and John Roach, "Global Warming Is Rapidly Raising Sea Levels, Studies Warn," *National Geographic News*, Mar. 23, 2006.

16. *The State of the World's Children 2005: Childhood Under Threat* (New York: UNICEF, Dec. 12, 2004). See www.unicef.org/publications/index_24432.html.

17. *Household Food Security in the United States, 2004* (Washington, D.C.: Department of Agriculture).

18. For more information, see the U.S. National Council on the Aging (NCOA) website: www.globalaging.org/health/us/2005/hungerus.htm.

19. A full copy of *Household Food Security in the United States, 2004*, is available at www.ers.usda.gov/publications/err11/. To obtain a bulletin of the analysis by the Center on Poverty and Hunger, visit www.centeronhunger.org.

20. For example, according to the U.S. Census Report published on Aug. 29, 2006, both men and women earned less in 2005 than in 2004. So while the nation's median household income rose slightly faster than inflation, census officials said it was because more family members were taking jobs to make ends meet and some people made more money from investments and other sources. Moreover, that slight increase of 1.1 percent in median household income did not make up for the fact that this figure fell 5.9 percent between the 2000 census and 2005, from $49,133 to $46,242. See Rick Lyman, "Census Reports Slight Increase in '05 Incomes," *New York Times*, Aug. 30, 2006, and the editorial, "Downward Mobility," *New York Times*, Aug. 30, 2006. For the astronomical rise in CEO salaries, see Holly Sklar, "Carving Up Our Economic Pie," *Knight Ridder/Tribune Information Services*, Nov. 22, 2005, in which she points out that by 2004 the ratio of CEO pay to worker pay had escalated to 362 to 1. See Ms Foundation for Women at http://ms.foundation.org/wmspage.cfm?parm1=329.

21. Latin American nations and other countries where family planning is discouraged on religious grounds have high abortion rates, with a high percentage of pregnancy-related deaths due to illegal abortions. Some of the highest abortion rates occur in countries where abortion is illegal. See Cicely Marston and John Cleland, "Relationship Between Contraception and Abortion: A Review of the Evidence," *International Family Planning Perspectives*, 2003, 29(1), 6–13. See www.guttmacher.org/pubs/journals/2900603.html. For example, 48 percent of maternal deaths in Uruguay are attributable to unsafe abortion. Lucia Rayas, Diane Catotti, and Ana Cortes, *Achieving ICPD Commitments for Abortion Care in Latin America: The Unfinished Agenda* (Chapel Hill, N.C.: Ipas, 2005); see www.ipas.org/publications/en/LACICPD_E05_en.pdf.

22. Net worth is defined by economists as marketable assets, such as real estate, stocks, and bonds, leaving aside consumer durables like cars and household items. When all debts, such as home mortgages and credit card debt, are subtracted, the result is net worth. Financial wealth is defined as net worth minus net equity in owner-occupied housing. For a comprehensive analysis, see G. William Domhoff, *Who Rules America? Power, Politics, & Social Change* (Annandale-on-Hudson, N.Y.: Levy Economics Institute, 1998) at http://sociology.ucsc.edu/whorulesamerica/. See also the United For A Fair Economy website: www.faireconomy.org/.

23. Reprinted with permission from G. William Domhoff, "Wealth, Income, and Power," Feb. 2006; http://sociology.ucsc.edu/whorulesamerica/power/wealth.html.

24. Reprinted with permission from G. William Domhoff, "Wealth, Income, and Power," Feb. 2006; http://sociology.ucsc.edu/whorulesamerica/power/wealth.html.

25. The Southern Poverty Law Center's Intelligence Project tracks the growth of hate groups in the United States. For information, see www.tolerance.org/maps/hate/. The Simon Wiesenthal Center's Task Force Against Hate and Terrorism provides information on hate groups worldwide. See www.wiesenthal.com/. Both show how the Internet has contributed to the growth of hate and terrorist groups through easy online communication and websites.

26. Although, clearly, all the benefits of caring and caregiving cannot be quantified, there is movement toward including some of these benefits in economic indicators, as I will discuss in chapter 4.

27. See chapter 8 for these proposals by both liberal and conservative economists.

28. See Eisler, *Tomorrow's Children*. This education is particularly urgent today, when it is estimated that in the United States the average child will have watched eight thousand screen murders and more than one hundred thousand acts of violence by the end of elementary school—a figure that will again double by the end of his or her teens. See David S. Barry, "Growing Up Violent: Decades of Research Link Screen Mayhem with Increase in Aggressive Behavior," *Media and Values*, Summer 1993, 62, 8–11. The University of Washington epidemiologist Dr. Brandon Centerwall's studies of epidemics of violence show that in the United States violent crimes increased almost 100 percent within a generation after television was introduced. See Brandon Centerwall, M.D., "Television and Violence: The Scale of the Problem and Where to Go from Here," *Journal of the American Medical Association*, June 1992, 267, 3059–3063. See also "A Tale of Three Countries: Homicide Rates Rise After Television's Arrival: An Interview with Brandon Centerwall, M.D.," *Media and Values*, Summer 1993, 62, 12–13. A particularly noteworthy finding is that parents who grew up watching television tend to use more violence in child rearing. The mass media even affect whether adults behave in hurtful ways. This was shown by a research project directed by social psychologist David Loye at the UCLA School of Medicine. Equally important was another finding from this study: after people watched programs that model caring and helpfulness, they acted in more caring and helpful ways. See David Loye, Roderic Gorney, and Gary Steele, "Effects of Television," *Journal of Communication*, 1977, 27(3), 206–216.

Chapter 3: It Pays to Care—in Dollars and Cents

1. For more details on SAS, see www.sas.com/jobs/USjobs/benefits.html.

2. For more details, see Sandra Burud and Marie Tumolo, *Leveraging the New Human Capital: Adaptive Strategies, Results Achieved, and Stories of Transformation* (Mountain View, Calif.: Davies-Black Publishing, 2004).

3. For more details, see www.winningworkplaces.org/bestbossesaward/previouswin _2004_fnl.php.

4. "The Retention Dilemma," 2001 survey by the Hay Group. Visit www.haygroup.com. Other studies estimate that turnover can cost a company anywhere from $10,000 per employee to as much as 200 percent of employee compensation. See "The Real Cost of Turnover," Nov. 6, 2003. www.staffing.org.

5. Linda H. Clever and Gilbert S. Omenn, "Hazards for Health Care Workers," *Annual Review of Public Health*, 1988, 9, 273–303.

6. Intermedics information from *Precious Time: Childcare That Works*; see http://ptcenters.com/employertestimonials.html. For Virginia Mason Medical Center information, see www.virginiamason.org/body.cfm?id=317. Johnson & Johnson information from http://govinfo.library.unt.edu/npr/library/reports/ hrm07.html.

7. See www.circadian.com/media/Release-03Aug12.html. Circadian's findings were based on a comprehensive review of existing literature and the firm's annu-

al survey, which encompasses data from 10,500 extended-hours employees in sixty companies and managers at more than a thousand companies representing approximately 150,000 employees across all major industry sectors.

8. For more information, see www.worklifelaw.org and www.pardc.org. See also Joan C. Williams, *Unbending Gender: Why Family and Work Conflict and What to Do About It* (New York: Oxford University Press, 2000); Gornick and Meyers, *Families That Work*. For a global perspective on this issue, see Jody Heymann, *Forgotten Families: Ending the Growing Crisis Confronting Children and Working Parents in the Global Economy* (New York: Oxford University Press, 2006). Indeed, as Harvard Business School professor Lynn Sharpe Paine points out, ethical and caring policies should be enacted even when, at least in the short run, they may to some extent reduce profits. See Lynn Sharpe Paine, *Value Shift: Why Companies Must Merge Social and Financial Imperatives to Achieve Superior Performance* (New York: McGraw-Hill, 2003).

9. Radcliffe Public Policy Center and Harris Interactive, Inc. *Life's Work: Generational Attitudes Toward Work and Life Integration* (Cambridge: Radcliffe Institute for Advanced Study, 2000). See www.Radcliffe.edu/research/pubpol/lifeswork.pdf.

10. *The Most Important Work/Life-Related Studies* (Minnetonka, Minn.: Work & Family Connection, 2005).

11. The Families and Work Institute (FWI) is a nonprofit research center that provides data to inform decision making on the changing workforce, changing family, and changing community. See www.familiesandwork.org/.

12. Burud and Tumolo, *Leveraging the New Human Capital*.

13. *The Most Important Work/Life-Related Studies*.

14. *Bright Horizons Child Care Trends*, 2002. See www.childcareinhealthcare.org/employer-sponsored-child-care.php.

15. Economic Policy Institute. See www.epinet.org/briefingpapers/1991_bp_new_policies.pdf

16. Christine Avery and Diane Zabel, *The Flexible Workplace: A Sourcebook of Information and Research* (Westport, Conn.: Quorum, 2000). I should add here that telecommuting not only helps with life-work balance but also eases traffic congestion and helps the environment, because it means less emissions from cars.

17. Burud and Tumolo, *Leveraging the New Human Capital*.

18. *The Most Important Work/Life-Related Studies*.

19. *The Most Important Work/Life-Related Studies*.

20. *The Most Important Work/Life-Related Studies*.

21. For the whole story of this bank, see Burud and Tumolo, *Leveraging the New Human Capital*.

22. Burud and Tumolo, *Leveraging the New Human Capital*.

23. These statistics are based on cost-benefit studies.

24. Positive organizational scholarship rose out of *positive psychology*, a concept introduced in 1998 by Martin Seligman, then-president of the American Psychological Association. Positive psychology looks at the organizational contexts that promote positive processes and states. Positive organizational scholarship draws heavily from the research at the Stone Center for Research on Women founded by Dr. Jean Baker Miller and others to examine what they call *relational psychology*. See, for example, Jean Baker Miller and Irene P. Stiver, *The Healing Connection: How Women Form Relationships in Therapy and in Life* (Boston: Beacon Press, 1997).

25. Jane Dutton and Emily Heaphy, "The Power of High-Quality Connections at Work," in Kim Cameron, Jane Dutton, and Robert. E. Quinn (eds.), *Positive Organizational Scholarship* (San Francisco: Berrett-Koehler, 2003).

26. Jane Dutton, *Energize Your Workplace* (San Francisco: Jossey-Bass, 2003).

27. Jane Dutton, Jacoba Lilius, and Jason Kanov, "The Transformative Potential of Compassion at Work." Paper presented at Weatherhead School of Management, Case Western Reserve University, Cincinnati, Aug. 2003.

28. Daniel Goleman, Richard Boyatzis, and Annie McKee, *Primal Leadership: Realizing the Power of Emotional Intelligence* (Boston: Harvard Business School Press, 2002); David L. Cooperrider and Suresh Srivastva, "Appreciative Inquiry in Organizational Life," *Research in Organizational Change and Development*, 1987, *1*, 129–169; Ronald Fry, Frank Barrett, Jane Seiling, and Diana Whitney (eds.), *Appreciative Inquiry and Organizational Transformation: Reports from the Field* (Westport, Conn.: Quorum, 2001).

29. Alice Isen, "Positive Affect, Cognitive Processes and Social Behavior," *Advances in Experimental Social Psychology*, 1987, *20*, 203–253; Barbara Fredrickson, "Positive Emotions and Upward Spirals in Organizations," in Cameron, Dutton, and Quinn, *Positive Organizational Scholarship*.

30. For a book extensively showing the benefits of a partnership-oriented organization, see Peter M. Senge, *The Fifth Discipline: The Art & Practice of the Learning Organization*, rev. ed. (New York: Doubleday, 2006).

31. Ontario Hospital Association. *OHA Executive Report*, *11*(32). See www.oha.com/client/OHA/OHA_LP4W_LND_WebStation.nsf/page/Archived+Executive+Report.

32. For more information on the Ontario program, see www.health.gov.on.ca/english/public/program/child/child_mn.html.

33. In 2001, Healthy Babies, Healthy Children staff made 31,479 formal referrals for 14,378 families who would benefit most from these services.

34. See www.health.gov.on.ca/english/public/pub/ministry_reports/healthy_babies_report/hbabies_report.html.

35. *The Economic Dimensions of Interpersonal Violence* (Geneva, Switzerland: Department of Injuries and Violence Prevention, World Health Organization, 2004). See also "Violence Creates Huge Economic Cost for Countries," a 2004 report; www.un.org/apps/news/story.asp?NewsID=11003&Cr=violence&Cr1=.

36. Gordon Cleveland and Michael Krashinsky, *The Benefits and Costs of Good Child Care: The Economic Rationale for Public Investment in Young Children—A Policy Study* (Scarborough: University of Toronto, Department of Economics, Mar. 1998).

37. Despite all the studies showing their benefits, child care programs have been vigorously opposed. For example, in Dec. 2005 a scathing critique of child care programs called "Universal Child Care, Maternal Labor Supply and Family Well-Being," was published by the U.S.–based National Bureau of Economic Research (NBER). It asserted that child care programs adversely affected children and families, and particularly criticized the Quebec program. Following the publicity the NBER report attracted, it was severely criticized by child development experts, including the director of the Human Early Learning Partnership, a Canadian interdisciplinary early child development research institute. In response to the NBER report, Dr. Clyde Herzman, Dr. Hillel Goelman, and Dr. Paul Kershaw of the University of British Columbia pointed out that, to begin with, it didn't actually study children who were enrolled in child care programs. "A careful reading of the report," they wrote, "reveals that they examined the possible effects of child care on children who were 'eligible' for Quebec's child care program but who were not necessarily enrolled in any child care programs at all." Herzman, Goelman, and Kershaw then criticized a second major flaw in the study: the authors "did not follow individual children over time, examining their development before, during, and after they were enrolled in child care" and therefore "have no direct way of knowing what influence child care had on any given child." In addition, Herzman, Goelman, and Kershaw pointed out that the study ignored the consistent findings of research that "it is the quality of the child care arrangement that is the most powerful predictor of child development," and did not include data on the quality of child care. In their Feb. 2006 letter to the Canadian newspaper *The Globe and Mail*, which had featured the NBER report, they wrote: "The article is seriously flawed, the conclusions misleading, and does a disservice to the national discussion on child care and family support programs."

38. Cleveland and Krashinsky, *Benefits and Costs of Good Child Care*.

39. As economist Peter Meyer-Dohm points out, the economic importance of investment in human capital first became a subject of discussion in the West when the U.S.S.R. sent its *Sputnik* into orbit before the United States could do it. This led to the development of a new branch of economics—the economics of education—and to heavy investments in higher education and the production of knowledge. As Meyer-Dohm notes, the main interest of the economics of education is the cost-benefit ratio of knowledge investment. But education (costs) and the quality of human capital measured by income (benefit) are a very narrow concept (Professor Meyer-Dohm, personal communication, Aug. 2006).

40. Burud and Tumolo, *Leveraging the New Human Capital*.

41. A few states have good programs focusing on young children and their parents. But because there is insufficient recognition of the importance of these programs, the essential services they provide are often among the first cut when there are budget shortfalls.

42. Richard Layard, *Happiness: Lessons from a New Science* (New York: Penguin Press, 2005).

43. The Structural Adjustment policies of the IMF and other international agencies require that government costs be severely cut to qualify a nation for loans. The result has been that governments have radically cut programs that support health, education, and welfare. Many studies show that this has extremely negative consequences for society at large and particularly for women caring for children, as well as for the children themselves. See, for example, Lois Woestman's paper, "Male Chauvinist SAPs: Structural Adjustment and Gender Policies," Dec. 1994–Jan. 1995. (For copies of Woestman's paper, write the secretariat of EURODAD or WIDE, Square Ambiorix 10, B-1040 Brussels, Belgium.)

44. In Canada, twelve months of partially paid maternity and parental leaves are available, and in 2001, 61 percent of new mothers were receiving maternity or parental leave benefits and 10 percent of husbands claimed or planned to claim paid parental benefits. Statistics Canada, "Life Stress." See www.statcan.ca. See also *Starting Strong: Early Childhood Education and Care* (Paris: Center of Excellence for Early Childhood Development, 2001). www.excellence-earlychildhood. ca/theme.asp?id=4&lang=EN.

45. Rob Stein, "U.S. Health Care Most Expensive, Error-Prone," *Monterey County Herald*, Nov. 4, 2005, p. A2. The survey—by Harris Interactive, commissioned by the Commonwealth Fund—was published in the journal *Health Affairs*.

46. Marcia K. Meyers and Janet C. Gornick, "The European Model: What We Can Learn from How Other Nations Support Families That Work," *American Prospect*, Nov. 1, 2004. For more details, see Janet C. Gornick and Marcia K. Meyers, *Families That Work: Policies for Reconciling Parenthood and Employment* (New York: Russell Sage Foundation Publications, 2003).

47. See *Labour Productivity: Data: GDP per Index and Percentage Change*, Aug. 12, 2005. www.oecd.org/searchResult/0,2665,en_2825_293564_1_1_1_1_1,00.html and www.oecd.org/dataoecd/30/14/29861140.xls. See also Meyers and Gornick, "The European Model."

48. *Child Health USA 2004* (Rockville, Md.: Health Resources and Services Administration, Maternal and Child Health Bureau. U.S. Department of Health and Human Services, 2004. www.mchb.hrsa.gov/mchirc/chusa_04/pages/ 0405iimr. htm.

49. Meyers and Gornick, "The European Model."

50. See Martha Burk, *Cult of Power: Sex Discrimination in Corporate America and What Can Be Done About It* (New York: Scribner's, 2005).

51. See Mona Harrington, *Care and Equality: Inventing a New Family Politics* (New York: Knopf, 1999), which shows how caregiving places an extra burden on women and explains the need for a new "family values" agenda to reduce the stress on U.S. families. Other works on this theme are Shirley Burggraf, *The Feminine Economy and the Economic Man: Reviving the Role of Family in the Post-Industrial Age* (New York: Perseus Books, 1999) and Anne Critterden, *The Price*

of Motherhood: Why the Most Important Job in the World Is Still the Least Valued (New York: Metropolitan Books, 2001).

52. "Message of the United Nations Secretary-General Kofi Annan for the International Day for the Eradication of Poverty," presentation by U.N. Secretary-General Kofi Annan on International Day for the Eradication of Poverty, Oct. 17, 2000. See www.oct17.org/archives/en/archiv_en/sout00e.htm.

53. Carol Bellamy's statement from the tenth annual UNICEF report on the state of the world's children, *The State of the World's Children 2005: Childhood Under Threat*. See www.medicalnewstoday.com/medicalnews.php?newsid=17670.

54. See www.cia.gov/cia/publications/factbook/rankorder/2091rank.html.

55. As Susan Kollin notes in her book *Nature's State* (Chapel Hill: University of North Carolina Press, 2001), the spill ultimately created a huge rise in U.S. GNP, because more than $2 billion was spent on cleanup and another $40 billion on other damages incurred as a result of air pollution.

56. Rather than take responsibility for the enormous environmental damage caused by the spill, at this writing Exxon continues to spend millions of dollars fighting the fines imposed for environmental crimes by the Justice Department as well as civil judgments, including $5.2 billion in punitive damages to Alaska Natives, property owners, and commercial fishers on Prince William Sound. See Ashley Shelby, "The Real Cost of Oil," *Alternet*, June 24, 2005. www.alternet.org/envirohealth/22260/.

57. See "Deaths from Air Pollution Now Triple Those from Traffic Accidents," Oct. 17, 2002. www.peopleandplanet.net/doc.php?id=1778.

58. See www.peopleandplanet.net/doc.php?id=1778.

59. http://edition.cnn.com/2005/WORLD/asiapcf/04/27/eyeonchina.environment/.

60. http://edition.cnn.com/2005/WORLD/asiapcf/04/27/eyeonchina.environment/.

61. Jenifer Warren, "Spare the Rod, Save the Child," *Los Angeles Times*, July 6, 2004. www.justicepolicy.org/article.php?id=429.

62. Warren, "Spare the Rod." The good news, as Daniel Weintraub writes, is that California is now also in process of moving toward changing its youth prisons to "more caring places where every kid gets a chance to go straight before it's too late." Though so far the overhaul is still mostly on paper, in 2006 the California budget included $100 million in new money to begin implementing basic changes (Daniel Weintraub, "Overhaul of Youth Prisons Just Might Give Kids a Chance," *Monterey County Herald*, Aug. 27, 2006, p. F2).

63. For the effects of maltreatment on the brain, see Bruce D. Perry, Ronnie A. Pollard, Toi A. Blakley, William L. Baker, and Domenico Vigilante, "Childhood Trauma, the Neurobiology of Adaptation, and 'Use-Dependent' Development of the Brain: How 'States' Become 'Traits,'" *Infant Mental Health Journal*, 1995, *16*, 271–291. For a national study of child maltreatment as a cause of crime as well as a survey of the literature showing a correlation between child abuse and crime, see Janet Currie and Erdal Tekin, "Does Child Abuse Cause Crime?"

Institute for the Study of Labor (IZA), 2006. The paper is Working Paper No. 12171 of the National Bureau of Economic Research, Inc. See an abstract at http://ideas.repec.org/p/nbr/nberwo/12171.html#provider.

64. The Perry Preschool Longitudinal Study, www.highscope.org/Research/ PerryProject/perrymain.htm.

Chapter 4: The Economic Double Standard

1. II Samuel, *The Dartmouth Bible* (Boston: Houghton Mifflin, 1950).

2. Deuteronomy 22:13–21.

3. Genesis 19.

4. Deuteronomy 22:28–29.

5. Augustine, quoted in Roy F. Baumeister, "How the Self Became a Problem: A Psychological Review of Historical Research," *Journal of Personality and Social Psychology*, 1987, 52(1), 169.

6. Susan Moller Okin, *Women in Western Political Thought* (Princeton: Princeton University Press, 1979), 200.

7. Rousseau, quoted in Okin, *Women in Western Political Thought*, 163–164.

8. See Christine de Pizan, *The Book of the City of Ladies* (Earl Jeffrey Richards, trans.) (New York: Persea Press, 1982). See also Gerda Lerner, *The Creation of Feminist Consciousness: From the Middle Ages to Eighteen-Seventy* (New York: Oxford University Press, 1993), and www.pinn.net/~sunshine/march99/pizan3.html.

9. Antoine Nicolas de Caritat, Marquis de Condorcet, "On the Admission of Women to the Rights of Citizenship," July 1790, in Lynn Hunt (trans., ed.), *The French Revolution and Human Rights: A Brief Documentary History* (Boston/New York: Bedford/St. Martin's, 1996).

10. William Thompson, for example, wrote that a married woman's lack of rights reduced her to become "an involuntary breeding machine and household slave." Quoted in Nancy Folbre, "Socialism, Feminist and Scientific," in Ferber and Nelson, *Beyond Economic Man*, p. 100.

11. Elizabeth Cady Stanton, *The Woman's Bible* (New York: European Publishing Co., 1885). Reprinted in *The Original Feminist Attack on the Bible*, by Elizabeth Cady Stanton, with a modern introduction by Barbara Welter (New York: Arno Press, 1974).

12. For more of Stanton's manifesto, see www.nps.gov/wori/address.htm.

13. Marx quoted in Folbre, "Socialism, Feminist and Scientific," p. 103.

14. While the effects on the overall quality of life of these generally ignored patterns of gender inequity are most dramatic in the developing world, they are hardly exclusive to it. The same patterns are evident in developed nations such as the United States, where they become most visible when families break up and the father's living standards generally rise while those of women and children drop.

15. Amartya Sen, "More Than 100 Million Women Are Missing," *New York Review of Books*, 1990, 37(20), 61–66.

16. *The World's Women: 1970–1990 Trends and Statistics* (New York: United Nations, 1991), 60.

17. Since the 1970s, many books have pointed out that economic development programs discriminate against women. Among them are Ester Boserup, *Women's Role in Economic Development* (London: Allen and Unwin, 1970); Devaki Jain and Nirmala Banerjee (eds.), *The Tyranny of the Household: Women in Poverty, Investigative Essays on Women's Work* (New Delhi: Shakti Books, a division of Vikas Publishing, 1985); Maria Mies, *Patriarchy and Accumulation on a World Scale: Women and the International Division of Labour* (London: Zed Books, 1986); Kathryn Ward (ed.), *Women Workers and Global Restructuring* (Ithaca, N.Y.: Cornell University Press, 1990); Jane Jaquette, *The Women's Movement in Latin America: Participation and Democracy*, 2nd ed. (Boulder, Colo.: Westview Press, 1994); Hale Afshar (ed.), *Women, Development, and Survival in the Third World* (New York: Longman, 1991); V. Spike Peterson and Anne Sisson Runyan, *Global Gender Issues: Dilemmas in World Politics*, 2nd ed. (Boulder, Colo.: Westview Press, 1999). For an analysis of the particularly severe impact of structural adjustment policies on women, see Woestman, "Male Chauvinist SAPs: Structural Adustment and Gender Policies." These works are part of a larger literature resulting from an explosion of research on gender roles and relations over the last several decades. For a work highlighting some of this research, see Linda L. Lindsey, *Gender Roles: A Sociological Perspective*, 2nd ed. (Englewood Cliffs, N.J.: Prentice Hall, 1994).

18. Marx used the term *alienation* in a number of ways. He argued that the labor of industrial workers was separated or alienated from its real value. That is, he argued that only labor creates value, and hence this value should all go to the worker and not to the owner of the machinery that the worker operates. He also argued that industrial labor was disconnected or alienated from meaning and purpose because it was broken down into mechanical assembly-line motions. Alienation thus had a number of meanings: separation, devaluation, and exploitation.

19. I want to credit the British biologist and feminist writer Hilary Rose for introducing the term *alienation of caring labor*. I cannot recall where she wrote about it, but it gave me a useful label for what I was observing, for which I am most grateful.

20. This view of women and women's work was still embedded in law as late as the nineteenth century. The view of women and women's work as male property was part of the British common law that was brought to the American colonies, and these laws changed only after they were challenged by the nineteenth-century feminist movement. For details, see Riane Eisler, *Dissolution: No-Fault Divorce, Marriage, and the Future of Women* (New York: McGraw-Hill, 1977).

21. In recent years in the United States women have entered medicine in significant numbers. At the same time, though still a high-income profession, some areas of medicine are becoming less lucrative, particularly those less technical ones where women tend to be more concentrated, such as pediatrics and obstet-

rics. This follows a classic pattern where, in accordance with the hidden gendered system of values characteristic of dominator economics, professions generally become less valued as women enter them in large numbers.

22. Riane Eisler, David Loye, and Kari Norgaard, *Women, Men, and the Global Quality of Life* (Pacific Grove, Calif.: Center for Partnership Studies, 1995). This study can be obtained at www.partnershipway.org.

23. According to the U.S. Census Bureau, among those ages sixty-five and over, 11.8 percent of women and 6.9 percent of men are poor. See *Country's Older Population Profiled by the U.S. Census Bureau*, June 1, 2001 (Public Information Office, CB01-96); www.census.gov/Press-Release/www/releases/archives/mobility_of_the_population/000335.html.

24. Joan A. W. Linsenmaier and Camille B. Wortman, "Attitudes Toward Workers and Toward Their Work: More Evidence That Sex Makes a Difference," *Journal of Applied Social Psychology*, Aug. 1979, 9(4).

25. See Eisler, *The Chalice and The Blade* and *Sacred Pleasure* for details on this shift in Western prehistory; see Min Jiayin (ed.), *The Chalice and The Blade in Chinese History: Gender Relations and Social Models* (Beijing: China Social Sciences Publishing House, 1995) for how it occurred in Asia; and June Nash, "The Aztecs and the Ideology of Male Dominance," *Signs*, Winter 1978, 4, 349–362, for a myth showing its occurrence in the Americas. Some of the most ancient myths of many cultures refer to a more peaceful and just time when women had high status. For example, the Chinese *Tao Te Ching*, as R. B. Blakney notes, refers to a time before the imposition of male dominance. (See R. B. Blakney [ed. and trans.], *The Way of Life: Tao Te Ching* [New York: Mentor, 1951].)

26. Bacon quote in Fritjof Capra, *The Turning Point* (London: Fontana Flamingo series, 1983). See www.lausd.k12.ca.us/North_Hollywood_HS/programs/thefarm/readings/capra.html.

27. Margaret G. Reid, *Economics of Household Production* (New York: Wiley, 1934).

28. Waring, *If Women Counted*. In this powerful book, Waring (a former member of the New Zealand legislature) shows how the exclusion of the "women's work" of caring and caregiving distorts economic indicators and how the devaluation of women and anything associated with women lies behind it, paving the way for a more thorough reexamination of economic measurements from a gendered perspective.

29. For a discussion of the methods proposed by OECD (Organisation for Economic Co-operation and Development), see Duncan Ironmonger, "Counting Outputs, Inputs, and Caring Labor: Estimating Gross Household Product," *Feminist Economics*, Fall 1996, 2(3), 37–64.

30. Ironmonger, "Counting Outputs."

31. Hilkka Pietila, "Non-Market Work in the Construction of Livelihood: The Work and Production at the Grass Roots Countervailing Globalization," presentation at the IGGRI Preparatory Meeting, Helsinki, Oct. 13–16, 1997.

32. www.sensiblepriorities.org/budget_analysis.php. For Korb's article, see www. sensiblepriorities.org/pdf/korb_report_Finalb.pdf. Business Leaders for Sensible Priorities is a nonpartisan, nonprofit organization of 650 top corporate executives from companies like Goldman Sachs, Hasbro, and Phillips-Van Heusen.

33. Julie Aslaksen and Charlotte Koren, "Unpaid Household Work and the Distribution of Extended Income: The Norwegian Experience," *Feminist Economics*, Fall 1996, 2(3), 65–80.

34. "Teure Haushaltproduktion" ["Expensive Household Production"].

35. *Human Development Report 1995*, United Nations Development Programme (New York: Oxford University Press, 1995), pp. 7, 6.

36. For a recent book dealing with happiness, see Layard, *Happiness*.

37. For example, the Adverse Childhood Experiences (ACE) study, an ongoing collaboration between Kaiser Permanente's Department of Preventive Medicine in San Diego, California, and the U.S. Centers for Disease Control and Prevention, has provided compelling evidence on the connection between early childhood trauma and emotional, social, and physical dysfunction later in life. For more information, see www.acestudy.org/pub-acereporter.php.

38. See, for example, "What the Research Shows."

39. For a discussion of this issue and studies shedding new light on it, see Julie A. Nelson, *Economics for Humans*, chapter 4.

40. Eisler, Loye, and Norgaard, *Women, Men, and the Global Quality of Life*. The link between gender equity and quality of life was confirmed at a very high level of statistical significance for correlational analysis. Sixty-one correlations at the .001 level and eighteen additional correlations at the .05 level were found, for a total of seventy-nine significant correlations in the predicted direction. This link was further confirmed by factor analysis. High factor loadings for gender equity and quality-of-life variables accounted for 87.8 percent of the variance. Regression analysis also yielded significant results. An R-square of .84, with statistical significance at the .0001 level, provided support for the hypothesis that gender equity is a strong indicator of the quality of life.

41. Eisler, Loye, and Norgaard, *Women, Men, and the Global Quality of Life*.

42. Eisler, Loye, and Norgaard, *Women, Men, and the Global Quality of Life*.

43. For information about the World Values Survey, see Ronald Inglehart, *Modernization and Postmodernization: Cultural, Economic, and Political Change in 43 Societies* (Princeton, N.J.: Princeton University Press, 1997).

44. Ronald F. Inglehart, Pippa Norris, and Christian Welzel, "Gender Equality and Democracy," *Comparative Sociology*, 2002, 1(3/4), 329.

45. Inglehart, Norris, and Welzel, "Gender Equality and Democracy." Using Freedom House scores on civil liberties and political rights, Inglehart and his colleagues also found "self-expression" values rising in societies moving toward democracy and gender equality. By contrast, societies that still emphasize "survival" values—which include traditional attitudes that severely limit women's life

options, intolerance toward out-groups, and low interpersonal trust—fall on the lower end of the civil liberties, political rights, and democracy scale. Most of Africa, the Muslim world, and the Catholic European and Latin American nations are still largely in the survival/traditional mode, which includes belief in gender inequality and more authoritarian institutions.

46. Inglehart, Norris, and Welzel, "Gender Equality and Democracy," p. 343. While the authors place great emphasis on economic development, they recognize that this development cannot be isolated from cultural changes—particularly changes in gender roles and relations.

47. Inglehart, Norris, and Welzel, "Gender Equality and Democracy," p. 343.

48. Eisler, Loye, and Norgaard, *Women, Men, and the Global Quality of Life.*

49. This finding for prevalence of contraception can be explained in a number of ways. But generally it seems to reflect a lessening of male control over women's sexuality, which could explain why it ranks so high in factor analysis.

50. Inglehart, Norris, and Welzel, "Gender Equality and Democracy," p. 335.

Chapter 5: Connecting the Dots

1. Systems self-organization is a term introduced by systems science, nonlinear dynamics, chaos theory, and other new approaches to the study of living systems. It does not focus on simple causes and effects, but on continual, mutually reinforcing interactions among the system's various components.

2. This failure to include early childhood relations was due in part to the fact that caring for children was viewed as "just women's work."

3. For example, a low-activity version of a gene called monoamine oxidase A (MAOA), has been implicated in a higher propensity for violence. But a study of men with this gene variant found that it alone does not predict who will become violent. Only those men who were mistreated as children (defined as having been physically or sexually abused, rejected by their mothers, or subjected to frequent changes in their primary caregivers) were more likely as adults to engage in antisocial behavior, including violent crime. See Avshalom Caspi, Joseph McClay, Terrie E. Moffitt, Jonathan Mill, Judy Martin, Ian W. Craig, Alan Taylor, and Richie Poulton, "Role of Genotype in the Cycle of Violence in Maltreated Children," *Science*, Aug. 2002, 297(5582), 851–854. See also Emily Singer, "Mistreatment During Childhood and Low Enzyme Activity May Make Men More Violent," *Los Angeles Times*, Aug. 2, 2002.

4. Theoretically, this could be the female half over the male half. But in practice, it has only been the ranking of the male half over the female half.

5. For an account of what happened to women when Hitler took over Germany, see Claudia Koonz, "Mothers in the Fatherland: Women in Nazi Germany," in Renate Bridenthal and Claudia Koonz (eds.), *Becoming Visible: Women in European History* (Boston: Houghton Mifflin, 1977), 445–473.

6. See, for example, Sheila Robotham, *Women, Resistance, and Revolution* (New York: Vintage, 1974).

7. See, for example, www.country-data.com/cgi-bin/query/r-14074.html.

8. See, for example, the Opacity Index, developed by PricewaterhouseCoopers, and Transparency International's Corruption Perception Index (CPI) for the prevalence of corruption worldwide. See "Global Corruption: Measuring Opacity" at www.helleniccomserve.com/opacity.html.

9. For example, in the Medicare prescription drug plan adopted in 2005, rather than requiring the government to negotiate with pharmaceutical companies for the best prices, the government was expressly prohibited from doing so.

10. Gifford Pinchot, *Intrapreneuring* (San Francisco: Berrett-Koehler, 2000). See also Gifford and Elizabeth Pinchot, *The Intelligent Organization* (San Francisco: Berrett-Koehler, 1994).

11. Stuart Schlegel, *Wisdom from a Rainforest* (Athens: University of Georgia Press, 1998), 111.

12. Schlegel, *Wisdom from a Rain Forest*, 244.

13. Schlegel, *Wisdom from a Rain Forest*, 249.

14. In her book *Women at the Center: Life in a Modern Matriarchy* (Ithaca, N.Y.: Cornell University Press, 2002), Peggy Reeves Sanday uses the term *matriarchy* to describe the Minangkabau because here men don't dominate women. But the Minangkabau are not ruled by women, as the term matriarchy (rather than patriarchy) implies. What Sanday describes is actually a society that orients to the partnership system.

15. Peggy Reeves Sanday, personal communication, Jan. 30, 2002.

16. Sanday, *Women at the Center*, 25.

17. See, for example, Layard, *Happiness*.

18. Sanday, *Women at the Center*, 22–24.

19. World Economic Forum, *Global Competitiveness Report, 2006–2007*. www.weforum.org/en/initiatives/gcp/Global%20Competitiveness%20Report/index.htm.

20. A higher status for women should not be confused with entry of women into "male" fields where dominator norms still prevail. Under these circumstances, the field is devalued as women enter. This happened to secretarial work in the nineteenth and early twentieth century, and is today happening to medicine in the United States.

21. This is not to say there is no violence against women in Nordic nations. This violence is unfortunately universal, because it is embedded in traditions of domination. As Jorgen Lorentzen and Per Are Lokke wrote in the paper they presented at the 1997 international seminar titled Promoting Equality: A Common Issue for Men and Women, "Many men have come to believe that violence against a woman, child, or another man is an acceptable way to control another person. . . . Domestic violence is a problem within existing masculinity and it is we, as men, who have to stop it" (Jorgen Lorentzen and Per Are Lokke, "Men's Violence Against Women: The Need to Take Responsibility," presentation at Promoting

Equality: A Common Issue for Men and Women, Strasbourg, France, June 17–18, 1997).

22. For more details, see www.copacgva.org/idc/copac-employment.doc.

23. Cooperatives have a long history that dates back to the eighteenth century, when Robert Owen applied the concept in Scottish cotton mills.

24. See, for example, Riccardo Lotti, Peter Mensing, and Davide Valenti, *The Cooperative Future*, Oct. 2005. www.boozallen.com.

25. Studies show that a combination of employee participation in ownership and participatory decision-making processes leads to greater effectiveness and higher company earnings. See "Employee Ownership and Corporate Performance" on the site of the National Center for Employee Ownership: www.nceo.org/library/corpperf.html.

26. Scholars studying networks have identified a number of different forms, such as hub, star, or wheel networks. See William M. Evan, "An Organization-Set Model of Interorganizational Relations," in Matthew Tuite, Roger Chisholm, and Michael Radnor (eds.), *Interorganizational Decision Making* (Chicago: Aldine, 1972).

27. For more details, see David Ronfeldt and John Arquilla, "Networks, Netwars, and the Fight for the Future," *First Monday*, Oct. 2001, 6(10). See also http://firstmonday.org/issues/issue6_10/ronfeldt/index.html.

28. Because our language does not offer any real alternative to the ranking of one half of humanity over the other, in *The Chalice and The Blade* I introduced the new term gylany. *Gy* derives from the Greek root word *gyne*, or woman. *An* derives from *andros*, or man. The letter *l* between the two has a double meaning. In English, it stands for the linking of both halves of humanity, rather than their ranking. In Greek, it derives from the verb *lyein* or *lyo*, which in turn has a double meaning: to solve or resolve (as in analysis) and to dissolve or set free (as in catalysis). In this sense, the letter l stands for the resolution of problems through the freeing of both halves of humanity from the stultifying and distorting rigidity of roles imposed by domination hierarchies.

Chapter 6: The Economics of Domination

1. For a more detailed description of Minoan culture, see Nicolas Platon, Crete (Geneva: Nagel Publishers, 1966); Nanno Marinatos, *Minoan Religion: Ritual, Image, and Symbol* (Columbia: University of South Carolina Press, 1993); R. F. Willetts, *The Civilization of Ancient Crete* (Berkeley: University of California Press, 1977); Eisler, *The Chalice and The Blade*. For even earlier more partnership-oriented cultures, see, for example, James Mellaart, *Çatal Hüyük* (New York: McGraw-Hill, 1967); Ian Hodder, "Women and Men at Catalhoyuk," *Scientific American*, Jan. 2004, pp. 77–83; Marija Gimbutas, *The Goddesses and Gods of Old Europe* (Berkeley: University of California Press, 1982); Eisler, *Sacred Pleasure*.

2. Platon, *Crete*, 148.

3. Platon, *Crete*, 69. Platon stresses that to explain the "Greek miracle" we must look to pre-Hellenic tradition. See also Jacquetta Hawkes, *Dawn of the Gods: Minoan and Mycenaean Origins of Greece* (New York: Random House, 1968).

4. J. V. Luce, *The End of Atlantis* (London: Thames & Hudson, 1968), 20, 137.

5. For details on Minoan and Athenian civilization, see Eisler, *The Chalice and The Blade*, especially chapters 3 and 8, and Eisler, *Sacred Pleasure*, part I.

6. Eva Keuls, *The Reign of the Phallus* (Berkeley: University of California Press, 1985), 7.

7. Keuls, *The Reign of the Phallus*, 6.

8. Keuls, *The Reign of the Phallus*, 206.

9. Aristotle, *Politics*, cited in Keuls, *The Reign of the Phallus*, 208.

10. As one ancient Greek bluntly put it, "We [Athenian men] keep *hetaerae* [courtesans] for pleasure, concubines for the daily care of our body, and wives for the bearing of legitimate children and to keep watch over our house" (*Against Neaera*, commonly attributed to Demosthenes, though probably not written by him), quoted in Keuls, *The Reign of the Phallus*, 99.

11. One way men legally enforced this control was by having sole management of women's property—even property they had inherited. See John Peradotto and John Patrick Sullivan, *Women in the Ancient World: The Arethusa Papers* (Albany: State University of New York Press, 1984), 33.

12. The protest against this *ius prima noctis* is one of the themes in Mozart's famous opera *The Marriage of Figaro*.

13. It is not coincidental that in the slaveholding American South the laws governing the status of slaves were modeled on the laws then governing the status of women.

14. As the German economist Peter Meyer-Dohm notes, these structures copied military organization, and companies were sometimes seen as being in a war against competitors.

15. In Rosabeth Moss Kanter, *When Giants Learn to Dance: Mastering the Challenge of Strategy, Management, and Careers in the 1990s* (New York: Random House, 1991). Kanter, a professor at Harvard Business School, notes how the traditional large, hierarchic corporation is not innovative or responsive; it becomes set in its ways, riddled with pecking-order politics, and closed to new ideas and outside influences.

16. See chapter 3 for some of the statistical data as well as studies in the positive organizational field. For an extensive review of the benefits of a partnership-oriented organization, see Peter M. Senge, *The Fifth Discipline: The Art & Practice of the Learning Organization*, rev. ed. (New York: Doubleday, 2006).

17. UNIFEM, Strengthening Women's Economic Capacity; World Development Indicators, 1997, Womankind Worldwide. See www.worldrevolution.org/projects/globalissuesoverview/overview2/briefenvironment.htm.

18. For information on the Hunger Project and its global work, see www.thp.org/.

19. Marjorie Kelly, "Reshaping the Language of Business: How New Language Helps Make the Case for Ethics," *Business Ethics*, Winter 2005, p. 6.

20. David Korten, *The Post-Corporate World* (San Francisco: Berrett-Koehler, 1999), 154.

21. Paul Scherrer, "The United States Has Highest Childhood Poverty Rate of Industrialized Countries," Mar. 14, 2001. www.wsws.org/articles/2001/mar2001/pov-m14.shtml. Twelve million American children live in poverty, or more than one in five children. The United States has the highest rate of childhood poverty among the nations included in the Organization for Economic Cooperation and Development (OECD). These findings are reported in the book *Child Well-Being, Child Poverty and Child Policy in Modern Nations*, which is the product of forty-five authors from three continents that make up the Luxembourg Income Study. It is the first time that child poverty levels have been measured taking into account taxes and benefits for individual U.S. states, which allows direct comparisons between U.S. states and other nations. An earlier report by the National Center for Children in Poverty (NCCP), comparing the five-year periods 1979 to 1983 and 1992 to 1996, revealed that the number of children under six living in poverty grew over that time by 1,456,284 to a yearly average of 5.9 million. See www.wsws.org/articles/2001/mar2001/pov-m14.shtml.

22. According to the U.S. Census Bureau, among those age sixty-five and over, 11.8 percent of women and 6.9 percent of men are poor. See "Country's Older Population Profiled by the U.S. Census Bureau," *U.S. Census Bureau News*, June 1, 2001 (Public Information Office, CB01-96). See www.census.gov/Press-Release/www/releases/archives/mobility_of_the_population/000335.html.

23. Moni Mukherjee, "Contributions to and Use of Social Product by Women," in Devaki Jain and Nirmala Banerjee (eds.), *The Tyranny of the Household: Women in Poverty, Investigative Essays on Women's Work* (New Delhi: Shakti Books, 1985), 270.

24. Daisy Dwyer and Judith Bruce (eds.), *A Home Divided: Women and Income in the Third World* (Stanford, Calif.: Stanford University Press, 1988), 526.

25. Judith Bruce and Daisy Dwyer, Introduction, in Dwyer and Bruce, *A Home Divided*. For a quantified analysis of time use in selected activities hours per week for some countries, see *The World's Women: 1970–1990* (New York: United Nations, 1991). For example, in Guatemala women spend 39.9 hours per week on unpaid housework and chores, while men spend 6.3. For child care in Guatemala the figures are 9.8 for women and 4.6 for men. In the United States in 1986 women spent 29.9 hours per week on unpaid household chores and men spent 17.4 hours. For child care, in the United States hours per week for women were two and for men 0.8 (*The World's Women*, p. 101).

26. Judith Bruce and Cynthia B. Lloyd, "Finding the Ties That Bind: Beyond Headship and Household," in Lawrence Haddad, John Hoddinott, and Harold Alderman (eds.), *Intrahousehold Resources Allocation in Developing Countries: Methods, Models, and Policy* (Baltimore: International Food Policy Research Institute and Johns Hopkins University Press, 1997).

27. Duncan Thomas, "Intra-Household Resource Allocation," *Journal of Human Resources*, Fall 1990, 25(4), 635.

28. Bruce and Lloyd, "Finding the Ties That Bind," pp. 8–9.

29. Dr. Anugerah Pekerti, chair of World Vision, Indonesia, states, "When the fathers are asked why they smoke cigarettes instead of buying food for their hungry children, they say, 'We can always make more children'" (Nicholas D. Kristof, "As Asian Economies Shrink, Women Are Squeezed Out," *New York Times*, June 11, 1998).

30. Ruth L. Sivard, *World Military & Social Expenditures* (Washington, D.C.: World Priorities, 1996).

31. *State of the World's Children 1996* (New York: UNICEF, 1996). See www.unicef.org/sowc96/.

32. "Iraq War Costlier Than Vietnam," in *The Iraq Quagmire*, Institute for Policy Studies (IPS) and Foreign Policy in Focus (FPIF), Aug. 31, 2005. http://news.bbc.co.uk/2/hi/americas/4201812.stm. See also Jamie Wilson, "Iraq War Could Cost U.S. Over $2 Trillion, Says Nobel Prize-Winning Economist; Economists Say Official Estimates Are Far Too Low; New Calculation Takes in Dead and Injured Soldiers," *The Guardian*/UK, Jan. 7, 2006. This article reported on a study by Joseph Stiglitz and Linda Bilmes estimating that the cost of the Iraq war is likely to be between $1 trillion and $2 trillion.

33. Randy Albelda, *Lost Ground: Welfare Reform, Poverty, and Beyond* (Cambridge, Mass.: South End Press, 2002).

34. Brian Griffith, *The Gardens of Their Dreams: Desertification and Culture in World History* (London and New York: Zed Books, 2003).

35. James DeMeo, "The Origins and Diffusion of Patrism in Saharasia, c. 4000 B.C.E.: Evidence for a Worldwide, Climate-Linked Geographical Pattern in Human Behavior," *World Futures*, 1991, 30(2), 247–271.

36. Griffith, *Gardens of Their Dreams*, 25.

37. Griffith, *Gardens of Their Dreams*, 26.

38. DeMeo, "The Origins and Diffusion of Patrism in Saharasia, c. 4000 B.C.E." For a cross-cultural study finding the same correlations, see Peggy Reeves Sandy, *Female Power and Male Dominance: On the Origins of Sexual Inequality* (Cambridge: Cambridge University Press, 1981).

39. Historian Ibn Khaldun, quoted in Griffith, *Gardens of Their Dreams*.

40. Griffith, *Gardens of Their Dreams*, 27.

41. Griffith, *Gardens of Their Dreams*, 30.

42. Griffith, *Gardens of Their Dreams*, 74

43. Griffith, *Gardens of Their Dreams*, 75.

44. For details, see www.millenniumassessment.org.

45. A 2005 report of British scientists from the Royal Society, quoted in Kenneth Chang, "Oceans Turning Acidic, Scientists Say," *New York Times News Service*, reprinted in *Monterey County Herald*, July 1, 2005, p. A8.

Chapter 7: The Economics of Partnership

1. Aristotle, *Aristotle's Politics* (Benjamin Jowett, trans.) (New York: Modern Library, 1943), 58.

2. Theories serve not only to explain "reality," but also to change it. Indeed, the stories theories tell us, be they religious or secular, be they about how the world was created or what kind of economic relations are natural, are powerful molders of consciousness, and hence of reality.

3. Adam Smith, *The Wealth of Nations* (New York: Modern Library, 1937). Adam Smith, *The Theory of Moral Sentiments*, 6th ed. (London: A. Millar, 1790 [originally published 1759]).

4. Robert Heilbroner, *The Worldly Philosophers: The Lives, Times, and Ideas of the Great Economic Thinkers*, 7th ed. (New York: Simon & Schuster, 1999). For more detail on these conditions, see chapters ii and iii.

5. Smith, *Wealth of Nations*, 460.

6. Smith, *Wealth of Nations*, 79.

7. Smith, quoted in Heilbroner, *The Worldly Philosophers*, 54.

8. Smith did not advocate the kind of concentration of wealth that is often justified in the name of a free market. His theory assumed a broad distribution of the ownership of productive assets in a market economy of small or medium-size firms, not the monopolies that resulted when his theory played out in a dominator framework.

9. Frederick Engels, *The Condition of the Working Class in England* (London: Panther Books, 1969 [originally published 1845].

10. For a website on utopian socialists, see http://cepa.newschool.edu/het/schools/utopia.htm.

11. John Stuart Mill also decried economic injustice, pointing out that while there may be economic laws of production, the laws of economic distribution are human-made, and must be changed. See John Stuart Mill, *Principles of Political Economy* (New York: Prometheus, 2004). An important aspect of Mill's work is how profoundly it was influenced by Harriet Taylor, his close friend and eventual wife. Mill even wrote that most of his famous book *On Liberty* was the work of Harriet Taylor, although he did not include her as his coauthor.

12. See http://en.wikipedia.org/wiki/Communist_Manifesto#Contents.

13. Nietzsche quoted in Aubery Castell, *An Introduction to Modern Philosophy* (New York: Macmillan, 1946), 340.

14. *The World Social Situation.*

15. *Human Development Report 2003*. United Nations Development Programme (New York: Oxford University Press, 2004).

16. See Heilbroner, *The Worldly Philosophers*, 214–217, for a vivid picture of the ruthlessness and "staggering dishonesty" of these and other capitalist robber barons in an age before there were government regulations of business practices.

17. It is sobering that with the switch to a capitalist system the dynamics of the underlying domination system again ensured that former Soviet commissars managed to buy up state-controlled assets at bargain-basement rates so that many of them accumulated great wealth as owners of private enterprises while the people's standard of living, and even their life expectancy rates, worsened.

18. In feudal economics, land was considered of primary importance. In capitalist economics, the focus shifted to industrial machinery. In socialist economics, the importance of labor was emphasized, but a major focus was still on control of the means of production—that is, of capital assets such as land and machinery.

19. Sen relates human capabilities to human well-being and proposes that monetary income be seen as only one of the means by which human capabilities are generated. See Amartya Sen, *Development as Freedom* (Oxford: Oxford University Press, 1999). Along similar lines, Chicago University law and ethics professor Martha Nussbaum proposes that the development of human capabilities should be central to social and economic policy. She argues for the development of a list of central human capabilities that includes not only physical ones but also emotional and spiritual ones, such as being able to use our senses and imagination and being able to form satisfying emotional attachments. See Nussbaum, *Sex and Justice*, and Martha Nussbaum, "Capabilities as Fundamental Entitlements: Sen and Social Justice," *Feminist Economics*, 2001, 9(2–3), 33–50.

20. Bruce D. Perry, "Childhood Experience and the Expression of Genetic Potential: What Childhood Neglect Tells Us About Nature and Nurture," *Brain and Mind*, 2002, 3(1), 79–100.

21. Strangely, autistic children seem to have accelerated brain growth in the early years.

22. For a discussion of how Darwin himself recognized these aspects of human evolution, see David Loye, *Darwin's Lost Theory, Who We Really Are and Where We're Going* (Carmel, Calif.: Benjamin Franklin Press, 2007). See www.benjaminfranklinpress.com.

23. Eisler, Loye, and Norgaard, *Women, Men, and the Global Quality of Life*.

24. Veblen, quoted in Ann L. Jennings, "Public or Private? Institutional Economics and Feminism," in Marianne A. Ferber and Julie A. Nelson (eds.), *Beyond Economic Man* (Chicago: University of Chicago Press, 1993), 113. Even earlier, August Bebel's 1879 best-seller *Women and Socialism* departed from Marx's theories to argue that the oppression of women must be addressed independently of the exploitation of working men. Bebel, *Women and Socialism* (New York: Schocken, 1971 [originally published 1879]). Charlotte Perkins Gilman, *Economics and Women* (Berkeley: University of California Press, 1998 [originally published 1898]).

25. See John Kenneth Galbraith, *Economics & The Public Purpose* (Boston: Houghton Mifflin, 1973). There were also socialist theorists such as André Gunder Frank, who harshly critiqued capitalist markets and the imperialistic expansion that has been required for their maintenance. See, for example, André Gunder Frank, *Capitalism and Underdevelopment in Latin America* (London: Penguin Books, 1971).

26. For an analysis of institutional economics, see Ann L. Jennings, "Public or Private? Institutional Economics and Feminism" in Ferber and Nelson (eds.), *Beyond Economic Man*. For a critique of the failure of most economic writings to look at the social context of economics, see Alberto Martinelli and Neil J. Smelser (eds.), *Economy and Society: Overviews in Economic Sociology* (Thousand Oaks, Calif.: Sage Publications, 1990).

27. The Arrow-Debreu economic model developed jointly by Kenneth Arrow and Gerard Debreu in the 1950s is a famous example.

28. Other economists, including Bina Agarwal, Nirmala Banerjee, Barbara Bergmann, Scott Burns, Marianne Ferber, Prue Hyman, Gita Sen, and Devaki Jain, have also made important contributions to expanding the purview of economic theory in this direction.

29. Julie A. Nelson, *Economics for Humans* (Chicago: University of Chicago Press, 2006).

30. Folbre, *The Invisible Heart*.

31. Hilkka Pietila, "Non-Market Work in the Construction of Livelihood: The Work and Production at the Grass Roots Countervailing Globalization," paper presented at IGGRI Preparatory Meeting, Helsinki, Oct. 13–16, 1997 (rev. Apr. 18, 1998). See also Hilkka Pietila "Cultivation and Households: The Basics of Nurturing Human Life," *EOLSS, Encyclopedia of Life Support Systems*, Section: Human Resources Policy and Management, UNESCO (Oxford, U.K.: Eolss Publishers, 2004). See www.eolss.net. Pietila notes: "'Family' or 'household' in this sense need not be a group of relatives, kindred persons. It could be any group of people who have decided to have a joint household, to 'eat out of the same refrigerator,' as it is sometimes said today."

32. Economics has always been composed of a number of theories and models in both what economists call *macroeconomics* (the study of relations among the various components of economic systems) and *microeconomics* (the study of these components and their behavior).

33. Most recently, Cahn founded the Time Dollar Youth Court, in which teen juries hear cases of teens arrested for the first time for nonviolent offenses and support them in rehabilitation through community service.

34. This approach is sometimes summed up with the term "triple bottom line"—people, planet, and profit.

35. There are well-documented cases, such as Nestlé executives who knowingly sold watered-down formula for children in the developing world; tobacco company executives who deliberately withheld findings that smoking causes lung

cancer; executives at petrochemical companies who failed to inform their employees that working in their plants was slowly killing them; and Pacific Gas & Electric executives who, as dramatized in the movie *Erin Brockovich*, deliberately deceived families about the health and environmental consequences of plant operations in a poor neighborhood. For an exposé of how giant oil companies kept denying their toxins-emitting storage plants were poisoning people living near them, see Jim Hightower, *There's Nothing in the Middle of the Road But Yellow Stripes and Dead Armadillos* (New York: HarperCollins, 1998).

36. Moises Naim, "Broken Borders," *Newsweek*, Oct. 24, 2005, pp. 57–62.

37. Ed Vulliamy, "Streets of Despair," *Amnesty International*, Winter 2005, pp. 12–16.

38. Interview with Randy Albelda. http://wfnetwork.bc.edu/The_Network_News/2-3/TNN2-3_Albelda.pdf. See also Albelda, *Lost Ground*.

39. For a discussion of happiness and how it relates to partnerist economic theory, see Layard, *Happiness*. For the connection between happiness and policies that support caring and caregiving, see particularly pp. 176–179. See also Nel Noddings, *Happiness and Education* (Cambridge: Cambridge University Press, 2003).

40. See Henderson, *Beyond Globalization*; Hazel Henderson, *Ethical Markets: Greening the Global Economy* (White River Junction, Vt.: Chelsea Green Publishing, 2006); and Inge Kaul, Isabelle Grunberg, and Marc Stern, *Global Public Goods: International Cooperation in the 21st Century* (New York: Oxford University Press, 1999).

41. Inge Kaul, Pedro Conceicao, Katell Le Goulven, and Ronald Mendoza (eds.), *Providing Public Goods* (New York: Oxford University Press, 2003).

42. Korten, *Post-Corporate World*, 76.

43. Korten, *Post-Corporate World*, 61.

44. Korten, *Post-Corporate World*. See also David Korten, *When Corporations Rule the World*, 2nd ed. (Bloomfield, Conn.: Kumerian Press and San Francisco: Berrett-Koehler, 2001).

45. See, for example, Thom Hartmann, *Unequal Protection: The Rise of Corporate Dominance and the Theft of Human Rights* (New York: Rodale Books, 2004).

46. See, for example, Jeff Gates, *Democracy at Risk: Rescuing Main Street from Wall Street* (Cambridge, Mass.: Perseus Publishing, 2000).

47. See, for example, Korten, *Post-Corporate World*.

48. See for example, John Cavanagh (ed.), *Alternatives to Economic Globalization: A Better World Is Possible* (San Francisco: Berrett-Koehler, 2002).

49. David Korten, private communication, Aug. 5, 2006.

50. For more information on child slavery, see among others, www.antislavery.com, globalmarch.org, www.hrw.org, and www.time.com/time/asia/features/slavery/cover.html.

51. Unfortunately, the global giants these local companies supply generally buy from the lowest bidder, so their pressure provides a justification for horrible practices. Organizations such as the Business Alliance for Local Living Economies (BALLE) are working to persuade local businesses to break away from these relationships and form cooperatives based on caring principles. For information on BALLE, see http://livingeconomies.org/.

52. A documentary graphically showing how in traditional Masai cultures young men's primary identity is still as warriors (even though they no longer raid their neighbors) and women are still brutally subordinated is the 1975 film *Masai Women*, by C. Curling and Melissa Llewelyn-Davies, distributed by Films Inc. See Women's Studies Films in the Media Resource Center at http://depts.drew. edu/wmst/StudentRes/filmbtable.htm.

Chapter 8: Technology, Work, and the Postindustrial Era

1. *The Independent*, Mar. 26, 2002.

2. See http://blog.taragana.com/index.php/archive/canine-robot/.

3. See www.rppi.org/outofcontrol/.

4. C/NET News.com Staff June 25, 2004.

5. C/NET News.com Staff June 25, 2004.

6. See http://news.com.

7. When economist Robert Theobald proposed a universal guaranteed income that would not be tied to acceptance of work in the early sixties—arguing that automation would continue to eliminate jobs and therefore income should be separated from employment—he was fiercely attacked. Later, President Richard Nixon proposed it as the Family Assistance Program, which did not pass Congress. In 1996, Theobald again argued for a guaranteed annual income. See Jim Smith, "Separating Survival from Work: The Quest for a Guaranteed Income," www.lalabor. org/GAI.html.

8. Economist Milton Friedman first proposed the negative income tax in 1962, and like Theobald's proposal, it was seriously considered during a period of much unrest in inner-city African-American ghettoes. As Jodie T. Allen wrote, "The negative income tax proposal basically reversed the current progressive tax scale." If, for example, the threshold for positive tax liability for a family of four was, say, $10,000, a family with only $8,000 in annual income would, given a negative tax rate of 25 percent, receive a check from the U.S. Treasury worth $500 (25 percent of the $2,000 difference between its $8,000 income and the $10,000 threshold). A family with zero income would receive $2,500. See Jodie T. Allen, "Negative Income Tax," in David R. Henderson (ed.), *The Concise Encyclopedia of Economics* (Indianapolis: Library of Economics and Liberty, Liberty Fund, 2001). www.econlib.org/library/Enc/ NegativeIncomeTax.html.

9. The vision of technology to free humans from backbreaking and mind-numbing work is not new. It was the vision of many of the "utopian" thinkers of the

nineteenth century. But within the confines of a culture orienting to the domination model, this vision came to be seen as nothing more than pie in the sky.

10. For some details on *Schmeiser v. Monsanto* and *Monsanto v. Schmeiser*, see www.percyschmeiser.com/conflict.htm. See also the Organic Consumer's Association website: www.purefood.org/monlink.html.

11. For a discussion of some of these risks, see Gordon Conway, president of the Rockefeller Foundation, "GM Food Safety: Facts, Uncertainties, and Assessment," address to the Conference on the Scientific and Health Aspects of Genetically Modified Foods, sponsored by the Organization for Economic Co-Operation and Development (OECD), Edinburgh, Scotland, Mar. 28, 2000.

12. The Center for Nonproliferation Studies (CNS) at the Monterey Institute of International Studies is the largest nongovernmental organization devoted to research and training on weapons nonproliferation issues.

13. See Jeremy Rifkin, *The Biotech Century* (New York: Tarcher, 1998).

14. Ker Than, "Brain Cells Fused with Computer Chip," *LiveScience*, Mar. 27, 2006. www.livescience.com/humanbiology/060327_neuro_chips.html.

15. Charles Q. Choi, "Transistor Flow Control: Forget Valves—Controlling Fluids with Electric Fields," *Scientific American*, Oct. 2005, 293(4), 26.

16. For more information on nanotubes, see www.pa.msu.edu/cmp/csc/nanotube.html.

17. Choi, "Transistor Flow Control."

18. See "Opposition to Nanotechnology," *New York Times*, Aug. 19, 2002. www.nytimes.com/2002/08/19/technology/19NECO.html.

19. James Bell, "Technotopia and the Death of Nature: Clones, Supercomputers, and Robots," *Earth Island Journal*, Nov.-Dec. 2001. See www.earthisland.org/.

20. David Noble, *A World Without Women: The Christian Clerical Culture of Western Science* (New York: Knopf, 1992). Also illustrative of this point is Margaret Wertheim's *Pythagoras Trousers: God, Physics, and the Gender Wars* (New York: Times Books, 1995). Other books that shed light on this problem are Ruth Bleier (ed.), *Feminist Approaches to Science* (New York: Pergamon Press, 1988) and Evelyn Fox Keller, *Reflections on Gender and Science* (New Haven, Conn.: Yale University Press, 1985).

21. For example, as scientists begin to move toward this more balanced style of observation, basing theories on observations that include not only precise quantitative measures but also value-laden qualitative descriptions, physicists are beginning to accept, and thus observe, ambiguity in nature.

22. Bill Joy, "Why the Future Doesn't Need Us," *Wired*, Apr. 2000. For a much more optimistic view of new technologies, see Joel Garreau, *Radical Evolution: The Promise and Peril of Enhancing Our Minds, Our Bodies and What It Means to Be Human* (New York: Doubleday, 2005).

23. See John Myers, "Birch Bark's 'Incredible' Potential: Extract May Serve as 'Medicine Chest for the World,'" Knight Ridder Newspapers, *Monterey County Herald*, Apr. 17, 2006, p. A2.

24. David S. Barry, "Growing Up Violent," *Media and Values*, Summer 1993, pp. 8–11.

25. See, for example, John De Graaf, *Take Back Your Time: Fighting Overwork and Time Poverty in America* (San Francisco: Berrett Koehler, 2003); Juliet Shore, *The Overworked American* (New York: Basic Books, 1993).

26. Gordon Johnson of the Pentagon's Joint Forces Command, in Tim Weiner, "A New Model Army Soldier Rolls Closer to the Battlefield," *New York Times*, Feb. 16, 2005.

27. Most of the demand for these technologies, the Economic Research Institute report noted, will take place in the developed world, particularly the G7 and other OECD countries. However, with OECD countries facing long-term population declines and with many current industries saturated, it also predicted that technology will be the driving force for economic growth in the developed world. See www.marubeni.co.jp/research/eindex/0212-2/.

28. *Global Trends 2015: A Dialogue About the Future with Nongovernment Experts* (Washington, D.C.: National Intelligence Council, U.S. Central Intelligence Agency, Dec. 2000).

29. *Converging Technologies for Improving Human Performance* (Washington, D.C.: National Science Foundation, June 2002). This report did acknowledge that its proposal to accelerate the development of these technologies will require an intense public relations effort to "prepare key organizations and societal activities for the changes made possible by converging technologies" and to counter concern over "ethical, legal and moral issues." In other words, it proposed effective public relations—when the real way to allay concerns must entail realistic planning guided by responsible and caring values.

30. *The World Social Situation.*

31. Lin Chew, "Women and Globalization in South East Asia: New Strategies for New Times," *Conscience*, Summer 2006, XXVII(2), 30. Chew also describes the successful efforts of new groups, such as the Domestic Workers Movement of Pune (PSMS) in India and the Sub-Contracting Cleaning Workers (SCCWS) in Hong Kong, to organize housecleaners and other women in the informal economy. These groups are using new strategies, such as forging alliances with other community groups, to improve working conditions for these women, help them with domestic violence and other family problems, and increase their participation in decision making.

32. *The State of the World's Children 2005: Childhood Under Threat.*

33. Interview with Augusto Lopez-Claros, chief economist and director, Global Competitiveness Network, Sept. 28, 2005. For more on the interview and the World Economic Forum's *Global Competitiveness Report 2005–06*, see www. weforum.org/site/homepublic.nsf/Content/Global+Competitiveness+Report+200

5-2006%3A+Interview. For David Korten's most comprehensive work, see *The Great Turning*.

34. See www.un.org/esa/desa/. See also Jan Knippers Black, *Inequity in the Global Village: Recycled Rhetoric and Disposable People* (Bloomfield, Conn.: Kumarian Press, 1999).

35. See www.peopleandplanet.net/.

36. The four "foundation" reports of the Millennium Ecosystem Assessment were released on Jan. 19, 2006. These reports can be purchased through Island Press (www.islandpress.org/books/), and summaries as well as individual chapters can be downloaded from www.millenniumassessment.org. For a brief summary of the findings from these reports, see Werner Fornos, "Homo Sapiens: An Endangered Species?" *POPLINE*, May-June 2005, p. 4.

Chapter 9: Who We Are and Where We Are

1. For more information on Ryan's Well, see www.ryanswell.ca/index.php?option=com_content&task=view&id=20&Itemid=50.

2. For more information on Clara Hale, see www.halehouse.org/biography.html.

3. For example, for sociobiologist Michael Ghiselin, the only motivation for caring behaviors is "man's" selfishness. He writes, "Scratch an 'altruist' and watch a 'hypocrite' bleed. No hint of genuine charity ameliorates our vision of society, once sentimentalism has been laid aside. What passes for cooperation turns out to be a mixture of opportunism and exploitation." See Michael Ghiselin, *The Economy of Nature and the Evolution of Sex* (Berkeley: University of California Press, 1974), 247. For the book that introduced the popular phrase *selfish gene*, see Richard Dawkins, *The Selfish Gene* (New York: Oxford University Press, 1976). For works refuting claims of genetic determinism, see for example, Richard Lewontin, *The Triple Helix: Gene, Organism, and Environment* (Cambridge, Mass. and London: Harvard University Press, 2000); John O'Manique, *The Origins of Justice: The Evolution of Morality, Human Rights, and Law* (Philadelphia: University of Pennsylvania Press, 2002); Hillary Rose and Stephen Rose (eds.), *Alas, Poor Darwin: Arguments Against Evolutionary Psychology* (New York: Harmony Books, 2000); Edward Deci and Richard Ryan, *Intrinsic Motivation and Self-Determination in Human Behavior* (Cambridge, Mass.: Perseus Books, 1985); Andrew W. Collins, Eleanor E. Maccoby, Laurence Steinberg, E. Mavis Hetherington, and Marc H. Bornstein. "Contemporary Research on Parenting: The Case for Nature and Nurture," *American Psychologist*, Feb. 2000, 55(2), 218–232; Perry, Pollard, Blakley, Baker, and Vigilante, "Childhood Trauma"; Steven R. Quartz and Terrence J. Sejnowski, "The Neural Basis of Cognitive Development: A Constructivist Manifesto," *Behavioral and Brain Sciences*, 1997, 20(4), 527–596.

4. Felix Warneken and Michael Tomasello, "Altruistic Helping in Human Infants and Young Chimpanzees," *Science*, Mar. 3, 2006, pp. 1301–1303. Other primates, apes in particular, display humanlike helpfulness, such as the gorilla who rescued a three-year-old boy who fell into her zoo enclosure. This shows that human helpfulness has deep evolutionary roots.

5. James K. Rilling, D. A. Gutman, T. R. Zeh, G. Pagnoni, G. S. Berns, and C. D. Kilts, "A Neural Basis for Social Cooperation," *Neuron*, 2002, 35, 395–405.

6. The study monitored the brains of eighteen pairs of young women playing a classic laboratory game called the Prisoner's Dilemma. The game offers each of two partners the option of defecting (acting solely for their own benefit) or cooperating (acting for mutual benefit).

7. Natalie Angier, "Why We're So Nice: We're Wired to Cooperate," *New York Times*, July 23, 2002. Berns also said that although they chose women for this research because so few brain studies have female subjects, there's no reason to believe the results would be different with men, even though women are socialized to focus more on relationships than men have been.

8. If both players chose to cooperate, each earned $2. If both opted to defect, each earned $1. But if one player defected and the other cooperated, the defector earned $3 and the cooperator nothing. So even though every round offered the possibility of getting an extra dollar by defecting, the motivation of mutualism often trumped the motivation of trying for that extra dollar.

9. These child brides were sometimes as young as eight years old, and their husbands were often men in their forties or fifties. Moreover, these children often became mothers at the age of eleven, and were sometimes considered fair sexual prey for other male members of their husband's household. But this brutal tradition persists to our day, and is still justified on moral and religious grounds. Three recent films that show the misery of Indian child brides are Neeraj Kumar's documentary *Child Marriage* (www.childmarriage.org/), Deepa Mehta's historical *Water* (www.imdb.com/title/tt0240200/ and http://water.mahiram.com/), and Cana Media's documentary *Child Brides* (www.canamedia.com/catalogue_dev_docu.html).

10. Debra Niehoff, *The Biology of Violence: How Understanding the Brain, Behavior, and Environment Can Break the Vicious Cycle of Aggression* (New York: Free Press, 1999), 185.

11. Bruce McEwen, quoted in Niehoff, *The Biology of Violence*, 186.

12. Niehoff, *The Biology of Violence*, 185.

13. I want to emphasize again that not all children born into such environments internalize these emotional and behavioral patterns. Some not only avoid abuse and violence in their own relations but grow up to work against patterns of abuse and violence they find around them. But many more people are affected negatively by early experiences of repression and violence.

14. See, for example, Joan Rockwell, *Fact in Fiction: The Use of Literature in the Systematic Study of Society* (London: Routledge & Kegan Paul, 1974).

15. Sociologist Milton R. Rokeach shows that values can be changed through the introduction of narratives that cause conflict between ostensible or consciously held values such as democracy and equality, and latent or unconsciously held values such as biases against people of different races or social groups. See Milton R. Rokeach, *The Nature of Human Values* (New York: Free Press, 1973).

16. Earlier researchers often cast families and peers as opposing forces vying for influence over a child's behavior. But as Collins, Maccoby, Steinberg, Hetherington, and Bornstein note in their survey of studies of parenting and peer influences ("Contemporary Research on Parenting"), socialization researchers are developing and testing models that examine how parents and peers exert conjoint influence on the developing child and her or his brain development. This research shows that although adolescent involvement in antisocial activity is often influenced significantly by relationships with antisocial peers, the chain of events that leads to antisocial peer groups often begins at home during childhood.

17. Else Frenkel-Brunswick, quoted in D. C. Beardslee and M. Wertheimer (eds.), *Readings in Perception* (New York: Van Nostrand Reinhold, 1958), 676.

18. For cross-cultural evidence confirming this pattern, see DeMeo, "The Origins and Diffusion of Patrism in Saharasia, c. 4000 B.C.E." See also Sanday, *Female Power and Male Dominance*.

19. Perry, Pollard, Blakley, Baker, and Vigilante, "Childhood Trauma."

20. Michael G. Marmot, G. Rose, M. Shipley, and P. J. Hamilton, "Employment Grade and Coronary Heart Disease in British Civil Servants," *Journal of Epidemiological Community Health*, 1978, *3*, 244–249.

21. Richard Wilkinson, *The Affliction of Inequality* (London: Routledge, 1996).

22. Robert Sapolsky, "Sick of Poverty," *Scientific American*, Dec. 2005, *293*(6), 98.

23. See, for example, Layard, *Happiness*.

24. There were intermittent attempts to inject partnership elements, such as the veneration of Mary as the compassionate mother of God and the courtly love and chivalry codes of the troubadours and their female counterparts, the trobaritzes. But for the most part, the Middle Ages conformed to the configuration of the authoritarian, male-dominated, economically inequitable, violent organization of the domination model.

25. In feudal Russia, as late as the mid-nineteenth century, this was common practice, as poignantly reported in the autobiography of the great Russian baritone Fiodor Chaliapin, whose childhood was a nightmare of brutality at the hands of both parents and the tradesmen to whom he was apprenticed. See *Chaliapin: An Autobiography As Told to Maxim Gorky* (Nina Froud and James Hanly, trans.) (New York: Stein and Day, 1967).

26. For accounts of severe child abuse in families, see Raffael Scheck, "Childhood in German Autobiographical Writings, 1740–1820," *Journal of Psychohistory*, Summer 1987, *15*(1), 391–422; Philippe Aries, *Centuries of Childhood: A Social History of Family Life* (Robert Baldick, trans.) (London: Cape, 1962); and Alice Miller, *For Your Own Good: Hidden Cruelty in Child-Rearing and the Roots of Violence* (Hildegarde and Hunter Hannum, trans.) (New York: Farrar, Straus & Giroux, 1983). For an account that focuses more on material conditions, see Frances and Joseph Gies, *Marriage and the Family in the Middle Ages* (New York: Harper & Row, 1987). For a documentation of the practice of child abandonment and the high death rates in orphanages, see John Boswell, *The Kindness of*

Strangers: The Abandonment of Children in Western Europe from Late Antiquity to the Renaissance (New York: Pantheon, 1988). For an account of the focus on pain in Christian mysticism, see Sara Maitland, "Passionate Prayer: Masochistic Images in Women's Experience," in Linda Hurcombe (ed.), *Sex and God: Some Varieties of Women's Religious Experience* (New York: Routledge and Kegan Paul, 1987). For an analysis of some partnership trends in families, see Anthony Giddens, *The Transformation of Intimacy: Sexuality, Love, and Eroticism in Modern Societies* (Stanford, Calif.: Stanford University Press, 1992).

27. See *William Blackstone's Commentaries on the Laws of England* (Oxford: Clarendon Press, 1765) on how the English common law treated women as basically male property.

28. I should add that just having an environmental agency is not enough. As Jane Anne Morris of the Program on Corporations, Law, and Democracy documents in "Sheep in Wolf's Clothing," government regulatory agencies are often pawns in the hands of the powerful corporate interests they were set up to regulate. POCLAD offers many articles, including writings by Richard Grossman, one of the pioneers in the movement to change corporate charters to be socially and environmentally responsible. See www.poclad.org.

29. As Sheldon Rampton and John Stauber show in *Trust Us, We're Experts: How Industry Manipulates Science and Gambles with Your Future* (New York: Putnam, 2000), billions are spent on PR agencies that put the right spin on policies designed to push us back to times when those on top essentially had the freedom to do as they please.

30. See Gates, *Democracy at Risk*.

31. IRS statistics quoted in Sklar, "Carving Up Our Economic Pie."

32. Sklar, "Carving Up Our Economic Pie."

33. See Scheck, "Childhood in German Autobiographical Writings."

34. Of course, women sometimes rule over men, but then they're seen as usurpers, as in the phrases "henpecking wife" and "she's wearing the pants in the family."

35. These "Christian" fundamentalists invoke the teachings of Jesus to fight equality between women and men, claiming it will destroy the family. They ignore the fact that when Jesus preached against divorce it was to protect women, since in his time only men could divorce women, and then by simply saying, "I divorce you," three times, as is still possible under Muslim family law today. We also know from the New Testament that many of the leaders in early Christian communities were women. For example, see Elizabeth Schussler Fiorenza, *In Memory of Her* (New York: Crossroad, 1983).

36. See Hanna Rosin, "A Tough Plan for Raising Children Draws Fire: 'Babywise' Guides Worry Pediatricians and Others," *Washington Post*, Feb. 27, 1999, p. A1, for a harrowing account of the damage done to children and parents by this approach. See also Hanna Rosin, "Critics Question Extreme Childrearing Method," *Washington Post*, reprinted in *Monterey County Herald*, Mar. 1, 1999, p. A10. For example, as the first *Washington Post* article reports: "Start early and

teach your baby 'highchair manners,'" parents are advised in [the 'Babywise'] series of popular books . . . on child rearing. A child as young as 8 months should sit with his hands on the side of his tray or in his lap. To avoid whining and fussing, the baby should learn hand signals to express 'please,' 'thank you' and 'I love you.' If the child disobeys, parents are told, the best thing is a moderate squeeze or swat to the hand. If the baby is older than 18 months, then it's time for 'chastisement' with a flexible instrument, such as a rubber spatula."

37. Michael Milburn and Sheree Conrad, *The Politics of Denial* (Cambridge, Mass.: MIT Press, 1996).

38. The Strategic Values Project survey of attitudes shows that a dramatic rise in the belief that fathers should control their families has occurred since 1992. As Ted Nordhaus and Michael Shellenberger wrote in their summary of the survey: "At a values level, the U.S. is looking more and more like the Deep South while Canada is looking increasingly like Western Europe. Of the more than 107 values that Environics tracks, perhaps no other value indicates as clearly the rightward shift in American life as the one labeled Patriarchy. In 1992, 42 percent of Americans agreed with the statement: "The father of the family is the master of the house." In 2004, 52 percent agreed. In contrast, today less than a third of Canadians agree with that statement, and only 20 percent of Europeans on average do. See Ted Nordhaus and Michael Shellenberger, *The Strategic Values Project*, (2005), 1. See www.thebreakthrough.org/files/Strategic_Values_Overview.pdf.

39. See Eisler, *Sacred Pleasure*, for an analysis of how the metaphor for the domination model is the punitive parent (stereotypically the father) and the metaphor for the partnership model is the nurturing parent (stereotypically the mother). The political scientist George Lakoff also equates liberal psychology with the nurturing parent and conservative psychology with the "strict father."

40. Among the most important early works on these phenomena is the research of psychologist Else Frenkel-Brunswick. See T. W. Adorno, Else Frenkel-Brunswick, Daniel Levinson, and R. Nevitt Stanford, *The Authoritarian Personality* (New York: Wiley, 1964).

41. These six companies are AOL/Time-Warner, Disney, Viacom-CBS-Paramount, Bertelsmann, General Electric, and Rupert Murdoch, whose media empire includes HarperCollins, Twentieth-Century Fox, the Fox Channel, 132 newspapers, twenty-five magazines, and a percentage of *TV Guide*. For details, see Ben Bagdikian, *The Media Monopoly*, 6th ed. (Boston: Beacon Press, 2000). As Bagdikian points out, the media mergers authorized by the 1996 Telecommunications Act have resulted in the most radical consolidation of media control in U.S. history, reversing more than sixty years of communications law. See also Richard McChesney, *Rich Media, Poor Democracy* (New York: New Press, 2000).

42. Smith's own motivation, as we saw in chapter 7, was a caring one: he wanted an economic system that works for the greater good of all.

43. See John Robbins, *Reclaiming Our Health* (Tiburon, Calif.: Kramer, 1996), and Christiane Northrup, *Women's Bodies, Women's Wisdom* (New York: Bantam, 2002).

44. For example, drawing from my research on ancient myths showing that with the shift to a domination system there was also a massive transformation of both religious and secular myths, in *The Chalice and The Blade* and *Sacred Pleasure* I trace the transformation of images and narratives showing women in positions of power to images and narratives where they are subordinate to men. See also Craig Barnes, *In Search of the Lost Feminine: Decoding the Myths That Radically Reshaped Civilization* (Golden, Colo.: Fulcrum Publishing, 2006).

45. For a detailed description of the Covenant, see Michael Lerner, *The Left Hand of God: Taking Back Our Country from the Religious Right* (San Francisco: Harper-SanFrancisco, 2006), particularly chapters 9 to 12. The Spiritual Covenant with America at www.spiritualprogressives.org/article.php?story=covenant begins with a call for policies that support partnership families, including legislation, tax policies, budgets, and social programs that support our capacities to be loving and caring for others.

46. As Marie Cocco writes about one of these companies in "Levi's Deserve a Teen's Support" (*Newsday* reprinted in *Monterey Herald*, Mar. 3, 1999, p. 7A), Levi-Strauss was "the first company to write a code of conduct for its network of subcontractors around the globe" and one of the few companies to worry "whether a 10-year-old girl in Mexico is getting a warped spine and going blind because she is stitching jeans all day and into the night."

47. See http://alt-e.blogspot.com/2004/09/germany-leads-way-using-energy-tariffs.html and www.germanyinfo.org/relaunch/info/publications/infocus/environment/ renew. html. See also Staffan Bengtsson, "Sweden's Renewable Energy Resources." For a good energy overview, see Michael Parfit, "Where on Earth Can Our Energy-Hungry Society Turn to Replace Oil, Coal, and Natural Gas?" *National Geographic*, Aug. 2005.

Chapter 10: The Caring Revolution

1. For an analysis of this issue, see Stephen A. Zarlenga, *The Lost Science of Money: The Mythology of Money—The Story of Power* (Valatie, N.Y.: American Monetary Institute Charitable Trust, 2002). For a look at how money takes over lives, see Lynne Twist, *The Soul of Money: Transforming Your Relationship with Money and Life* (New York: Norton, 2003).

2. See H. Anisman, M. D. Zaharia, M. J. Meaney, and Z. Merali, "Do Early-Life Events Permanently Alter Behavioral and Hormonal Responses to Stressors?" *International Journal of Developmental Neuroscience*, 1998, *16*, 149–164; Riane Eisler and Daniel S. Levine, "Nurture, Nature, and Caring: We Are Not Prisoners of Our Genes," *Brain and Mind*, 2002, *3*(1), 9–52; W. T. Greenough, C. S. Wallace, A. Alcantara, B. J. Anderson, N. Hawrylak, A. M. Sirevaag, I. J. Wiler, and G. Withers, "Development of the Brain: Experience Affects the Structure of Neurons, Glia, and Blood Vessels," in N. J. Anastasiow and S. Harel (eds.), *At-Risk Infants: Interventions, Families, and Research* (Baltimore: Paul H. Brookes, 1993); J. P. Henry and S. Wang, "Effects of Early Stress on Adult Affiliative Behavior," *Psychoneuroendocrinology*, 1998, *23*, 863–875.

3. Compared to the United States, China now consumes nearly twice as much meat (67 million tons compared with 39 million tons) and more than twice as much steel (258 million to 104 million tons).

4. Lester R. Brown, *Plan B 2.0: Rescuing a Planet Under Stress and a Civilization in Trouble* (New York: W.W. Norton, 2006).

5. Brown, *Plan B 2.0.*

6. Brown quoted in Jim Lobe, "China's Upward Mobility Strains World Resources," *Energy Bulletin*, Mar. 9, 2005.

7. See, for example, Vandana Shiva, *Water Wars* (Cambridge, Mass.: South End Press, 2000), for a discussion of the privatization of water.

8. For a review of these and other important developments, see Hazel Henderson, "21st Century Strategies for Sustainability," *Foresight*, Feb. 2006.

9. See http://swz.salary.com/momsalarywizard/htmls/mswl_momcenter.html. Salary.com used information from *Dream Job: Stay at Home*, by Regina O'Brien, and *Working Moms* to determine the top ten jobs that make up a mother's job description, from janitor to teacher to CEO and psychologist.

10. See Duncan Ironmonger, "Counting Outputs, Inputs, and Caring Labor: Estimating Gross Household Product," Fall 1993, *Feminist Economics*, 2(3), 37–64.

11. A report by Joseph Stiglitz, who won a Nobel prize for economics in 2001, and Linda Bilmes, a Harvard budget expert, estimated that the cost of the Iraq war is likely to be between $1 trillion and $2 trillion. See Wilson, "Iraq War Could Cost U.S. Over $2 Trillion." *The Guardian/UK*, Jan. 7, 2006.

12. For data from neuroscience, see Perry, Pollard, Blakley, Baker, and Vigilante, "Childhood Trauma." For data from psychology, see Penelope Leach, *Your Baby and Child* (New York: Knopf, 1997). Popular magazines such as *Child* and *Parenting* also highlight the ineffectiveness of dominator child rearing and offer partnership alternatives. For a pioneering book on the importance of caring touch, see Ashley Montagu, *Touching: The Human Significance of the Skin*, 3rd ed. (New York: Harper & Row, 1986). On the importance of teaching parenting, see also Nel Noddings, *Critical Lessons: What Our Schools Should Teach* (Cambridge, Cambridge University Press, 2006).

13. Eisler, Loye, and Norgaard, *Women, Men, and the Global Quality of Life.*

14. Ronald F. Inglehart, Pippa Norris, and Christian Welzel, "Gender Equality and Democracy," *Comparative Sociology*, 2002, 1(3/4), 321–346. Based on their findings, they write, "It is not surprising to find that gender issues constitute such a central component—arguably, *the* most central component—of value change in postindustrial societies."

15. Inglehart, Norris, and Welzel, "Gender Equality and Democracy," 330.

16. Ann Crittenden, *The Price of Motherhood: Why the Most Important Job in the World Is Still the Least Valued* (New York: Metropolitan Books, 2001).

17. See, for example, Bina Agarwal, *A Field of One's Own: Gender and Land Rights in South Asia* (Cambridge: Cambridge University Press, 1995), and Jane S. Jaquette and Gale Summerfield (eds.), *Women and Gender Equity in Development Theory and Practice: Institutions, Resources, and Mobilization* (Durham, N.C.: Duke University Press, 2006).

18. See Bruce and Lloyd, "Finding the Ties That Bind."

19. There has been only a marginal increase in female representation rates after decades of work in national assemblies or parliaments around the world, from 10.9 percent in 1975 to 16.3 percent in 2005 (New York: U.N. Commission on the Status of Women, Statement on International Women's Day, 2006).

20. See Raffi Cavoukian and Sharna Olfman (eds.), *Child Honoring: How to Turn This World Around* (New York: Praeger, 2006).

21. See Riane Eisler, "Toward an Integrated Theory of Human Rights," *Human Rights Quarterly*, 1987, 9(3), 287–308, and Riane Eisler, "Human Rights and Violence: Integrating the Private and Public Spheres," in Lester Kurtz and Jennifer Turpin (eds.), *The Web of Violence* (Urbana: University of Illinois Press, 1996).

22. For an analysis of this, see Eisler, Loye, and Norgaard, *Women, Men, and the Global Quality of Life*.

23. Lauralee Alben, *Navigating a Sea Change*. See www.albendesign.com.

24. As Margaret Wheatley points out, there is great power in conversation. See Margaret Wheatley, *Turning to One Another: Simple Conversations to Restore Hope to the Future* (San Francisco: Berrett-Koehler, 2002).

25. There is some movement in this direction. For example, the Bainbridge Graduate Institute MBA program (see www.bgiedu.org/) combines traditional approaches with a focus on social and environmental responsibility. The Presidio School of Management in San Francisco offers another such program (see www.presidiomba.org/). In addition, MBA programs at some traditional universities are also moving in this direction—for example at the Weatherhead School of Management at Case Western Reserve University (http://weatherhead.case.edu/mba/) and the Stephen M. Ross Business School at the University of Michigan (www.bus.umich.edu/).

26. Caring economics will be explored not only in the theoretical but also in the practical spaces of lived reality through conferences and other meetings that bring together academics, policymakers, practitioners, and other concerned citizens. For general information, see www.partnershipway.org.

27. Those of us living in the United States can lobby our senators to ratify the United Nations Convention to Eliminate All Forms of Discrimination Against Women (CEDAW) and the United Nations Convention on the Rights of the Child, which have been ratified by almost every other nation except the United States. Grassroots organization packets and other information on CEDAW can be obtained from the National Committee on UN/CEDAW; 310/271-8087. For information on the Convention on the Rights of the Child, see www.unicef.org/crc/.

28. I co-founded an organization to bring together spiritual and religious leaders to take a strong stand against intimate violence: the Spiritual Alliance to Stop Intimate Violence (SAIV). See www.saiv.net.

29. For a discussion of this, see Noddings, *The Challenge to Care in Our Schools*.

30. See David Loye (ed.), *The Great Adventure: Toward a Fully Human Theory of Evolution* (Albany: State University of New York Press, 2004); David Loye, *Darwin's Lost Theory: Who We Really Are and Where We're Going* (Carmel, Calif: Benjamin Franklin Press, 2007); David Loye, *Measuring Evolution: A Guide to the Health and Wealth of Nations* (Carmel, Calif.: Benjamin Franklin Press, 2007); and David Loye, *Darwin's Lost Theory of Love* (iuniverse.com, 2000). See also John O'Manique, *The Origins of Justice: The Evolution of Morality, Human Rights, and Law* (Philadelphia: University of Pennsylvania Press, 2003); and Ervin Laszlo, *The Creative Cosmos* (Edinburgh: Floris Books, 1993).

31. Eisler, *Tomorrow's Children*. See also David Grossman and Gloria Degaetano, *Stop Teaching Our Kids to Kill: A Call to Action Against TV, Movie and Video Game Violence* (New York: Crown, 1999).

BIBLIOGRAPHY

Achieving ICPD Commitments for Abortion Care in Latin America: The Unfinished Agenda. Chapel Hill, N.C.: Ipas, 2005.

Afshar, Hale (ed.). *Women, Development, and Survival in the Third World.* New York: Longman, 1991.

Adorno, T. W., Else Frenkel-Brunswick, Daniel Levinson, and R. Nevitt Stanford. *The Authoritarian Personality.* New York: John Wiley, 1964.

Agarwal, Bina. *A Field of One's Own: Gender and Land Rights in South Asia.* Cambridge: Cambridge University Press, 1995.

Albelda, Randy. *Lost Ground: Welfare Reform, Poverty, and Beyond.* Cambridge, Mass.: South End Press, 2002.

Angier, Natalie. "Why We're So Nice: We're Wired to Cooperate," *New York Times,* July 23, 2002.

Anisman, H., M. D. Zaharia, M. J. Meaney, and Z. Merali. "Do Early-Life Events Permanently Alter Behavioral and Hormonal Responses to Stressors?" *International Journal of Developmental Neuroscience,* 1998, *16,* 149–164.

Aries, Philippe. *Centuries of Childhood: A Social History of Family Life.* (Robert Baldick, trans.). London: Cape, 1962.

Aristotle. *Aristotle's Politics* (Benjamin Jowett, trans.). New York: Modern Library, 1943.

Aslaksen, Julie, and Charlotte Koren. "Unpaid Household Work and the Distribution of Extended Income: The Norwegian Experience," *Feminist Economics,* Fall 1996, 2(3), 65–80.

Avery, Christine, and Diane Zabel. *The Flexible Workplace: A Sourcebook of Information and Research.* Westport, Conn.: Quorum Books, 2000.

Bagdikian, Ben. *The Media Monopoly* (6th ed.). Boston: Beacon Press, 2000.

Barnes, Craig. *In Search of the Lost Feminine: Decoding the Myths That Radically Reshaped Civilization.* Golden, Colo.: Fulcrum, 2006.

Barry, David S. "Growing Up Violent: Decades of Research Link Screen Mayhem with Increase in Aggressive Behavior," *Media and Values,* Summer 1993, 62, 8–11.

Baumeister, Roy F. "How the Self Became a Problem: A Psychological Review of Historical Research," *Journal of Personality and Social Psychology,* 1987, 52(1), 163–176.

Beardslee, David C., and Michael Wertheimer. *Readings in Perception*. Princeton, N.J.: Van Nostrand Reinhold, 1958.

Bebel, August. *Women and Socialism*. New York: Schocken, 1971. (Originally published 1879)

Black, Jan Knippers. *Inequity in the Global Village: Recycled Rhetoric and Disposable People*. Bloomfield, Conn.: Kumarian Press, 1999.

Blackstone, William. *Commentaries on the Laws of England*. Oxford: Clarendon Press, 1765.

Blades, Joan, and Kristin Rowe-Finkbeiner. *The Motherhood Manifesto*. New York: Nation Books, 2006.

Blakney, R. B. (ed. and trans.). *The Way of Life: Tao Te Ching*. New York: Mentor, 1951.

Bleier, Ruth (ed.). *Feminist Approaches to Science*. New York: Pergamon Press, 1988.

Blumberg, Rae Lesser. "A Women-in-Development Natural Environment in Guatemala: The Alcoa Agribusiness Project in 1980 and 1985." Mimeo report, 1986. Cited in Daisy Dwyer and Judith Bruce (eds.), *A Home Divided: Women and Income in the Third World*. Stanford, Calif.: Stanford University Press, 1988.

Boserup, Ester. *Women's Role in Economic Development*. London: Allen and Unwin, 1970.

Boswell, John. *The Kindness of Strangers*. New York: Pantheon, 1988.

Brandt, Barbara. *Whole Life Economics: Revaluing Daily Life*. Philadelphia: New Society Publishers, 1995.

Brown, Lester R. *Plan B 2.0: Rescuing a Planet Under Stress and a Civilization in Trouble*. New York: W.W. Norton, 2006.

Bruce, Judith, and Cynthia B. Lloyd. "Finding the Ties That Bind: Beyond Headship and Household," in Lawrence Haddad, John Hoddinott, and Harold Alderman (eds.), *Intrahousehold Resources Allocation in Developing Countries: Methods, Models, and Policy*. Baltimore: International Food Policy Research Institute and Johns Hopkins University Press, 1997.

Bruce, Judith, Cynthia B. Lloyd, and A. Leonard. *Families in Focus*. New York: Population Council, 1995.

Burggraf, Shirley. *The Feminine Economy and the Economic Man: Reviving the Role of Family in the Post-Industrial Age*. New York: Perseus Books, 1999.

Burud, Sandra, and Marie Tumolo. *Leveraging the New Human Capital*. Mountain View, Calif.: Davies-Black, 2004.

Cadoret, Remi J., T. W. O'Gorman, E. Troughton, and E. Heywood. "Alcoholism and Antisocial Personality. Interrelationships, Genetic and Environmental Factors," *Archives of General Psychiatry*, 1985, 42, 161–167.

Cahn, Edgar. *No More Throwaway People: The Co-Production Imperative.* Washington, D.C.: Essential Books, 2004.

Cai, Junsheng. "Myth and Reality: The Projection of Gender Relations in Prehistoric China," in Yiayin Min (ed.), *The Chalice and The Blade in Chinese Culture: Gender Relations and Social Models.* Beijing: China Social Sciences Publishing House, 1995.

Cameron, Kim, Jane Dutton, and Robert E. Quinn (eds.). *Positive Organizational Scholarship.* San Francisco: Berrett-Koehler, 2003.

Caspi, Avshalom, Joseph McClay, Terrie E. Moffitt, Jonathan Mill, Judy Martin, Ian W. Craig, Alan Taylor, and Richie Poulton. "Role of Genotype in the Cycle of Violence in Maltreated Children," *Science,* Aug. 2002, *297*(5582), 851–854.

Castell, Aubery. *An Introduction to Modern Philosophy.* New York: Macmillan, 1946.

Cavanagh, John. (ed.). *Alternatives to Economic Globalization: A Better World Is Possible.* San Francisco: Berrett-Koehler, 2002.

Cavoukian, Raffi, and Sharna Olfman. (eds.). *Child Honoring: How to Turn This World Around.* New York: Praeger, 2006.

Centerwall, Brandon, M.D. "Television and Violence: The Scale of the Problem and Where to Go from Here," *Journal of the American Medical Association,* June 1992, *267,* 3059–3063.

Chaliapin: An Autobiography as Told to Maxim Gorky. (Nina Froud and James Hanly, trans.). New York: Stein and Day, 1967.

Chang, Kenneth. "Oceans Turning Acidic, Scientists Say," *New York Times News Service,* reprinted in *Monterey County Herald,* July 1, 2005, p. A8.

Chew, Lin. "Women and Globalization in South East Asia: New Strategies for New Times," *Conscience,* Summer 2006, *XXVII*(2), 30–32.

Child Health USA 2004. Rockville, Md.: U.S. Department of Health and Human Services, Health Resources and Services Administration, Maternal and Child Health Bureau, 2004.

Chisholm, K. "A Three-Year Follow-Up of Attachment and Indiscriminate Friendliness in Children Adopted from Romanian Orphanages," *Child Development,* 1998, *69,* 1092–1106.

Choi, Charles Q. "Transistor Flow Control: Forget Valves—Controlling Fluids with Electric Fields," *Scientific American,* Oct. 2005, *293*(4), 26.

Cleveland, Gordon, and Michael Krashinsky. *The Benefits and Costs of Good Child Care: The Economic Rationale for Public Investment in Young Children—A Policy Study.* Scarborough: University of Toronto, Department of Economics, Mar. 1998.

Clever, Linda H., and Gilbert S. Omenn. "Hazards for Health Care Workers," *Annual Review of Public Health,* 1988, *9,* 273–303.

Cocco, Marie. "Levi's Deserve a Teen's Support," *Newsday* reprinted in *Monterey Herald*, Mar. 3, 1999, p. 7A.

Collins, Andrew W., Eleanor E. Maccoby, Laurence Steinberg, E. Mavis Hetherington, and Marc H. Bornstein. "Contemporary Research on Parenting: The Case for Nature and Nurture," *American Psychologist*, Feb. 2000, 55(2), 218–232.

Coltrane, Scott. "Father-Child Relationships and the Status of Women: A Cross-Cultural Study," *American Journal of Sociology*, Mar. 1988, 93(5).

Cooperrider, David L., and Suresh Srivastva. "Appreciative Inquiry in Organizational Life," *Research in Organizational Change and Development*, 1987, 1, 129–169.

Crittenden, Ann. *The Price of Motherhood: Why the Most Important Job in the World Is Still the Least Valued.* New York: Metropolitan Books, 2001.

Currie, Janet, and Erdal Tekin. "Does Child Abuse Cause Crime?" *IZA Discussion Papers 2063.* Bonn, Germany: Institute for the Study of Labor (IZA), 2006.

Daly, Herman E., and John B. Cobb. *For the Common Good : Redirecting the Economy Toward Community, the Environment, and a Sustainable Future* (2nd ed.). Boston: Beacon Press, 1994.

Dawkins, Richard. *The Selfish Gene.* New York: Oxford University Press, 1976.

de Caritat, Antoine Nicolas, Marquis de Condorcet. "On the Admission of Women to the Rights of Citizenship," in Lynn Hunt (trans. and ed.), *The French Revolution and Human Rights: A Brief Documentary History.* Boston/New York: Bedford/St. Martin's Press, 1996. (Originally published July 1790)

Deci, Edward, and Richard Ryan. *Intrinsic Motivation and Self-Determination in Human Behavior.* Cambridge, Mass.: Perseus Books, 1985.

De Graaf, John. *Take Back Your Time: Fighting Overwork and Time Poverty in America.* San Francisco: Berrett-Koehler, 2003.

DeMeo, James. "The Origins and Diffusion of Patrism in Saharasia, c. 4000 B.C.E.: Evidence for a Worldwide, Climate-Linked Geographical Pattern in Human Behavior," *World Futures*, 1991, 30(2), 247–271.

de Pizan, Christine. *The Book of the City of Ladies* (Earl Jeffrey Richards, trans.). New York: Persea Press, 1982.

De Soto, Hernando, *The Mystery of Capital.* New York: Basic Books, 2003.

Domhoff, G. William. (2005). *Who Rules America? Power, Politics, & Social Change* (5th ed.). New York: McGraw-Hill.

Dutton, Jane. *Energize Your Workplace.* San Francisco: Jossey-Bass, 2003.

Dutton, Jane, and Emily Heaphy. "The Power of High-Quality Connections at Work," in Kim Cameron, Jane Dutton, and Robert E. Quinn (eds.), *Positive Organizational Scholarship.* San Francisco: Berrett-Koehler, 2003.

Dutton, Jane, Jacoba Lilius, and Jason Kanov. "The Transformative Potential of Compassion at Work," presentation at Weatherhead School of Management, Case Western Reserve University, Cincinnati, Aug. 2003.

Dwyer, Daisy, and Judith Bruce (eds.). *A Home Divided: Women and Income in the Third World.* Stanford, Calif.: Stanford University Press, 1988.

Edwards, Valerie J., George W. Holden, Vincent J. Felitti, and Robert F. Anda. "Relationship Between Multiple Forms of Childhood Maltreatment and Adult Mental Health in Community Respondents: Results from the Adverse Childhood Experiences Study," *American Journal of Psychiatry*, Aug. 2003, *160*,1453–1460.

Eisler, Riane. *Dissolution: No-Fault Divorce, Marriage, and the Future of Women.* New York: McGraw-Hill, 1977.

Eisler, Riane. "Toward an Integrated Theory of Human Rights," *Human Rights Quarterly*, Aug. 1987, *9*(3), 287–308.

Eisler, Riane. *The Chalice and The Blade: Our History, Our Future.* San Francisco: Harper & Row, 1987.

Eisler, Riane. "Technology, Gender, and History: Toward a Nonlinear Model of Social Evolution," in Ervin Laszlo, Ignazio Masulli, Robert Artigiani, and Vilmos Csanyi (eds.), *The Evolution of Cognitive Maps: New Paradigms for the Twenty-First Century.* Langhorne, Penn.: Gordon and Breach Science Publishers, 1993.

Eisler, Riane. *Sacred Pleasure: Sex, Myth, and the Politics of the Body.* San Francisco: HarperCollins, 1995.

Eisler, Riane. "Human Rights and Violence: Integrating the Private and Public Spheres," in Lester Kurtz and Jennifer Turpin (eds.), *The Web of Violence.* Urbana: University of Illinois Press, 1996.

Eisler, Riane. "Cultural Transformation Theory: A New Paradigm for History," in Johan Galtung and Sohail Inayatullah (eds.), *Macrohistory and Macrohistorians.* Westport, Conn.: Praeger, 1997.

Eisler, Riane. *Tomorrow's Children: A Blueprint for Partnership Education in the 21st Century.* Boulder, Colo.: Westview Press, 2000.

Eisler, Riane. *The Power of Partnership: Seven Relationships That Will Change Your Life.* Novato, Calif.: New World Library, 2002.

Eisler, Riane. "Culture, Technology, and Domination/Partnership," in David Loye (ed.), *The Great Adventure.* Albany: State University of New York Press, 2003.

Eisler, Riane. "Spare the Rod," *YES: A Magazine of Positive Futures*, Winter 2005, pp. 30–32.

Eisler, Riane, and Daniel S. Levine. "Nurture, Nature, and Caring: We Are Not Prisoners of Our Genes," *Brain and Mind*, 2002, *3*(1), 9–52.

Eisler, Riane, David Loye, and Kari Norgaard. *Women, Men, and the Global Quality of Life.* Pacific Grove, Calif.: Center for Partnership Studies, 1995.

Elkins, Paul. (ed.). *The Living Economy.* New York: Routledge & Kegan Paul, 1986.

Encyclopedia of World Problems and Human Potential (4th ed.). Brussels: Union of International Associations, 1994–95.

Engels, Frederick. *The Condition of the Working Class in England*. London: Panther Books, 1969. (Originally published 1845)

Eron, Leonard D., and L. Rowell Huesmann. *Advances in the Study of Aggression*. Orlando: Academic Press, 1984.

Evan, William M. "An Organization-Set Model of Interorganizational Relations," in Matthew Tuite, Roger Chisholm, and Michael Radnor (eds.), *Interorganizational Decision Making*. Chicago: Aldine, 1972.

Ferber, Marianne A., and Julie A. Nelson (eds.). *Beyond Economic Man: Feminist Theory and Economics*. Chicago: University of Chicago Press, 1993.

Fiorenza, Elizabeth Schussler. *In Memory of Her*. New York: Crossroad, 1983.

Flannery, Tim. *The Weather Makers: How Man Is Changing the Climate and What It Means for Life on Earth*. New York: Atlantic Monthly Press, 2006.

Folbre, Nancy. "Socialism, Feminist and Scientific," in Marianne A. Ferber and Julie A. Nelson (eds.), *Beyond Economic Man: Feminist Theory and Economics*. Chicago: University of Chicago Press, 1993.

Folbre, Nancy. *The Invisible Heart: Economics and Family Values*. New York: New Press, 2001.

Fornos, Werner. "Homo Sapiens: An Endangered Species?" *POPLINE*, May-June 2005, p. 4.

Frank, Andre Gunder. *Capitalism and Underdevelopment in Latin America*. London: Penguin, 1971.

Fredrickson, Barbara. "Positive Emotions and Upward Spirals in Organizations," in Kim Cameron, Jane Dutton, and Robert E. Quinn (eds.), *Positive Organizational Scholarship*. San Francisco: Berrett-Kohler, 2003.

Fry, Ronald, Frank Barrett, Jane Seiling, and Diana Whitney (eds.). *Appreciative Inquiry and Organization Transformation: Reports from the Field*. Westport, Conn.: Quorum Books, 2002.

Galbraith, John Kenneth. *Economics & the Public Purpose*. Boston: Houghton Mifflin, 1973,

Garreau, Joel. *Radical Evolution: The Promise and Peril of Enhancing Our Minds, Our Bodies, and What It Means to Be Human*. New York: Doubleday, 2005.

Gates, Jeff. *Democracy at Risk: Rescuing Main Street from Wall Street*. Cambridge, Mass.: Perseus Publishing, 2000.

Ghiselin, Michael. *The Economy of Nature and the Evolution of Sex*. Berkeley: University of California Press, 1974.

Giddens, Anthony. *The Transformation of Intimacy: Sexuality, Love, and Eroticism in Modern Societies*. Stanford, Calif.: Stanford University Press, 1992.

Gies, Frances, and Joseph Gies. *Marriage and the Family in the Middle Ages*. New York: Harper & Row, 1987.

Gilligan, Carol. *In a Different Voice: Psychological Theory and Women's Development*. Cambridge, Mass.: Harvard University Press, 1982.

Gilman, Charlotte Perkins. *Economics and Women*. Berkeley: University of California Press, 1998. (Originally published 1898)

Gimbutas, Marija. *The Goddesses and Gods of Old Europe*. Berkeley: University of California Press, 1982.

Global Trends 2015: A Dialogue About the Future with Nongovernment Experts. Washington, D.C.: National Intelligence Council (U.S. Central Intelligence Agency), Dec. 2000.

Goleman, Daniel, Richard Boyatzis, and Annie McKee. *Primal Leadership: Realizing the Power of Emotional Intelligence*. Cambridge, Mass.: Harvard Business School Press, 2002.

Gornick, Janet C., and Marcia K. Meyers. *Families That Work: Policies for Reconciling Parenthood and Employment*. New York: Russell Sage Foundation, 2003.

Greenough, W. T., C. S. Wallace, A. A. Alcantara, B. J. Anderson, N. Hawrylak, A. M. Sirevaag, I. J. Wiler, and G. Withers (1993). "Development of the Brain: Experience Affects the Structure of Neurons, Glia, and Blood Vessels," in N. J. Anastasiow and S. Harel (eds.), *At-Risk Infants: Interventions, Families, and Research*. Baltimore: Paul H. Brookes, 1993.

Griffith, Brian. *The Gardens of Their Dreams: Desertification and Culture in World History*. London and New York: Zed Books, 2003.

Grossman, David, and Gloria Degaetano. *Stop Teaching Our Kids to Kill: A Call to Action Against TV, Movie, and Video Game Violence*. New York: Crown, 1999.

Harrington, Mona. *Care and Equality: Inventing a New Family Politics*. New York: Knopf, 1999.

Hartmann, Heidi. "Thirty Years from Today: Visions of Economic Justice," *Dollars & Sense*, Nov. 1, 2004.

Hartmann, Thom. *Unequal Protection: The Rise of Corporate Dominance and the Theft of Human Rights*. New York: Rodale Books, 2004.

Hawken, Paul, Amory Lovins, and L. Hunter Lovins. *Natural Capitalism: Creating the Next Industrial Revolution*. Boston: Back Bay Books, 2000.

Hawkes, Jacquetta. *Dawn of the Gods: Minoan and Mycenaean Origins of Greece*. New York: Random House, 1968.

Heilbroner, Robert. *The Worldly Philosophers: The Lives, Times, and Ideas of the Great Economic Thinkers* (rev. 7th ed.). New York: Simon & Schuster, 1999.

Heim, Christine, D. Jeffrey Newport, Andrew H. Miller, and Charles B. Nemeroff. "Long-Term Neuroendocrine Effects of Childhood of Maltreatment," *JAMA*, 2000, *284*, 2321.

Held, Virginia (ed.). *Justice and Care: Essential Readings in Feminist Ethics*. Boulder, Colo.: Westview Press, 1995.

Henderson, Hazel. "Changing Paradigms and Indicators: Implementing Equitable, Sustainable and Participatory Development," in Jo Marie Griesgraber and Bernhard G. Gunter (eds.), *The World Bank: Lending on a Global Scale (Rethinking Bretton Woods)*. Vol. 2. London: Pluto Press, 1996.

Henderson, Hazel. *Beyond Globalization*. Bloomfield, Conn.: Kumarian Press, 1999.

Henderson, Hazel. *Ethical Markets: Greening the Global Economy*. White River Junction, Vt.: Chelsea Green Publishing, 2006.

Henderson, Hazel. "21st Century Strategies for Sustainability," *Foresight*, Feb. 2006.

Henry, J. P. and S. Wang. "Effects of Early Stress on Adult Affiliative Behavior," *Psychoneuroendocrinology*, 1998, 23, 863–875.

Heymann, Jody. *Forgotten Families: Ending the Growing Crisis Confronting Children and Working Parents in the Global Economy*. New York: Oxford University Press, 2006.

Hightower, Jim. *There's Nothing in the Middle of the Road But Yellow Stripes and Dead Armadillos*. New York: HarperCollins, 1998.

Hodder, Ian. "Women and Men at Catalhoyuk," *Scientific American*, Jan. 2004, pp. 77–83.

Hoddinott, John, and Lawrence Haddad. "Understanding How Resources Are Allocated Within Households," presentation at the Canadian Economic Association meeting, Ottawa, Canada, 1993.

Human Development Report 1990. United Nations Development Programme (UNDP). New York: Oxford University Press, 1990.

Human Development Report 1995. United Nations Development Programme (UNDP). New York: Oxford University Press, 1995.

Human Development Report 2003. United Nations Development Programme (UNDP). New York: Oxford University Press, 2004.

Hyman, Prue. *Women and Economics: A New Zealand Feminist Perspective*. Wellington, New Zealand: Bridget Williams Books, 1996.

Inglehart, Ronald. *Modernization and Postmodernization: Cultural, Economic, and Political Change in 43 Societies*. Princeton, N.J.: Princeton University Press, 1997.

Inglehart, Ronald F., Pippa Norris, and Christian Welzel. "Gender Equality and Democracy," *Comparative Sociology*, 2002, 1(3/4), 321–346.

Ironmonger, Duncan. "Counting Outputs, Inputs, and Caring Labor: Estimating Gross Household Product," *Feminist Economics*, Fall 1996, 2(3), 37–64.

Isen, Alice. "Positive Affect, "Cognitive Processes, and Social Behavior," *Advances in Experimental Social Psychology*, 1987, 20, 203–253.

Jaggar, Alison M. (ed.). *Living with Contradictions: Controversies in Feminist Social Ethics*. Boulder, Colo.: Westview Press, 1994.

Jain, Devaki, and Nirmala Banerjee (eds.). *The Tyranny of the Household: Women in Poverty, Investigative Essays on Women's Work*. New Delhi: Shakti Books, 1985.

James, William. *Principles of Psychology*. Mineola, N.Y.: Dover Publications, 1955. (Originally published 1890)

Jaquette, Jane S. *The Women's Movement in Latin America: Participation and Democracy* (2nd ed.). Boulder, Colo.: Westview Press, 1994.

Jaquette, Jane S., and Gale Summerfield (eds.). *Women and Gender Equity in Development Theory and Practice: Institutions, Resources, and Mobilization*. Durham, N.C.: Duke University Press, 2006.

Jennings, Ann L. "Public or Private? Institutional Economics and Feminism," in Marianne A. Ferber and Julie A. Nelson (eds.), *Beyond Economic Man*. Chicago: University of Chicago Press, 1993.

Joy, Bill. "Why the Future Doesn't Need Us," *Wired*, Apr. 2000.

Kantor, Rosabeth Moss. *When Giants Learn to Dance: Mastering the Challenge of Strategy, Management, and Careers in the 1990s*. New York: Random House, 1991.

Kaul, Inge, Pedro Conceicao, Katell Le Goulven, and Ronald Mendoza (eds.). *Providing Public Goods*. New York: Oxford University Press, 2003.

Kaul, Inge, Isabelle Grunberg, and Marc Stern. *Global Public Goods: International Cooperation in the 21st Century*. New York: Oxford University Press, 1999.

Keller, Evelyn Fox. *Reflections on Gender and Science*. New Haven, Conn.: Yale University Press, 1985.

Kelly, Marjorie. "Reshaping the Language of Business: How New Language Helps Make the Case for Ethics," *Business Ethics*, Winter 2005, p. 6.

Keuls, Eva. *The Reign of the Phallus*. Berkeley: University of California Press, 1985.

Kluger, Jeffrey. "The Tipping Point," *Time*, Apr. 3, 2006.

Kolbert, Elizabeth. *Field Notes from a Catastrophe: Man, Nature, and Climate Change*. London: Bloomsbury Publishing, 2006.

Kollin, Susan. *Nature's State*. Chapel Hill: University of North Carolina Press, 2001.

Koonz, Claudia. "Mothers in the Fatherland: Women in Nazi Germany," in Renate Bridenthal and Claudia Koonz (eds.), *Becoming Visible: Women in European History*. Boston: Houghton Mifflin, 1977.

Korten, David C. *The Post-Corporate World: Life After Capitalism*. San Francisco: Berrett-Koehler and West Hartford, Conn.: Kumarian Press, 1999.

Korten, David C. *When Corporations Rule the World* (2nd ed.). Bloomfield, Conn.: Kumerian Press and San Francisco: Berrett-Koehler, 2001.

Korten, David C. *The Great Turning: From Empire to Earth Community*. San Francisco: Berrett-Koehler, 2006.

Kristof, Nicholas D. "As Asian Economies Shrink, Women are Squeezed Out," *New York Times*, June 11, 1998.

Krugman, Paul. *The Great Unraveling: Losing Our Way in the New Century*. New York: W.W. Norton, 2004.

Laszlo, Ervin. *The Creative Cosmos*. Edinburgh, Scotland: Floris Books, 1993.

Layard, Richard. *Happiness: Lessons from a New Science*. New York: Penguin, 2005.

Leach, Penelope. *Your Baby and Child*. New York: Knopf, 1997.

Lerner, Gerda. *The Creation of Feminist Consciousness: From the Middle Ages to Eighteen-Seventy*. New York: Oxford University Press, 1993.

Lerner, Michael. *The Left Hand of God: Taking Back our Country from the Religious Right*. San Francisco: Harper San Francisco, 2006.

Lewontin, Richard. *The Triple Helix: Gene, Organism, and Environment*. Cambridge, Mass., and London: Harvard University Press, 2000.

Linden, Eugene. *The Winds of Change: Climate, Weather and the Destruction of Civilizations*. New York: Simon & Schuster, 2006.

Lindsey, Linda L. *Gender Roles: A Sociological Perspective* (2nd ed.). Englewood Cliffs, N.J.: Prentice Hall, 1994.

Linsenmaier, Joan A. W., and Camille B. Wortman. "Attitudes Toward Workers and Toward Their Work: More Evidence That Sex Makes a Difference," *Journal of Applied Social Psychology*, Aug. 1979, 9(4).

Lobe, Jim. "China's Upward Mobility Strains World Resources," *Energy Bulletin*, Mar. 9, 2005.

Loye, David. *Darwin's Lost Theory of Love*. New York: iUniverse, 2000.

Loye, David (ed.). *The Great Adventure: Toward a Fully Human Theory of Evolution*. Albany: State University of New York Press, 2004.

Loye, David. *Darwin's Lost Theory: Who We Really Are and Where We're Going*. Carmel, Calif.: Benjamin Franklin Press, 2007.

Loye, David. *Measuring Evolution: A Guide to the Health and Wealth of Nations*. Carmel, Calif.: Benjamin Franklin Press, 2007.

Loye, David, Roderik Gorney, and Gary Steele. "Effects of Television: An Experimental Field Study," *Journal of Communications*, 1977, 27(3), 206–216.

Luce, J. V. *The End of Atlantis*. London: Thames & Hudson, 1968.

Lux, Kenneth. *Adam Smith's Mistake: How a Moral Philosopher Invented Economics and Ended Morality*. Boston: Shambhala, 1990.

Maitland, Sara. "Passionate Prayer: Masochistic Images in Women's Experience," in Linda Hurcombe (ed.), *Sex and God: Some Varieties of Women's Religious Experience*. New York: Routledge and Kegan Paul, 1987.

Marinatos, Nanno. *Minoan Religion: Ritual, Image, and Symbol*. Columbia: University of South Carolina Press, 1993.

Marmot, Michael G., G. Rose, M. Shipley, and P. J. Hamilton. "Employment Grade and Coronary Heart Disease in British Civil Servants," *Journal of Epidemiological Community Health*, 1978, 3, 244–249.

Marston, Cicely, and John Cleland. "Relationship Between Contraception and Abortion: A Review of the Evidence," *International Family Planning Perspectives*, 2003, 29(1), 6–13.

Martinelli, Alberto, and Neil J. Smelser (eds.). *Economy and Society*. Newbury Park, Calif.: Sage, 1990.

Marx, Karl, and Friedrich Engels. *Werke*. Vol. 8. Berlin: Dietz Verlag, 1960. (Originally published in the 1800s)

Maslow, Abraham. *Toward a Psychology of Being*. New York: Van Nostrand Reinhold, 1968.

McChesney, Richard. *Rich Media, Poor Democracy*. New York: New Press, 2000.

Mellaart, James. *Çatal Hüyük*. New York: McGraw-Hill, 1967.

Meyers, Marcia K., and Janet C. Gornick. "The European Model: What We Can Learn from How Other Nations Support Families That Work," *American Prospect*, Nov. 1, 2004.

Mies, Maria. *Patriarchy and Accumulation on a World Scale: Women and the International Division of Labour*. London: Zed Books, 1986.

Milburn, Michael, and Sheree Conrad. *The Politics of Denial*. Cambridge, Mass.: MIT Press, 1996.

Mill, John Stuart. *Principles of Political Economy*. New York: Prometheus, 2004. (Originally published 1848)

Miller, Alice. *For Your Own Good: Hidden Cruelty in Child-Rearing and the Roots of Violence* (Hildegarde and Hunter Hannum, trans.). New York: Farrar, Straus and Giroux, 1983.

Miller, Jean Baker, and Irene P. Stiver. *The Healing Connection: How Women Form Relationships in Therapy and in Life*. Boston: Beacon Press, 1997.

Min, Jiayin (ed.). *The Chalice and The Blade in Chinese Culture: Gender Relations and Social Models*. Beijing: China Social Sciences Publishing House, 1995.

Montagu, Ashley. *Touching: The Human Significance of the Skin* (3rd ed.). New York: Harper & Row, 1986.

Morris, David. *Measuring the Condition of the World's Poor*. New York: Pergamon Press, 1979.

Mukherjee, Moni. "Contributions to and Use of Social Product by Women," in Devaki Jain and Nirmala Banerjee (eds.), *The Tyranny of the Household: Women in Poverty, Investigative Essays on Women's Work*. New Delhi: Shakti Books, 1985.

Myers, John. "Birch Bark's 'Incredible' Potential: Extract May Serve as 'Medicine Chest for the World,'" Knight Ridder Newspapers, *Monterey County Herald*, Apr. 17, 2006, p. A2.

Naim, Moises. "Broken Borders," *Newsweek*, Oct. 24, 2005, pp. 57–62.

Nash, June. "The Aztecs and the Ideology of Male Dominance," *Signs*, Winter 1978, 4, 349–362.

Nelson, Julie A. *Economics for Humans*. Chicago: University of Chicago Press, 2006.

Niehoff, Debra. *The Biology of Violence: How Understanding the Brain, Behavior, and Environment Can Break the Vicious Circle of Aggression*. New York: Free Press, 1999.

Noble, David. *A World Without Women: The Christian Clerical Culture of Western Science*. New York: Knopf, 1992.

Noddings, Nel. *Caring: A Feminine Approach to Ethics & Moral Education*. Berkeley: University of California Press, 1984.

Noddings, Nel. *Starting at Home: Caring and Social Policy*. Berkeley: University of California Press, 2002.

Noddings, Nel. *Happiness and Education*. Cambridge: Cambridge University Press, 2003.

Noddings, Nel. *Critical Lessons: What Our Schools Should Teach*. Cambridge: Cambridge University Press, 2006.

Nord, Mark, Margaret Andrews, and Steven Carlson. *Household Food Security in the United States, 2004*. USDA-ERS Economic Research Report No. 11. Washington, D.C.: U.S. Department of Agriculture, Oct. 2005.

Nussbaum, Martha. *Sex and Justice*. New York: Oxford University Press, 2000.

Nussbaum, Martha. "Capabilities as Fundamental Entitlements: Sen and Social Justice," *Feminist Economics*, 2001, 9(2–3), 33–50.

Okin, Susan Moller. *Women in Western Political Thought*. Princeton, N.J.: Princeton University Press, 1979.

O'Manique, John. *The Origins of Justice: The Evolution of Morality, Human Rights, and Law*. Philadelphia: University of Pennsylvania Press, 2002.

Ornstein, Robert. *The Psychology of Consciousness*. New York: Viking, 1972.

Peradotto, John, and J. P. Sullivan (eds.). *Women in the Ancient World: The Arethusa Papers*. Albany: State University of New York Press, 1984.

Perry, Bruce D. "Childhood Experience and the Expression of Genetic Potential: What Childhood Neglect Tells Us About Nature and Nurture," *Brain and Mind*, 2002, 3(1), 79–100.

Perry, Bruce D., Ronnie A. Pollard, Toi A. Blakley, William L. Baker, and Domenico Vigilante. "Childhood Trauma, the Neurobiology of Adaptation, and 'Use-

Dependent' Development of the Brain: How 'States' Become 'Traits,'" *Infant Mental Health Journal*, 1995, *16*, 271–291.

Peterson, V. Spike, and Anne Sisson Runyan. *Global Gender Issues: Dilemmas in World Politics* (2nd ed.). Boulder, Colo.: Westview Press, 1999.

Pietila, Hilkka. "Non-Market Work in the Construction of Livelihood: The Work and Production at the Grass Roots Countervailing Globalization," paper presented at IGGRI Preparatory Meeting, Helsinki, Oct. 13–16, 1997 (rev. Apr. 18, 1998).

Pietila, Hilkka. "Nordic Welfare Society—A Strategy to Eradicate Poverty and Build Up Equality: Finland as a Case Study," *Journal Cooperation South*, 2001, 2, 79–96.

Pietila, Hilkka. "Cultivation and Households: The Basics of Nurturing Human Life," *EOLSS, Encyclopedia of Life Support Systems,* Section: Human Resources Policy and Management, UNESCO. Oxford, United Kingdom: Eolss Publishers, 2004.

Pinchot, Gifford. *Intrapreneuring*. San Francisco: Berrett-Koehler, 2000.

Pinchot, Gifford, and Elizabeth Pinchot. *The Intelligent Organization*. San Francisco: Berrett-Koehler, 1994.

Platon, Nicholas. *Crete*. Geneva: Nagel Publishers, 1966.

Polanyi, Karl. *The Great Transformation*. Boston: Beacon Press, 1941

Quartz, Steven R., and Terrence J. Sejnowski. "The Neural Basis of Cognitive Development: A Constructivist Manifesto," *Behavioral and Brain Sciences*, 1997, *20*(4), 527–596.

Rampton, Sheldon, and John Stauber. *Trust Us, We're Experts: How Industry Manipulates Science and Gambles with Your Future*. New York: Putnam, 2000.

Rayas, Lucia, Diane Catotti, and Ana Cortes. *Achieving ICPD Commitments for Abortion Care in Latin America: The Unfinished Agenda*. Chapel Hill, N.C.: Ipas, 2005.

Reich, Robert. *I'll Be Short: Essentials for a Decent Working Society*. Boston: Beacon Press, 2003.

Reid, Margaret G. *Economics of Household Production*. New York: Wiley, 1934.

Report on the World Social Situation: The Inequality Predicament. New York: United Nations and Division for Social Policy and Development, U.N. Department of Economic and Social Affairs, 2005.

Rifkin, Jeremy. *The Biotech Century*. New York: Tarcher, 1998.

Rilling James K., D. A. Gutman, T. R. Zeh, G. Pagnoni, G. S. Berns, and C. D. Kilts. "A Neural Basis for Social Cooperation," *Neuron*, 2002, 35, 395–405.

Roach, John. "Greenland Glaciers Losing Ice Much Faster, Study Says," *National Geographic News*, Feb. 16, 2006.

Roach, John. "Global Warming Is Rapidly Raising Sea Levels, Studies Warn," *National Geographic News*, Mar. 23, 2006.

Robbins, John. *Reclaiming Our Health*. Tiburon, Calif.: H.J. Kramer, 1996.

Robotham, Sheila. *Women, Resistance, and Revolution*. New York: Vintage, 1974.

Rockwell, Joan. *Fact in Fiction: The Use of Literature in the Systematic Study of Society*. London: Routledge & Kegan Paul, 1974.

Roco, Mihail C., and William Sims Bainbridge (eds). *Converging Technologies for Improving Human Performance*. Arlington, Va.: National Science Foundation, June 2002.

Rokeach, Milton. *The Nature of Human Values*. New York: Free Press, 1973.

Ronfeldt, David, and John Arquilla. "Networks, Netwars, and the Fight for the Future," *First Monday*, Oct. 2001, 6(10).

Rose, Hillary, and Stephen Rose. (eds.). *Alas, Poor Darwin: Arguments Against Evolutionary Psychology*. New York: Harmony Books, 2000.

Rosin, Hanna. "A Tough Plan for Raising Children Draws Fire: 'Babywise' Guides Worry Pediatricians and Others," *Washington Post*, Feb. 27, 1999, p. A1.

Rosin, Hanna. "Critics Question Extreme Childrearing Method," *Washington Post*, reprinted in *Monterey County Herald*, Mar. 1, 1999, p. A10.

Sachs, Jeffrey. *The End of Poverty: Economic Possibilities for Our Time*. New York: Penguin, 2006.

Sanday, Peggy Reeves. *Female Power and Male Dominance: On the Origins of Sexual Inequality*. Cambridge: Cambridge University Press, 1981.

Sanday, Peggy Reeves. *Women at the Center: Life in a Modern Matriarchy*. Ithaca, N.Y.: Cornell University Press, 2002.

Sapolsky, Robert. "Sick of Poverty," *Scientific American*, Dec. 2005, 293(6), 93–99.

Scheck, Raffael. "Childhood in German Autobiographical Writings, 1740–1820," *Journal of Psychohistory*, Summer 1987, 15(1), 391–422.

Schlegel, Stuart A. *Wisdom from a Rain Forest*. Athens: University of Georgia Press, 1998.

Sen, Amartya. "More Than 100 Million Women Are Missing," *New York Review of Books*, 1990, 37(20), 61–66.

Sen, Amartya. *Development as Freedom*. Oxford: Oxford University Press, 1999.

Sharpe Paine, Lynn. *Value Shift: Why Companies Must Merge Social and Financial Imperatives to Achieve Superior Performance*. New York: McGraw-Hill, 2003.

Shelby, Ashley. "The Real Cost of Oil," *AlterNet*, June 24, 2005.

Shiva, Vandana. *Water Wars*. Cambridge, Mass.: South End Press, 2000.

Shore, Juliet. *The Overworked American*. New York: Basic Books, 1993.

Sivard, Ruth Leger. *World Military and Social Expenditures 1991*. Washington, D.C.: World Priorities, 1991.

Sklar, Holly. "Carving Up Our Economic Pie," *Knight Ridder/Tribune Information Services*, Nov. 22, 2005.

Smith, Adam. *The Theory of Moral Sentiments* (6th ed.). London: A. Millar, 1790. (Originally published 1759)

Smith, Adam. *The Wealth of Nations*. New York: Modern Library, 1937.

Stanton, Elizabeth Cady. *The Woman's Bible*. New York: European Publishing Company, 1885. Reprinted in *The Original Feminist Attack on the Bible* by Elizabeth Cady Stanton, with a modern introduction by Barbara Welter. New York: Arno Press, 1974.

Stein, Rob. "U.S. Health Care Most Expensive, Error-Prone," *Monterey County Herald*, Nov. 4, 2005, p. A2.

Stiglitz, Joseph. *Globalization and Its Discontents*. New York: W. W. Norton, 2003.

"Teure Haushaltproduktion" ["Expensive Household Production"], *Neue Zürcher Zeitung*, Nov. 11, 2004.

Than, Ker. "Brain Cells Fused with Computer Chip," *LiveScience*, Mar. 27, 2006.

The Dartmouth Bible. Boston: Houghton Mifflin, 1950.

The Economic Dimensions of Interpersonal Violence. Geneva, Switzerland: Department of Injuries and Violence Prevention, World Health Organization, 2004.

The Most Important Work-Life-Related Studies. Minnetonka, Minn.: Work & Family Connection, 2005.

The State of the World's Children 1996. New York: UNICEF, 1996.

The State of the World's Children 2005: Childhood Under Threat. New York: UNICEF, 2004.

The World Social Situation: The Inequality Predicament. New York: United Nations, 2005.

The World's Women: 1970–1990 Trends and Statistics. New York: United Nations, 1991.

Thomas, Duncan. "Intra-Household Resource Allocation," *Journal of Human Resources*, Fall 1990, 25(4), 635.

Tong, Rosemarie. *Feminist Thought: A Comprehensive Introduction*. Boulder, Colo.: Westview Press, 1989.

Twist, Lynne. *The Soul of Money: Transforming Your Relationship with Money and Life*. New York: Norton, 2003.

Vaughan, Genevieve. *For-Giving: A Feminist Criticism of Exchange*. Austin, Tex.: Plain View Press, 1997.

Veblen, Thorsten. *The Theory of the Leisure Class*. New York: Signet, 1970.

Vulliamy, Ed. "Streets of Despair," *Amnesty International*, Winter 2005, pp. 12–16.

Ward, Kathryn (ed.). *Women Workers and Global Restructuring*. Ithaca, N.Y.: Cornell University Press, 1990.

Waring, Marilyn. *If Women Counted: A New Feminist Economics*. San Francisco: Harper & Row, 1988.

Warneken, Felix, and Michael Tomasello. "Altruistic Helping in Human Infants and Young Chimpanzees." *Science*, Mar. 3, 2006, pp. 1301–1303.

Warren, Jenifer. "Spare the Rod, Save the Child," *Los Angeles Times*, July 6, 2004.

Watson, Robert, A. H. Zakri, Angela Cropper, Harold Mooney, and Walter Reid (co-chairs and director). *Millennium Ecosystem Assessment: Current State and Trends; Scenarios; Policy Responses; and Multi-Scale Assessments* (Vols. 1–5). Washington, D.C.: Island Press, 2005.

Weiner, Tim. "A New Model Army Soldier Rolls Closer to the Battlefield," *New York Times*, Feb. 16, 2005.

Weintraub, Daniel. "Overhaul of Youth Prisons Just Might Give Kids a Chance," *Monterey County Herald*, Aug. 27, 2006, p. F2.

Wertheim, Margaret. *Pythagoras Trousers: God, Physics, and the Gender Wars*. New York: Times Books, 1995.

Wheatley, Margaret. *Turning to One Another: Simple Conversations to Restore Hope to the Future*. San Francisco: Berrett-Koehler, 2002.

Wilkinson, Richard. *The Affliction of Inequality*. London: Routledge, 1996.

Willetts, R. F. *The Civilization of Ancient Crete*. Berkeley: University of California Press, 1977.

Williams, Joan C. *Unbending Gender: Why Family and Work Conflict and What to Do About It*. New York: Oxford University Press, 2000.

Wilson, Jamie. "Iraq War Could Cost U.S. Over $2 Trillion, Says Nobel Prize Winning Economist," *The Guardian* (U.K.), Jan. 7, 2006.

Woestman, Lois. "Male Chauvinist SAPs: Structural Adjustment and Gender Policies," EURODAD/WIDE briefing paper, Dec. 1994-Jan. 1995. Brussels: European Network on Debt and Development/Women in Development Europe.

Zarlenga, Stephen A. *The Lost Science of Money: The Mythology of Money—The Story of Power*. Valatie, N.Y.: American Monetary Institute Charitable Trust, 2002.

Acknowledgments

This book has truly been a collaborative effort, and I am most grateful to all the people who have contributed to it.

First, I want to thank the wonderful people at Berrett-Koehler. It has been a pleasure working with my editor Steve Piersanti. His faith in this project has meant a great deal to me, and his excellent ideas have greatly enriched this book. Jeevan Sivasubramaniam's caring support has been invaluable, as has Dianne Platner's creativity in the design and production of the book and its cover. Linda Jupiter, James Maxwell, and Naomi Schiff made important creative contributions to the book's design, Karen Marquardt matched the meaning of the book with the perfect visual and type design for the cover, and Sandra Beris's copyediting review, Henri Bensussen's proofreading, and Medea Minnich's indexing are greatly appreciated. I am also grateful to the fine BK marketing team of Maria Jesus Arguilo, Ian Bach, Marina Cook, Michael Crowley, Robin Donovan, Kristen Frantz, Tiffany Lee, Catherine Lengronne, and Ken Lupoff.

In addition, I want to thank my superb literary agent, Ellen Levine, and her assistant Alanna Ramirez, as well as Claire Roberts and others at Trident Media for their long-standing commitment to my work and their efforts on its behalf.

Closer to home, my husband David Loye has, as always, been of indispensable, unflaggingly loving support, as well as an amazing information and editing resource. My daughter Andrea Eisler has been a most talented, creative, and supportive editorial consultant, and a pleasure to work with. Her sister Loren Alison has also given me her sage advice and good ideas. So also has my wonder-woman assistant Leah Gowron, whose general support plays such a large part in all my efforts and in both David's and my life.

I am immensely grateful to the pre-publication readers of this book for their important comments at various stages. I particularly want to thank Josh Blivens, Helen Knode, David Korten, Jeff Kulick, Peter Meyer-Dohm, Julie Nelson, Nel Noddings, Patrick O'Heffernan, Barbara Stanbridge, and Mal Warwick, who read the whole manuscript from cover to cover, and whose suggestions were invaluable. I also want to thank the friends and colleagues who read parts of the manuscript for their good ideas and wise suggestions. Again in alphabetical order, these include Lauralee Alben, Chandra Alexandre, Doug Autenrieth, Charlyn Beluzzo, Marianna Bozesan, Hilary Bradbury, Sandy Burud, Edgar Cahn, Susan Carter, Nancy Folbre, Bob Graham, Christine Gray, Heidi Hartman, Hazel Henderson, Matt Hudson, Sylvia Johnson, Mara Keller, Matthew King, Marci Koblenz, Regula Langemann, Tracy Leighton, Alex Loeb, Deborah Nelson, Gina Ogden, Joseph Chilton Pearce, Russell Precious, Martin Rausch, Alan Rosenblith, Barbara Schaefer, and Suna Yamaner.

In addition, I want to thank Stuart Silverstone, whose Graphics News electronic clipping service has been of much help in my research. As always, I am very grateful to Victor Henry, Doug Holtzman, Joe Johnson, Inga Labeaune, Joanne May, Bridget McConnell, Steve Parker, Debbie Reagan, Janis Rodman, and the other Monterey librarians who are always so helpful to me in my research.

Finally, I am most grateful to the board and staff of the Kalliopeia Foundation for their grant in support of the research and writing of this book.

Index

About the Author

RIANE EISLER is an eminent social scientist, attorney, and social activist best known as author of the international best-seller *The Chalice and The Blade: Our History, Our Future*, hailed by Princeton anthropologist Ashley Montagu as "the most important book since Darwin's *Origin of Species*" and by novelist Isabel Allende as "one of those magnificent key books that can transform us." This was the first book reporting the results of Eisler's study of human cultures spanning thirty thousand years, and is now available in twenty-two languages, including most European languages as well as Arabic, Chinese, Russian, Korean, Hebrew, and Japanese.

Eisler was born in Vienna, fled from the Nazis with her parents to Cuba, and later emigrated to the United States. She obtained degrees in sociology and law from the University of California, taught pioneering classes on women and the law at UCLA, and is a founding member of the General Evolution Research Group (GERG) and the Alliance for a Caring Economy (ACE), a fellow of the World Academy of Art and Science and World Business Academy, and a commissioner of the World Commission on Global Consciousness and Spirituality, along with the Dalai Lama, Archbishop Desmond Tutu, and other spiritual leaders. She is also co-founder of the Spiritual Alliance to Stop Intimate Violence (SAIV). She is president of the Center for Partnership Studies, which is dedicated to research and education.

Eisler has received many honors, including selection as the only woman among twenty great thinkers including Hegel, Adam Smith, Marx, and Toynbee for inclusion in *Macrohistory and Macrohistorians* in recognition of the lasting importance of her work as a cultural historian and evolutionary theorist.

Her books include the award-winning *The Power of Partnership* and *Tomorrow's Children*, as well as *Sacred Pleasure*, a daring reexamination of sexuality and spirituality, and *Women, Men, and the Global Quality of Life*, which statistically documents the key role of the status of women in a nation's general quality of life. She is the author of over two hundred essays and articles in publications ranging from *Behavioral Science, Futures, Political Psychology*, and the *UNESCO Courier* to *Brain and Mind, YES!, The Human Rights Quarterly*, the *International Journal of Women's Studies*, and the *World Encyclopedia of Peace*.

Eisler is sought after to keynote conferences worldwide, and is a consultant to business and government on applications of the partnership model introduced in her work. International venues have included Germany at the invitation of Professor Rita Suessmuth, President of the Bundestag (the German Parliament), and Daniel Goeudevert, Chair of Volkswagen International; Greece at the invitation of First Lady Margarita Papandreou; Colombia, invited by the Mayor of Bogota; and the Czech Republic, invited by Vaclav Havel, President of the Czech Republic.

Her pioneering work in human rights expanded the focus of international organizations to include the rights of women and children. Her work in economics introduces a new holistic model for government and business. Her research has had an impact on many fields, including history, sociology, education, and evolutionary systems science, and her books are required reading in many courses.

Riane Eisler is widely recognized as a visionary pragmatist whose books, speeches, and leadership have inspired people worldwide. *The Real Wealth of Nations: Creating a Caring Economics*, her latest book, proposes a new economics that gives visibility and value to the most essential human work: the work of caring for people and planet.

Riane Eisler can be contacted at center@partnershipway.org or through www.realwealthbook.net.

About the Center for Partnership Studies

THE CENTER FOR PARTNERSHIP STUDIES (CPS) is a 501c(3) nonprofit public benefit corporation that offers information and tools to promote the shift from domination to partnership in all aspects of life—from families and education to economics and politics. Since its establishment in 1987, CPS has worked with individuals and organizations to change consciousness, promote positive personal action, encourage social advocacy, and influence policy. Many CPS initiatives focus on equal partnership between women and men as a major component of the partnership system. CPS initiatives advance a way of life based on harmony with nature, nonviolence, and gender, racial, and economic equity. The Center's current projects include:

- *The Spiritual Alliance to Stop Intimate Violence (SAIV):* an initiative to make ending violence against women and children a top social, religious, and political priority. The SAIV Council includes Nobel Peace laureates Archbishop Desmond Tutu and Betty Williams, Queen Noor and Prince El Hassan bin Talal of Jordan, Ela Ghandi, Jane Goodall, Deepak Chopra, Robert Muller, and other global leaders. SAIV gives small grants to grassroots organizations in Africa, Asia, Latin America, and the Middle East, and the SAIV Sourcebook offers violence prevention resources on SAIV's website (www.saiv.net) and on CD.

- *The Caring Family Policy Agenda:* proposing policies designed to implement:

  A Bill of Rights for Children that includes the right to loving care, shelter, nutrition, education, health care, freedom from violence, and a clean environment.

Caring Family Values based on partnership, mutual respect, nonviolence, and a high valuing of caring and caregiving.

Family-Friendly Governments and Workplaces needed for healthy, prosperous families and a healthy, prosperous, postindustrial economy.

- *The Alliance for a Caring Economy (ACE):* to influence leaders and policymakers to move to a partnership economics where caring and caregiving work are adequately valued and rewarded, with the first stage focusing on changing measures of economic productivity to include this socially essential work.

For more information on the Center for Partnership Studies, as well as for articles, other resources, and how to support the Center's work, visit us at www.partnershipway.org.

Information on how to form a partnership book discussion group or create a partnership center in your community is available at www. partnershipway.org/html/subpages/centermanual.htm. *Information on how to contact a member of the CPS Speakers Bureau* is available at www. partnershipway.org/html/subpages/speaking.htm.

About Berrett-Koehler Publishers

BERRETT-KOEHLER is an independent publisher dedicated to an ambitious mission: Creating a World That Works for All.

We believe that to truly create a better world, action is needed at all levels—individual, organizational, and societal. At the individual level, our publications help people align their lives with their values and with their aspirations for a better world. At the organizational level, our publications promote progressive leadership and management practices, socially responsible approaches to business, and humane and effective organizations. At the societal level, our publications advance social and economic justice, shared prosperity, sustainability, and new solutions to national and global issues.

A major theme of our publications is "Opening Up New Space." They challenge conventional thinking, introduce new ideas, and foster positive change. Their common quest is changing the underlying beliefs, mindsets, institutions, and structures that keep generating the same cycles of problems, no matter who our leaders are or what improvement programs we adopt.

We strive to practice what we preach—to operate our publishing company in line with the ideas in our books. At the core of our approach is stewardship, which we define as a deep sense of responsibility to administer the company for the benefit of all of our "stakeholder" groups: authors, customers, employees, investors, service providers, and the communities and environment around us.

We are grateful to the thousands of readers, authors, and other friends of the company who consider themselves to be part of the "BK Community." We hope that you, too, will join us in our mission.

A BK CURRENTS BOOK

This book is part of our BK Currents series. BK Currents books advance social and economic justice by exploring the critical intersections between business and society. Offering a unique combination of thoughtful analysis and progressive alternatives, BK Currents books promote positive change at the national and global levels. To find out more, visit www.bkcurrents.com.

Be Connected

VISIT OUR WEBSITE

Go to www.bkconnection.com to read exclusive previews and excerpts of new books, find detailed information on all Berrett-Koehler titles and authors, browse subject-area libraries of books, and get special discounts.

SUBSCRIBE TO OUR FREE E-NEWSLETTER

Be the first to hear about new publications, special discount offers, exclusive articles, news about bestsellers, and more! Get on the list for our free e-newsletter by going to www.bkconnection.com.

GET QUANTITY DISCOUNTS

Berrett-Koehler books are available at quantity discounts for orders of ten or more copies. Please call us toll-free at (800) 929-2929 or email us at bkp.orders@ aidcvt.com.

HOST A READING GROUP

For tips on how to form and carry on a book reading group in your workplace or community, see our website at www.bkconnection.com.

JOIN THE BK COMMUNITY

Thousands of readers of our books have become part of the "BK Community" by participating in events featuring our authors, reviewing draft manuscripts of forthcoming books, spreading the word about their favorite books, and supporting our publishing program in other ways. If you would like to join the BK Community, please contact us at bkcommunity @bkpub.com.